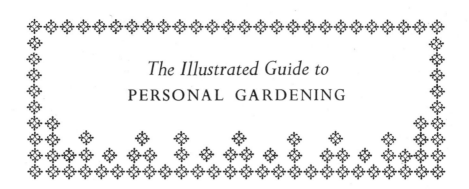

The Illustrated Guide to
PERSONAL GARDENING

The
Illustrated Guide to
PERSONAL
GARDENING

by

JOSEPHINE VON MIKLOS

Prentice-Hall, Inc., Englewood Cliffs, New Jersey

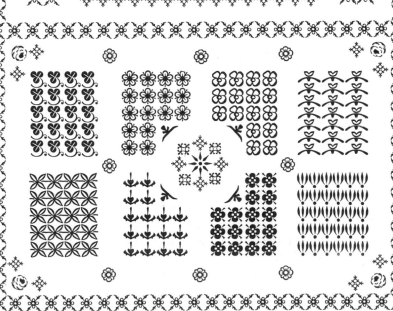

The Illustrated Guide to Personal Gardening by Josephine von Miklos

Copyright © 1972 by Josephine von Miklos
All rights reserved. No part of this book may be
reproduced in any form or by any means, except
for the inclusion of brief quotations in a review,
without permission in writing from the publisher.
ISBN 0-13-450965-X
Library of Congress Catalog Card Number: 70-160357
Printed in the United States of America T
Prentice-Hall International, Inc., London
Prentice-Hall of Australia, Pty. Ltd., North Sydney
Prentice-Hall of Canada, Ltd., Toronto
Prentice-Hall of India Private Ltd., New Delhi
Prentice-Hall of Japan, Inc., Tokyo
ERRATUM—Caption for photograph on page 11 of second color insert should
read: Fringed orchis, one of the multiple-headed wild orchids
Full color illustrations printed in Japan.
Photographs by the author unless otherwise credited
Design by Janet Anderson

Acknowledgments ✦✦✦✦✦✦✦✦✦✦✦✦✦✦✦✦✦✦✦✦✦✦✦✦✦✦✦

I owe much to many people—young and old, experienced and novice—who have helped with this project and even supplied some of the photographs. Here I can name only a few who perhaps have helped the most: Muriel Hinerfeld, horticulturist par excellence, who keeps on advising me in the more or less esoteric ways of making things come out of the earth, and who has identified some of the photographs I have taken here and abroad.

Helen Federico, whose ungardened rock garden remains one of the most beautiful spots I have ever seen anywhere. Her young daughter Gina, who has been my scout for several seasons and has discovered all sorts of exciting places for me to photograph. Frances Merriam of hawthorn, primrose, and shrub geranium fame. Claudine Hurwitz, specialist in African violets whose beauty she has helped me discover. Anne and John Straus, and Carol and Jerry Soling who always allowed me to roam their beautiful places.

Also Pat Medvecky, who has not only shown me her own bountiful ways with plants, but has also taken me to see other people's gardens and works of art. The owners of Bluemount Nurseries in Monkton, Maryland, who have introduced me to ornamental grasses and all their stunning beauty. Lisa Federico, who drew the flowers in Chapter Two and, fence in Chapter Three. Sarah Weintz, who drew the lovely plan of the herb gardens in Mystic, Connecticut, for Chapter Seven.

And my friends Jimmy Baker of New Canaan, Connecticut, Sue Koch of Stamford, Connecticut; Stephen Simon of Monkton, Maryland, and J. Lawrence Starke of San Francisco, California, who made important photographic contributions. Tom Gieseler of South Salem, New York, and Scott Weinert of New Canaan, Connecticut, who in their darkroom and mine sweated out most of the black-and-white prints reproduced on these pages.

Last but certainly not least, Walter and Stephen Weintz of Pound Ridge, New York, to whose loving labors in the past several seasons I owe many of the pleasures of my own small garden.

This book belongs to them all, for their patience, interest, and love and never-failing readiness to help toward its completion.

Josephine von Miklos
Pound Ridge, N.Y.

CONTENTS

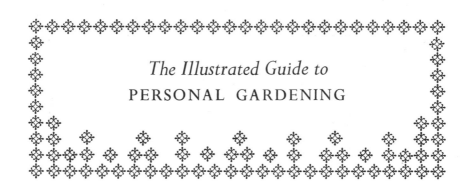

The Illustrated Guide to
PERSONAL GARDENING

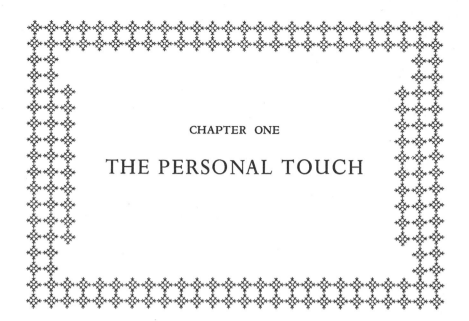

CHAPTER ONE

THE PERSONAL TOUCH

I have often thought that if heaven had given me
choice of my position and calling, it should have
been on a rich spot of earth. . . . No occupation
is so delightful to me as the culture of the earth,
and no culture comparable to that of the garden.
Such a variety of subjects, some one always com-
ing to perfection, the failure of one thing repaired
by the success of another, and instead of one har-
vest, a continued one through the year.
THOMAS JEFFERSON, 1811

THIS book attempts to be a specific, undidactic, leisurely conversation about a very special kind of gardening. It will not tell
you that you must have a bed of roses in front of your house
to fill your friends and neighbors with envy; it will not suggest
exact patterns for your patch of herbs; it will not try to tell you
that you *must* have a lawn on your property, or that you ab-
solutely need even to have flowers. Rather it will try to help you
with ways of *thinking* about gardens.

A friend of mine thinks about gardening five days a week, winter and summer. To get to work, he takes perhaps a fifteen-minute drive through the suburbs. During his drive there are enough stop signs and red lights for him to slow down and observe what is growing on either side of the road. The region was almost wholly forest only twenty years ago; though large sections of virgin wood still remain, new office buildings and developments are springing up with increasing frequency. Isolated among older backroads are the older houses, often built close to the road so as to make it easier to get to the horsedrawn carriages that moved quietly along streets then unpaved.

"It's astonishing," my friend wrote me recently, "to see how the owners' personalities—really their whole attitude toward life—are reflected in what they've done with the land immediately around their houses. I suppose many gardeners get pleasure from all their greenery.

"At one extreme are the suburban split-levels where the premium seems to be put on neatness. There's nothing but grass. clipped too short, a few shrubs snuggled up against the house for 'foundation planting,' perhaps one or two uncomfortable-looking trees left from when the builders went through. The lawn is just an outdoor version of wall-to-wall carpeting. Sometimes you see a juniper that has been planted to fill in the appalling emptiness, but even it has been pruned and hacked at because, deep in his heart, the owner doesn't *want* his pristine expanse ruined by any shrub that might get out of control.

"At the other extreme are the older houses whose owners seem afraid to disturb history. Evergreens that must have been charming when small have loomed over the rooftops. The entire backyard is in pitch-darkness, winter and summer, because of the towering rhododendrons and hemlocks. And I can spot newer, smaller shrubs that are drowning and being crowded out.

"Still other gardeners strike a fairly good balance—but their

2

gardens are as unnatural as a patchwork quilt. In spring, tulips of different colors are blooming in isolated clumps; later geraniums or roses are simply spaced every two feet. Azaleas and boxwoods are planted mechanically on either side of the path, next to the house itself, and everything else is grass. There is no design, only an attempt to fill empty space. All these gardens I have begun to overlook—they're relentlessly the same, the work of people who don't trust themselves enough to risk the unusual and—just possibly—the truly stunning.

"There are other houses I slow down for, however, each time I pass them. One of them has a large outcropping of natural rock in the backyard. Rather than plant flowers, the owners have left a number of the original oaks and birches that soar upward from cracks in the stone. They have also planted a number of rhododendrons and mountain laurel and other broad-leafed evergreens. The whole effect is that of an unexpected, lovely chunk of woodland set down in the midst of an immaculate lawn. The contrast is arresting. In the winter, these broad-leafed evergreens keep their color. The owner has even stopped raking leaves at the border of his 'rockery.' It's the obvious, perfect solution to a problem that could have been an eyesore if treated differently.

"Another home has the usual assortment of azaleas and rhododendrons around the front walk—but not in a strictly straight line. Starting at the edge of the road, the shrubs curve back in semicircles to the house, forming a funnel that welcomes you to the front door. And instead of bare, raked earth and sickly grass, underneath these plantings is a lush bed of pachysandra which remains evergreen, swallowing up each year's fallen leaves and mulching them for these shrubs' nourishment. Again, these garden elements make use of the available space, soothing the eye and making sure there is something that looks halfway decent each season of the year.

"Still another house I often pass is on the top of a hill, and

3

the owner has managed to terrace the slope and grow a garden. A zigzag path laid with fieldstone is set among low shrubs, laurel, and azaleas which in turn are underplanted with wild-flowers and ferns. There is no grass growing up the slope. But wherever the ground is bare, other small evergreens are planted surrounded by pine bark. At intervals, flat stones are laid against the earth to hold it. To keep this neat and trim all the time may take some doing—though not nearly so much as a culti-vated flower garden does, let alone a lawn."

None of these ideas my friend describes is particularly origi-nal. The island-of-rusticity technique goes back to eighteenth-century England, to the sweeping avenue of evergreens to Versailles, where the famed garden architect Le Nôtre planted splendid specimens for the pleasure of the kings of France—he is said to have abhorred flowers—and even further back to Renaissance Italy. (One cannot help wondering whether these enormous and dramatic displays were meant to create horticul-tural pleasure or merely envy among lesser mortals!) But even the overgrown splendor of that age had not invented anything.

The Egyptians had tightly planted gardens, often walled in to protect them from the wind. A famed king of Assyria built terraces of cascading shrubbery and trees that reached down from the top of a ziggurat (like the Tower of Babel) for his queen who was forever pining for the trees of her native Persia; the Cretans painted lilies and roses on their walls and pottery, and the Greeks were such proficient growers of violets, their favorite flowers, that they took them to sell at the Agora, the marketplace of old Athens. Homer has left us the following description of a Hellenistic garden:

> *Outside the palace yard, stretching out*
> *From the gates, lies a fine four-acre orchard with a hedge*
> *On either side. Here tall trees are thriving,*
> *Heavy with pears and pomegranates, with glossy apples,*

4

Sweet figs, and luscious plum olives. Here too
His fruitful vineyard is planted, in one part of which
Is a level spot where grapes are drying. . . . Beyond
The last row of vines, trim vegetable beds are laid out,
Green and growing all year long. . . .

And since time immemorial mountain people have *had* to plant their gardens on terraces, and they still do—in Peru, in Austria, in Switzerland, even in Colorado. There were private, statue-filled gardens in Pompeii in which the wealthy Romans enjoyed the sun and their leisure. The great emperor Charlemagne (768–814) had a kitchen garden in which grew more than seventy culinary herbs and vegetables. Medieval monks had herb and flower gardens even though the Church frowned on the pleasure the flowers gave to the monks, who enjoyed violets and daisies just as much as they did their herb cookery. St. Francis of Assisi, in the thirteenth century, knew better:

Praised be my Lord for our sister, mother earth,
That which sustains and keeps us
And brings forth diverse fruit with grass and flowers
bright.

No, the only real difference between the gardeners my friend praises and those he faults is their choice of model: the run-of-the-mill, forgettable, unimaginative gardeners have simply borrowed from one another, feeling that what is good enough for their neighbors is also good enough for them. In the past, each style of architecture came to influence a style of gardening so that now we can associate the layout and choice of plants on an estate in Europe, for example, with a specific period in time. And although few early twentieth-century architects designed innovations beyond the front porch, today, all over the country new work is combining contemporary architecture with the de-

5

sign of the space surrounding it. Much new dynamic and imaginative work is also being done in the planned communities emerging around the great centers of the country. We must begin to learn that in our own personal efforts to create effects that make passersby and visitors grateful and intrigued, we can come up with simple but dramatic and appealing ideas which take no more hard labor and complicated contortions than any ordinary, conventional, humdrum pattern. Usually less. I know some people who scour their natural outcropping of rocks (to make them look neat and clean, no doubt!) and plant lots and lots of annuals which may give them spots of color but which also need assiduous weeding, and who do far more backbreaking and thankless labor than the anonymous property owner who lets oaks, rhododendrons, and birches do his mulching and weed-prevention for him.

There is no question that beauty often requires work. But doesn't it make better sense to work *with* nature rather than fight a continuous uphill battle?

The accompanying illustration shows one extreme of horticulture where the mind of man is seen as all-important, and the living plants of a garden are considered merely as components of architecture. All spontaneity is denied them; some gardeners even clipped off the buds so that a rosebush would have no more flowers on one side than the other: better no flowers at all than asymmetry.

The other extreme was reached only one hundred and fifty years later when an eighteenth-century Englishman, Lancelot "Capability" Brown, attempted to redesign the English landscape and reintroduce what today we would call the "natural look." His work illustrates the one thing that has distinguished one school of gardening from another—the degree to which the gardener has felt compelled to control nature. Following Brown's lead, the rich made every effort to reproduce natural chaos on their estates, even to the point of constructing artfully decaying

6

A Dutch garden design—formal, designed and maintained for the pleasure of those who could afford them. (Hans Friedman De Vries, Antwerp, 1583. Courtesy of Hunt Botanical Library, Carnegie-Mellon University, Pittsburgh, Pennsylvania.)

Gothic ruins and paying hermits to come and live in artificial grottos.

7

One gardener I have seen is out every weekend, trimming a vast rectangular privet hedge that is always going out of shape. The privet bushes of which this hedge is composed never heard of a right angle; they were genetically programmed to grow as large, towering blobs of shrubbery. The only thing that is going to restrain them is constant clipping from April through October . . . when the "privacy" hedge promptly drops its leaves and becomes transparent.

I would admire that hedger's efforts far more if I hadn't seen the *two* hedges which belong to a neighbor of his. One hedge is of Korean boxwood, which naturally forms neat, compact egg-shaped bundles of green. The other is of arbor vitae, which have grown into a neat, dense, columnar curtain of attractive evergreen foliage. Neither drops its leaves in the fall. Both appear immaculately groomed, but neither has ever required a single clipping. They never will.

I have known Long Island gardeners who did a valiant job of keeping sad-looking hemlocks alive under the constant mist of salt spray that threatens to kill them. But I have seen other seaside gardens whose beach roses, sea buckthorn, bayberry, goldenrod (yes—*Solidago*), jack pine, and wild (now cultivated) sweet peas thrive and grow riotously even when seawater washes over their roots. The difference, again, is the source of inspiration plus the owners' willingness to trade familiarity for beauty.

In this book I am not going to promise you that junipers, rhododendrons, or azaleas will grow on your property. But I do suggest that out of the over 600,000 species of cultivated and wild plants there are more than enough that are perfectly right for your particular garden. They may be at the corner nursery, or even in a vacant lot or along the roadsides, or you may have to grow them laboriously from seed or even climb New Hampshire or Colorado's taller mountains to find and transplant them. But I do promise you they are there.

I am not assuring you, either, that to make your garden look even halfway decent you will be able to use the same layout your next-door neighbor does. As John Parkinson said in *Paradisi in Sole, Paradisus Terrestris:* "To prescribe one forme for every man to follow, were too great presumption and folly: for every man will please his owne fancie, according to the extent he designeth out for that purpose, be it orbicular or round, triangular or three-square, quadrangular or four-square, or more long than broad. I will only shew you here the severall forms that many men have taken and delighted in. Let every man choose which he liketh best, or may most fitly agree to that proportion of ground he hath set out for that purpose."

I do assure you that with at least a cursory acquaintance with what the gardeners of Egypt, Mesopotamia, Greece, Ancient Rome, Persia, China, and Japan have accomplished, you will have new ideas that suddenly will make a great deal more sense. I have a friend in New Jersey who is seriously attempting to reproduce the effect enjoyed by Louis XIV at Versailles, where avenues of horse chestnut lead the eye into dark woods at their end. No matter if my friend has only a third of an acre! He is using trees such as green Japanese maples, gray birch, and American red maples (even though the maples are not exactly small trees), and whose fall colors are remarkable to behold. Already you cannot imagine his property planted any other way. And it is this sense of "just rightness," the unique and *seemingly* original touch that is often not apparent to the eye, that makes a garden something to take your breath away. In each case the *effect,* not the *fact,* is what is important.

Though I am hopelessly in love with wildflowers, I cannot say whether you will need or even want flowers in your garden. The answer may well lie in the remarkable dwarfed evergreens which are now on the market, in delicate sedums and succulents cascading in torrents through the cracks of an artificially re-created mountain scree—or even in an expanse of sea-rounded pebbles and rocks with no green vegetation whatever. There are delights in other things as well as in flowers. While Americans line the Blue Ridge Mountains in spring to watch the wild azaleas in their seasonal triumph, the Japanese take to the mountains each fall to observe the colors of fall foliage just as we do in New England. The Egyptians were often far more interested in the mythological connotations of their plantings than they were in the blossoms. To them, even the lotus was not just a pretty face but a symbol of something greater. Many friends of mine share a parallel attitude in their herb gardens, neat expanses of fragrant greenery whose culinary uses balance their visual appeal.

But I can also assure you that if you already love flowers you can begin to appreciate their foliage, the locations they need to do their best, and the background they need to set them off. You will become increasingly aware of the marvelous subtleties, infinite variety, and constant challenge in making a garden *yours*—not a seedy, woebegone carbon copy of a flowerbed you saw growing in different soil, different exposures, and with essentially different purposes and tastes in mind.

This book is really a collection of good—and possible—solutions to the challenge of bare ground. Some go back five thousand years; others have recently been worked out in New England arboretums. It would be impossible for you to use all of them but you can begin to understand the factors that make every garden a special case, with its own problems and advantages. And, hopefully, you will find that the final answers you choose *must* be different from the everyday, and that they *will* cut down on needless work, and *can* make you the envy of your neighborhood. This book is in no way a substitute for shovel, trowel, and hose, but is rather a catalogue of unusual (and often necessary) ideas that should start you thinking— if not of new solutions of your own, then of what you can

Details of cultivated plants: the blossoms of bleeding heart, the dew-spotted leaves of lupine.

"borrow" for your own elegant and breathtaking resplendent purposes. The problems nature has provided for you are unique in their combinations, and so must also be your response.

Now, when there are so few private moments left, so little time for peace and quiet contemplation, the pursuit of inner values and personal freedom, there is almost nothing like a garden one designs, builds, and tends oneself. As everyone knows, we are living in the midst of several great and inter-dependent revolutions: social, psychological, spiritual and, above all, overwhelmingly technological. No matter how eager we are to help preserve the green and blooming world, the Army Corps of Engineers, real-estate developers, and ever-growing "industrial parks" are constantly encroaching on the land, the woods, and the waters. Everywhere waste and pollution are threatening the good rich earth which literally feeds us and gives us life. The personal garden is our last chance to preserve a vestige of the blooming world that once was, and to create our own small patch of Paradise.

Nor can we find—or afford—much professional help for our gardens. Fewer and farther between are the skillful men who really cherish the soil and make it respond with bloom. Richer or poorer, you must "do your own thing" if you want any kind of green world at your door.

There never is any true guarantee that a plant will do well (or even survive) just because you want it to do so. But if you remember a few basic facts, it probably will succeed. You will discover that nature has her own mysterious devices; you cannot dictate to her or trick her. You can allow yourself to experiment with this or that, here and there. And if you really love a plant, it might just find a way to stay with you and give forth leaf and blossom. Although old knowledge and tradition play an important part in gardening, isn't it more satisfying to plant with new ideas, make your own discoveries, in your own manner of doing things, your own dreaming, planning, playing?

Do what a friend of mine did. She wanted a hawthorn in front of her house—which was considered impossible and sheer lunacy by every experienced gardener she knew and the several nursery men she consulted. "There never was a hawthorn in this kind of soil or with that exposure," some said. Be she did insist and planted one; it grew and flourished, perhaps only because she loved it so. Today it is the miracle of the neighborhood, year after year when it comes into ever more spectacular bloom.

This is not to say you cannot obtain much help from friends with well-established gardens, that is, if they are not like the many cooks who never share a recipe. Some nurserymen are always ready to talk and make suggestions and won't sell you a flowering shrub which has no chance in the wrong kind of soil or exposure. Ask, experiment, dare. You may suspect that you have a "brown" rather than a "green thumb." But if you care enough and think enough, you will eventually come through.

As far back as in the sixteenth century, Sir Francis Bacon wrote: "God almighty first planted a garden. And indeed it is the purest of human pleasures. It is the greatest refreshment to the spirit of man; without which buildings and palaces are but gross handiworks: and a man shall ever see that when ages grow into civility and elegancy, men come to build stately sooner than to garden finely; as if gardening were the greater perfection."

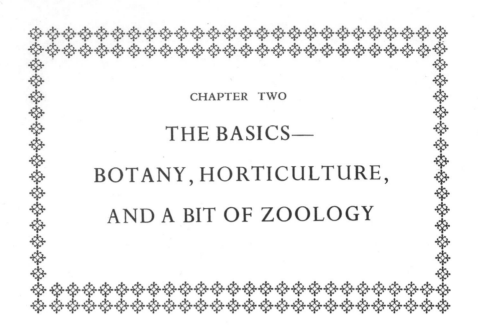

CHAPTER TWO

THE BASICS—
BOTANY, HORTICULTURE,
AND A BIT OF ZOOLOGY

*. . . That our sons may be as plants grown up
in their youth . . .*
PSALMS 144:12

I. BOTANY

The science that deals with the life, structure, growth and classification of plants is as old as history—probably much older. The first botanist was the individual who took a closer look at a few plants, compared them with other plants, and found them different in color, shape, scent, and manner of their growth. And they were wondrous things, coming up from the earth by themselves, without any discernible power pushing them. That individual may have wondered and puzzled and then picked them, and eaten one or the other, or used its juice for the cooling of a wound. He did not find them wanting.

Several thousand years before the Christian era, Egyptians and Assyrians had made lists of plants they had studied and collected for their medicinal and cosmetic properties. But the first true

14

botanists were Theophrastus (c. 372–287 B.C.) and Dioscorides (flourished about A.D. 50) who not only traveled far and wide to collect plants and study them (even Alexander the Great sent Theophrastus some of the strange plants he found on his campaigns) and put their newly found knowledge into basic botanical works. Theophrastus wrote *On the History of Plants* and *On the Causes of Plants;* Dioscorides' *De Materia Medica* is the most famous and often-translated botanical work of all time. The earliest known copy of his manuscript in Greek and Arabic, dating from 512, was found in Turkey in the sixteenth century by the Austrian ambassador de Busbequ and is now one of the greatest treasures of the Vienna National Library.

What makes Dioscorides' work so extraordinary is that he had laid the foundation of all herbal and much medical knowledge. Most later herbalists referred to him, for his works were translated and retranslated into Greek, Italian, Spanish, Arabic, and other languages. And although we don't know whether he gained some knowledge from the Egyptian and Middle-Eastern works or experimented totally on his own, some of the plants he cited are still used in modern pharmacoepeas.

Not much new botanical knowledge was gathered until the Renaissance, when new herbals appeared in almost all European countries; but they still only *described* plants rather than classified them. Although there had been an earlier attempt, it was Carl von Linné of Sweden (1707–1778) who really became the first to set about exploring and systematically noting the attributes of the plants he found, and grouped them according to their characteristics. Thus he created the botanical system that still forms the basis of present-day botanical science. But although Linné knew a scant 5,950 species, (among which were hundreds and perhaps thousands that have been discovered in North America) today over 300,000 species are known, and every year, nearly 4,000 new plants are found and classified all over the

world. I mention these early pioneers because I'll be talking about
them in later chapters.

The average gardener need not, and indeed cannot know all
the scientific facts about his flowers, trees, shrubs, vines, and
ferns. To enjoy his labors, he does not need to know much about
plant morphology (which deals with the structure of plants; or
cytology, the science of the cell). None of this is an essential
part of an amateur gardener's knowledge; although a studious
mind will always want to know more, curiosity usually takes
one far from the basics.

For our purpose, it is enough to say that in many ways plants
are like men: They are born, they live, breathe, suffer, and
flourish; they sicken, they weaken, they die. The mechanics of
their reproduction, at least among the "higher" plants (the
"lower" plants reproduce by spores in a somewhat different way)
are quite like those of human beings, although plants need the
help of insects, wind, water—and gardeners. In many ways, so
is their physiology, and so are their likes and dislikes, their power
of adaptability, their resistance to enemies, their harmony with
friends, their will to fight for their comfort, their success, their
very survival.

I used to make light of the Greek and Latin names flung about
by more knowledgeable gardeners; the common names sounded
so much nicer and cozier and seemed to fit so much better into
the everyday common world. Often they add a feeling of poetry
to the landscape. Doesn't bouncing Bet sound prettier and more
amusing than *Saponaria officinalis,* or isn't devil's paintbrush
more vivid than *Hieracium aurantiacum,* or blue-eyed grass much
sweeter than *Sisyrinchium campestre?*

But I soon found out that a Greek described Queen Anne's
lace when he said *Daucus carota;* or that an Austrian meant cob-
webbed houseleek, which grows in altitudes up to 9,600 feet in

the Alps, when he mentioned *Sempervivum arachnoidum*, whose relative I had just planted at the edge of a path at a much lower altitude. Botanical names are often descriptive and explain much about a plant, for *carota* means carrot and thus describes the family of Queen Anne's lace; and *Sempervivum* stands for living forever, which the houseleek practically does. Knowing botanical names not only helps achieve a universal language and build more bridges to more people, but it brings those who love nature and gardeners even closer to their subject.

Nor did I really care how many pistils and stamens a flower had, or whether it reproduced itself vegetatively (the plant being able to send out roots from cuttings, a method first described by Theophrastus) or sexually (the union of male and female germ cells for the creation of a new genetic species). But as I became ever more passionately interested in the unbelievable riches around me, it dawned on me that it would help in the discoveries I was constantly making—in the woods, in the meadows, and in and around waters—if I knew more about the plants: how they fitted into the scheme of things; and why and how they got along with their neighbors and in their specific piece of earth.

I *had* to try to identify the plants, their names, their families, and at least some of the facts which surrounded their existence. How else could I learn how to match and mix them and transplant them into my own piece of ground to save them from the next bulldozer that was making noises right around the corner? If I had fallen in love with a flower or a fern, its color, its design, its scent, and wanted very much to save it and transplant it, how else could I know what kinds of roots it had, what soil it needed, what food, what location it preferred in sun or shade or filtered sun and partial shade, and how it reproduced itself? How else could I understand its needs and make sure that I would see it again after the first year and the year after that?

17

As there are no two fingerprints alike in all mankind, so in the world of plants, even within the same species, there are no two roots, no two leaves, no two fruits alike—not even on the same flower on the same tree. There is an infinity of design, a total individuality of each specimen. Although there are common characteristics within each group—all pines, for example, are evergreen and have needles—the individual detail in all places and at all times varies. It is in this sense that an understanding of botany is essential to the gardener, for he must learn to *see* and not just look.

All plants have roots to anchor them in the soil and absorb the needed food. In addition, some plants also have storage chambers for the food, called bulbs (hyacinths, tulips, fritillaria) or corms which have no scales such as bulbs have and differ in shape (crocuses, gladioli); or rhizomes, underground stems with rootlets and "eyes" out of which next year's growth will come (Solomon's-seal, lily of the valley).

All plants have stems which are the pipelines to the leaves and flowers, and there are as many forms of stems (round, triangular, oval, square) as there are shapes of flowers. Leaves serve for breathing or, as it is called, transpiration, according to the need of the plant and the changing weather—another of those highly complicated, almost mysterious processes which the gardener can help (by watering) but not totally control. Again there are many forms of leaves, kinds, types of margins, shapes, bases, tips, and designs of venation. Observing the growth of leaves also serves to determine the plant's need for food and water.

The leaves' most important function, photosynthesis, is the process by which plants manufacture starch and sugar with the help of light. Sunlight acts on food and the green substance in all leaves, chlorophyll. Although the details of this process are understood by scientists—they are merely words to the layman—the process itself has never been duplicated in a laboratory. Per-

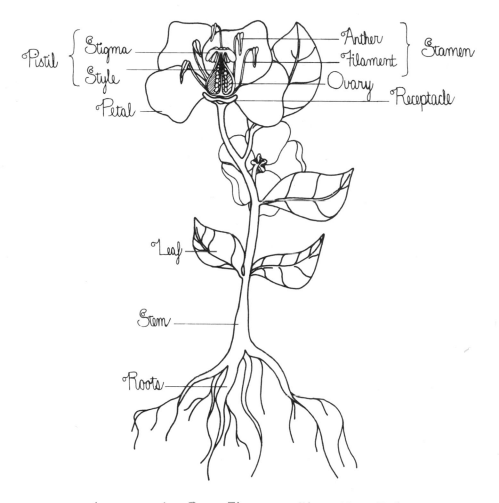

Anatomy of a Basic Flowering Plant (Lisa Federico)

haps as scientists come closer and closer to creating the essence of all life, the day may not be too far off when they might also be able to mimic the function of sunlight in the life of plants.

Finally there is the flower, the crowning glory of a plant, whose real purpose is not to please but to display the plants' organs of reproduction and to facilitate the production of pollens and seeds. There are several types of flower "construction," single heads, rays, racemes, umbels, and panicles, in all colors of the rainbow, and hues and shades in between, produced in infinite variety. But in the final analysis the color, shape, and scent of the flowerhead are nothing more or less than devices to attract the agents of propagation—wind, bee, beetle, fly, even bird and bat.

The arrangement of the seeds inside a flower's ovaries also varies and is a cause of wonder—in straight lines, in a marvelous display of symmetry, or in random design—though who are we to call anything that nature does is without rhyme or reason? The minute male reproductive material, the pollens, also made in great variety, are strewn over the earth by the wind or birds or insects, or man, as are the final mature seeds. It is astonishing

Umbel (Saint-John's-wort). (Lisa Federico)

Raceme (snapdragon). (Lisa Federico)

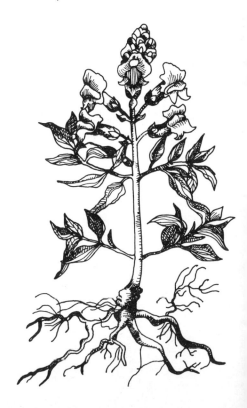

to watch the maturing of a milkweed flowerhead, the transformation of a bud into the pod full of seeds which are then carried into the world by wispy wings.

II. HORTICULTURE

> *For the seed shall be prosperous; the vine shall*
> *give her fruit, and the ground shall give her in-*
> *crease, and the heavens shall give their dew . . .*
> ZECHARIAH 8:12

Horticulture might be called botany in practice. It is the application of botanical facts to the growing, tending, and, sometimes, creating plants in the field or garden. The meaning of the word horticulture lies in the name itself, for *hortus* is Latin

Rays (ox-eye daisy). (Lisa Federico)

Microphotograph of mixed flower pollens. (Ross Hutchins)

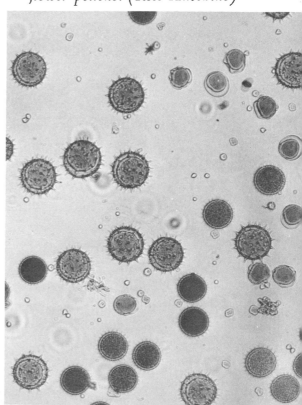

for garden; and although it is also applied in the large commercial production of vegetables and other plants, here it is used only in the sense of the needs of basic gardening. Each garden club, for instance, has a horticulture section in which club members grow plants from seeds or cuttings, ordinary or unusual, but in all instances proudly display the *quality* of the plants they have grown. They constantly experiment, indoors and out, in hothouse or cold frame, in pots, in dishes, even in paper cups. They know about watering, composition of soil, exposure to light, fertilizers, tools. They are, in many ways, the prototype of good gardeners, God-given green thumb or not. They *try*.

Once you have designed and laid out your garden in your own way and decided what to do with existing plants—leave them alone and love them, or rip them out to make room for better things to come—you will have to deal with several basic horticultural facts. Whatever your taste, there are certain forces of nature which you have to have on your side.

First, there is the soil: too many people take it for granted, not realizing that it has taken millions of years to make it. It is composed, in varying degrees, of mineral and vegetative matter, the result of the lives and deaths of plants and animals by the billion. In the *Handbook on Soils,* published by the Brooklyn Botanic Garden (all their handbooks are my favorite botanical and horticultural reading matter) you can find the following short glossary of soil terms:

Aggregate: a mass of soil particles, also called granule or crumb.

Hardpan: a layer of soil that is compacted and cemented by iron oxide, silica, or other substances.

Horizon: if a hole is dug in any well-drained upland soil, there can be seen on its walls a series of horizontal layers of soil in varying thickness, color, texture, etc. The layers are called horizons.

Leaching: removal of dissolved materials by water.

Marl: soft, earthy material consisting of large amounts of calcium carbonate with various impurities alkaline in reaction.

Profile: the succession of horizons from the surface down to and including the underlying rock or other parent material.

Puddle: to destroy the granular structure of a soil.

Subsoil: the part of the soil below topsoil and above the underlying rock or other parent material.

Tilth: a general term indicating the physical condition and workability of the soil.

Topsoil· the surface layer of soil, i.e., the living soil containing organic matter and teeming with microorganisms.

Topsoil is the medium in which you can plant a garden. But an important consideration is the pH factor (the symbol for the hydrogen ion concentration) which indicates the degree of acidity or alkalinity of the soil and allows you to judge where and what to plant. A pH factor of 3.5 means that the soil is very acid (swamplands, forests); a factor of 7 means that the soil is neutral (and good for most garden plants); and a factor of 9 denotes great sweetness which is not really necessary. Rhododendrons, laurels, and many wildflowers and ferns like acid soil; cultivated plants, herbs, flowers, and vegetables need "sweet" soil. Before you go into any elaborate kind of planting— or transplant any fussy, specialized species—you had best test your soil either with one of the available kits, or by sending samples to government agricultural stations.

Luckily we are able to change the pH factor of the soil either way: if the soil should be more acid, you can add muck from swamps, leaf mold—preferably from oak leaves, spaghnum moss, rotted wood chips, chemicals, and so on. If you need sweeter soil, spread hydrated lime—the product of lime rock—over the surface, and work it well into the earth to make sure that even plants with long roots get the proper conditions. Lime is available in many nurseries and in farm and hardware stores which sell garden equipment. The details of application are usually printed on the packages.

Once I was lazy about all this sweet-versus-acid and, much to my amazement, a small patch of garden in which I had planted several kinds of perennials (including small shrubs such as daphne and blue mist, my special favorites) began to support baneberry, thimbleweed, and other wild plants. In other words, I neglected to sweeten the soil at regular intervals and allowed it to become acid enough by itself to allow wildflowers to do well.

It's not always as simple as that, however; many plants which *should* grow only in one type of soil seem to have built into them a margin of accommodation or adaptability—as was proved to me by several different *cultivated* plants of columbine which continue to bloom happily next to the wild variety. Perhaps this is just another proof that Man does not always know best and that in gardening, as in so many other things in life, there is a constant element of chance.

Garden soil must be maintained crumbly to allow water to penetrate and be retained around the roots, and so that fertilizers dissolve and do their job properly. Also tiny bubbles of air are needed, or the roots may "drown." Indoors or in potted plants, mica material such as vermiculite keeps open spaces for air and water when mixed with top or potting soil.

Nature provides plenty of food for wild plants, since they are almost always growing in and among the decaying remnants of other vegetable matter. In a sense, our woodland wildflowers grow in a perennial compost heap, supplied each fall with a fresh layer of leaves, rotting wood, twigs, and branches. But in our own more or less artificially created garden spots—where weeds are pulled up, leaves are raked out, and grass clippings removed—usually more food is needed than even the best topsoil provides. The more plants you grow, the more food you must add, for many cultivated plants are voracious eaters. Some are even gourmets. But just like children never overfeed them.

Talking about raking leaves, another gardener I know has told me of a terrific new idea: he gets a few 50-lb. cardboard cartons, fills them with leaves and stamps them down between fillings. In time they compact further, the cardboard dissolves and disappears, and he is left with neat squares of composted leaves.

For many years a great controversy has raged over the kind of fertilizers to use: natural or artificial. Natural fertilizers include bonemeal, compost (which is made of leaves, grass cuttings, and even kitchen garbage that has decomposed over a period of time) and manure. This is the old-fashioned, conservative way. A woman physician in whose hothouse I have photographed the most astonishing plants, including vegetables grown for year-round food for a large family, told me with fire in her eyes that she *despised* chemical fertilizers and only the organic food she could compost was good enough for her plants. Looking at the miraculous growth, the stunning shapes and colors she had conjured up from her pots and flats, I believed her.

On the other hand, there are available today commercial chemical fertilizers, whether in powder or tablet form, that seem to do quite well. And so long as they contain sufficient amounts of nitrogen (chemical symbol N) phosphorus (P_2O_5) and potassium (K_2O) in the recommended combination for the plants you wish to grow (5-10-5, or 5-10-10, or whatever combination is suitable) they may be just as helpful as compost or other organic means of gardening. Certain compost materials may be deficient in a given mineral, and you may wish to add, say, chelated iron, the way a parent supplements orange juice with vitamins. At any rate, chemicals work much faster and in our day of haste, waste, and nervous tension they have certain advantages. If you have a small decorative garden, a window "hothouse" and no vast expanse of anything resembling a luxury garden on which years of work have been expended, then perhaps, you might be just as well off with contemporary fertilizers which come in packages with detailed instructions. But remember the stories of DDT and cyclamates, which proved that even government-accepted chemicals and procedures sometimes turn sour. Read, read, and read some more; ask questions of your friends who have more experience, and then go ahead and plant, fertilize, and watch.

In any case you should also "mulch" your soil. At least allow dead leaves to stay for a while, give them time to do their job, prevent weeds from invading your flowerbeds, and help retain the all-important moisture the soil needs to give forth with bloom. Some mulches are better-looking than others. Again, commercially-bagged types are usually preferred by landscape architects, but not all are recommended for all areas in your garden. Most of them are available in local garden supply stores.

Buckwheat hulls have good color, long life, pleasant texture, and are suitable around roses and other ornamental plantings.

Cocoa-bean hulls are available from chocolate and candy manufacturers. They may pack together, so it is best to mix them with sawdust. Use under ornamentals, for they have very good texture and color.

Crushed stone and gravel come from lumberyards or building contractors. They're best for alpine plants, but I have also seen gravel used for roses. If you do use gravel, be sure to use it only when the plants get some shade; otherwise there will be too much reflection from the sun, and moisture will disappear. Gravel, of course, does not decompose but will eventually sink into the ground, and so will need replenishing. Marble chips will act

26

a bit like lime and will sweeten your soil; be aware of this if you plant them under rhododendrons or any plant that loves a low pH.

Hay comes from farm and feed stores or your own meadow, decays fast, and supplies nitrogen—good around roses for winter protection.

Lawn clippings are good for the lawn, if not matted and other non-ornamental areas of garden (vegetable garden, for example).

Leaf mold results when fallen leaves are allowed to rot in compost heap or where they fall; useful the following year over wildflowers, under rhododendron, laurel, and so on. Unrotted maple leaves sometimes mat like the pages of a wet book and have to be loosened with rake or fork. Oak leaves curl and thus make a light, springy mat that is good protection for winter.

Manure from farms or stables should be used carefully because its chemicals may burn plants. It has some nutritive value.

Peat moss has fine texture and good color, comes either loose or compacted in small bales. It is the most commonly used mulch, good for keeping weeds down, but loses its value if too dry. Attractive brown color makes it suitable for most garden areas.

Pine bark comes in two sizes commercially (or directly off the dead tree) and is better than peat moss because its rougher texture helps to better retain water. It is my favorite mulch for ferns, and almost all shrubs and flowers.

Pine needles and those of other conifers are obtainable wherever evergreens grow, and are very useful for wild plants, particularly trailing arbutus, lady's-slippers, trillium, other wildflowers.

Plastic film is excellent for the vegetable garden, but not very good-looking for ornamental plants. Retains moisture, prevents weeds, and does not rot.

Salt hay is an excellent general-purpose mulch, especially for covering plants for the winter.

Straw, coarser and more durable than hay, is good between rows of vegetables.

Wood chips are sometimes available from tree surgeons, but easily made from your own fallen branches and twigs and prunings—if you can rent or borrow a wood chipper or have good muscles—is coarser than sawdust, and approaches chipped bark.

Water, the most common compound on earth, supplies food and refreshment to your plants, and is perhaps the single most important factor to success in your garden. Mulches will help to keep up the water table—the level of saturated soil, usually several feet below the surface—so that constant watering of plants is not needed even in a dry spell.

If you live in a dry and sandy area you will, of course, have to water much more than where humidity is high and rains are frequent. The success of English gardens is in large part due to the fog and rain, which help English gardeners to win many of their battles and maintain the greenness of their thumbs. But remember not to place your finest plants under the drip line of your roof or your trees.

Try to build your beds and borders in such a way that they are slightly raised toward the front so that rainwater and water from your house does not run off into your paths and terraces or drown your plants.

These rollers can be "planted" wherever needed to keep your hose away from planted areas.

When you plant laurels, rhododendrons, or azaleas, leave a ring of soil around the plant so that the water goes into the earth and will not run off. I have seen this done even with garden flowers where the space permits, and the dike lasts at least for the first few days.

In indoor planting, the problem of watering is somewhat different; unless you have a hothouse with the proper watering devices, your plants will suffer from the heat and dryness in your rooms. But some plants need more water than others. Impatiens, for example, will need watering every day; cyclamen, perhaps twice a week; and your Christmas cactus will need frequent watering only when it blooms. Spider plants and begonias need more water than geraniums, modest plants which can be quite happy if you forget to water them on occasion. And so it goes. You will have to judge the needs of your plants as you go along; they will let you know soon enough through wilted leaves and bone-dry soil. Misting from an atomizer is a good idea for most plants because it allows the leaves to drink. This is particularly important if you have planted seeds and the first shoots are coming up; strong watering may drown them or encourage "browning off"—a fungus that attacks delicate shoots.

You need tools for working with soil, planting, cultivating, cleaning up, cutting, pruning, and trimming; the best are made of stainless steel which do not rust and stay shiny for many years with just a minimum of care; however, they are quite expensive. The run-of-the-mill tools are made of iron and they do rust, but if kept covered with machine oil during the winter they will last for quite a while. Good tools make gardening easier; the right tools make it more successful. Here are suggestions for a basic collection.

For turning over soil, mixing and distributing mulches and working them into the soil, removing boulders and large stones: Short-

and long-handled shovels; forks with flat, thin, and pointed tines; large metal rake. Also very useful is a crowbar for testing soil for rocks and helping to remove them.

For digging holes for small trees, shrubs (don't try to move large ones yourself, nurseries can do a safer job) *and large plants:* Shovels as described above; spade with square blade; hoes. A fork is also useful for digging up plants with large or long roots.

For small holes for smaller plants; planting: Small long-handled shovel; trowel, if possible also a slender kind which has inches marked, very good for planting bulbs; small weeding fork; small metal rake for smoothing out soil after planting.

For loosening soil, removing weeds, etcetera: Curved draw and Dutch hoes, small fork.

For pruning and clipping: Tree saw; pruning shears; clippers (English ones are best).

For "manicuring" lawn: Edger; old kitchen knife to remove dandelion and crabgrass, mowers, rake.

For raking leaves: Flexible fan rake, metal and bamboo. Also small bamboo rake for raking between plants.

And: Wheelbarrow (with tire; much easier to use); hose; watering can; basket for weeds (plastic is best); fertilizer spray gun (for leaf feeding); gun for spraying insects; burlap (for transplanting larger plants, keeping a sufficient amount of earth around the roots); flats; carrier for seedlings. Stakes and "Twist 'ems" for containing plants; stakes; wall nails for training vines; light plastic pails for bringing home wild plants from woods and roadsides.

For Indoors (short of hothouse culture): Flats; trays or other bases for pellet growing media and pots; tiny cultivating tools; waterbottle with "mister" attached. Saucers for pots when taking plants indoors.

Also: Twine for laying out rows for vegetables; a stick for making rows; stakes or pieces of wood to attach twine. And an assort-

An open porch at the end of Nancy Cook's garden in New Canaan, Conn., in which she kept those tools most needed. They are all made of stainless steel . . . expensive but indestructible, and therefore a very good bargain.

Never be without a watering can. This is a particularly good-looking French or Italian design.

ment of everyday tools, such as a hammer and screwdriver, nails, pliers, and the like.

Above all, you need hands, arms, a head that can think, and a strong back that can bend. And then, of course, if you aspire to become a real horticulturist, you will start with seeds—those miraculous small things which are the beginning and the end of everything in the garden, as they are in all living matter. Or, you will "propagate" with cuttings, by division, or by layering. All this is more interesting than just buying plants and a great deal less expensive.

Naturally, if you want any kind of showing the very first year, you will have to start with plants from nurseries, and, hopefully, generous friends. But in subsequent years you will be able to greatly increase your enjoyment and the appearance of your garden if you take seeds from your columbines and dianthus, for example, root them in sand or soil, and then, after the first true leaves have appeared, transplant them first into larger pots, or into flats, or, when the danger of frost is over, into cold frames, and finally into the garden.

If you have a hothouse, even if it is just a built-out window frame at the south side of your house, you can winter over many of your potted plants and increase them by cuttings. You can also grow a great deal in the winter under fluorescent light (also see Chapter Nine) in flats, in pots, and in the media which have lately come on the market—complete peat pellets or planting mixes into which everything needed for the growth of seedlings has been compressed. Then, when the first true leaves appear, the plants can be put into larger pots without disturbing the root system, and, finally, into flats until the time comes for outdoor planting.

If you get carried away with the whole idea of propagating as a great many people do, then by all means get yourself a cold frame, or build one with boards for the sides and removable storm sash (by far the least expensive way) for cover. A cold frame can be used the year round: in the winter to protect small or delicate plants which might otherwise die under heavy snow or under the heaving ice; in spring to start seed and seedlings of many annuals, including vegetables, and to "harden off" indoor plants before they are set outside; to start plants like mums and other chrysanthemum for autumn planting.

Cold-frame with flats of seedlings open for ventilation. Although a minimum amount of ventilation—a slight raising of the storm sash—should be done even in cold days in the winter, more and more ventilation and even complete uncovering can be allowed on sunny days as soon as days of frost are passed. Annuals and vegetables can be set out earlier than perennial seedlings.

Professional growers use slats for partial shade all summer long. This picture was taken at the Blue Mount nurseries in Maryland, a much warmer part of the country than New England.

III. FRIENDS AND ENEMIES

Hearing thee flute, who pines and grieves
For vernal smiles and showers?
Thy voice is greener than the leaves,
And fresher than the flowers.
Scorning to wait for tuneful May
When every throat can sing,
Thou floutest Winter with thy lay,
And art thyself the Spring.
ALFRED AUSTIN, DESCRIBING THE THRUSH
IN HIS BOOK, "THE GARDEN THAT I LOVE"

Although some plants reproduce themselves asexually and others bear their sex organs in proximity on the same plant, most of our flowers, herbaceous or otherwise, and the woody plants, are pollinated by outside agents such as bees and birds, butterflies and other insects, winds and men who carry the ripe seeds, usually unwittingly, to other places. Some insects come to flowers for their nectar; but inevitably, if the anthers are ripe, some pollen grains will attach themselves to wings and other parts of an insect's body and later dropped at some point in the insect's flight—hopefully on a receptive pistil.

Thus the marvelous process of pollination and fertilization goes on. As soon as seeds and pods are mature, the mysterious cycle of life is carried on again. Butterflies, bees, and birds are desirable visitors in your garden not only for their beauty and their song, but also for the all-important function they serve in helping to create new plant life.

There are several ways in which we can attract birds and entice them to live closer by. Water in birdbaths, shelter by way of birdhouses, and food, not only sunflower seeds, cakes of seeds and suet, but also berry-bearing shrubs and trees which you can plant,

On a summer evening the pron-
uba moth obtains a mass of
pollen from one of the six stamens and then flies with it to
the central stigma of another
yucca blossom, thus assuring
cross-pollination. Then she lays
her eggs in the ovary, which is
seen there inside the circle of six
stamens. (Ross Hutchins)

A black-capped chickadee takes
its meal from a glass tube with
metal openings. A mixture of
seeds is inside. This feeder hangs
in front of a kitchen window and
gives its owner much pleasure
while she is cooking.

such as wild cherries, bush honeysuckles, wild grapes, dogwood, roses, viburnums, ashes, or holly. All will attract bluebirds, thrushes, chickadees, wrens and woodpeckers, to mention just a few. But there are other birds which can become a nuisance in devouring the berries we plant for our own delight; straw- and blueberries, among others, which must be protected by nets or small mesh wires. Seedbeds too must be safeguarded by netting fastened at some distance above them.

To attract a population of desirable birds, several designs of birdhouses are available in garden stores. You can usually fabricate them more cheaply at home. Always determine which edifice is most desirable for the specific living habits of specific birds. But remember that birds use birdhouses mainly for nesting, not for shelter. It's the squirrels and mice who may want to take up permanent residence.

I discovered that birds are almost sacrosanct to many people, when a close friend who had just bought a house asked the gas company to remove a tank she no longer needed. After a while the men arrived to take the tank—but left without removing it. They did leave a note at the front door, however, which read: "We were here to remove the gas tank but found a nest of swallows at the top. Please call us when the birds have hatched." My friend did—and after another wait, the tank was finally gone.

But don't be too much in a hurry to feed birds during the summer months. Let them eat their natural diet in the form of the many insects which are a nuisance and a danger to vegetation.

Bees are some of the most desirable insects to have around, for as we know, it is their job in life to pollinate plants and to make honey. The nectar of clover, milkweed, foxglove as well as buttonbush, lindens, tulip trees, wisterias and apple trees, among many other plants, provide the substance for honey—that sweet and healthy food especially beloved by small children the world over.

36

There are other beneficial creatures living in and on our land. Among the most important are earthworms, those slinky and somewhat slimy things my young fishermen friends stick at the end of their fishhooks. Worms burrow through the soil and bring tiny bits of decaying matter down from the surface, thereby continually helping to fertilize the subsoil. Sometimes there are so many of them that they loosen the soil too much, in which case you can get rid of them with some exterminant. But I, for one, hate to exterminate anything (with the exception of rodents, beetles, and inchworms) and somehow prefer to let nature take its course.

Although not all birds are beautiful and their song not always reminiscent of Schubert or Brahms, and even harmless bees are not necessarily nature's most excitingly beautiful creations, there *are* insects so delicate and intricate in design and movement that we can thoroughly enjoy their dances in the sun. Dragonflies, fireflies (actually a kind of beetle) and even daddy longlegs are quite harmless to man and plant. And if we could only remember that repulsive caterpillars, which eat some of our leaves and flowers, eventually turn into gorgeous butterflies, that the clumsy, funny-looking larva of the lunar moth is only an intermediate step before great beauty, we wouldn't be quite so unhappy with the plump ugly creatures that waddle along on the ground and up and down our plants.

Planting butterfly bush, a friend of mine told me, will attract many bright-winged visitors; but you may also select specific plants which feed the adult or larval forms of your favorite kind of butterflies and moths. Honeysuckle attracts hummingbirds, and also the weirdly beautiful hawkmoths. To furnish fodder for the hawkmoth caterpillars, you can plant tomatoes. The saddleback caterpillar feeds usually on the underside of the leaves of dahlia, ivy, roses, and many other plants. It looks exotic, but beware of touching it, as it can cause severe skin irritation that lasts for several hours. The adult monarch—an unforgettable

37

tapestry of black and orange—prefers zinnias for sipping; but its young feed exclusively on the milkweed. Violets play host to the fritillary, the underside of whose wings are inlaid with silvery plates. The larvae of the deep brown, almost black, skippers feed on black locust.

Weeping willow feeds the mourning-cloak larva; the adult is a black and brown, gaudy ragamuffin with naturally tattered wings. And just a stand of fairly tall grass will supply you with some of the most attractive Lepidoptera—the miniature hair-streak butterflies whose wingspread is often barely half an inch, and the larger, but still modest, white cabbage butterfly whose wings seem made of gauze.

Parsley and carrots feed the larvae of the black swallowtail, an elegant large butterfly in velvet black, with blue irridescent spots on its tailed hindwings. And wild cherry will assure you the huge, strong tiger swallowtail, a spectacular yellow and black giant. It seems a small sacrifice to give up some of your foliage in order to have these dazzlingly beautiful creatures.

Dragonflies need only a pool of water to keep them happy: they will lay their eggs, breed, and their young will keep your water free of mosquito larvae while the adult dragonflies attack the adult mosquitoes.

And though few have ever seen the katydids whose tick-tick-tick supposedly announces the coming of cold weather and dying gardens, or the tiny peepers which loudly proclaim the coming of spring, somehow the accompaniment of music to the growing and fading world seems to bless all nature's mysterious handi-work. Even the cicadas' metallic howl seems a fitting noise for the heat of the dog days.

But there also *are* many pesty creatures which make the gardener's life miserable all through the growing season, almost as though it had been decreed that there shall be no joy without sorrow. Aphids, often carried by ants, carpet the new growth of trees and bushes. Borers leave gaping, bleeding holes in the bark of flowering trees. Leafhoppers and miners, mealybugs and millipedes, mites, scale insects, snails, slugs, and spittlebugs ruin foliage and defoliate evergreens. Saddlebacks and other caterpillars, flies and midges, wasps and hornets, weevils and whiteflies are a nuisance. Others attack specific plants—the rose chafer and beetle ruin roses; the red-banded leaf rollers roll up leaves and devour them; the garden fleahopper and hornwork attack flowering tobacco (*Nicotiana*).

Most of us have learned in bitter experience what to do about ants and beetles outdoors, and aphids and mealybugs on our indoor plants. (Usually they can be picked off by hand and drowned in kerosene.) These last few years we have battled the cankerworms which have been eating the leaves off our most precious maples, oaks, and other deciduous trees until we had almost no shade and green at all—and the gypsy moth which attacks and kills fruit trees, ornamentals and even evergreens, and the millions of inchworms which fell on our hair and neck and shoulders as soon as we took a step outside.

Sprays and specific poisons help. Although it is best to spray trees *before* the leaves appear, to catch the larvae before they hatch, there are measures which gardeners can take to reduce insect damage on their plants. There are sprays and dusts for roses, for example, and other available pesticides will do much against many bugs but must be used with care because some can be absorbed through the skin. (Do *not* use DDT or any poison the compounds of which do not break down naturally—or you may well eliminate all your songbirds and butterflies too.)

Other sprays and dusts are available in garden stores, and much has been done in horticultural and agricultural stations to produce pest-free seeds and plants. Above all, follow the practices suggested by the U.S. Department of Agriculture in its booklet *Controlling Insects on Flowers:*

❧ Use adequate fertilizers.

❧ Grow only the plants and varieties best suited to your particular soil and climate.

❧ Select vigorous, healthy plants which are free of insects. Avoid plants that are unusually susceptible to insect attack; avoid invalid types that require special care.

❧ Keep your garden or nursery free of weeds and grass. Keep it clean. Bury or otherwise dispose of trash, mature and dead plants and fallen leaves except materials intended for composting.

❧ In dry weather, and in arid regions, water thoroughly once a week instead of sprinkling daily. You can use mulches in summer to conserve soil moisture and keep plants healthy.

❧ If you are establishing a garden in a recently woodland area, treat the soil for lawns and garden flowers with some pesticide.

Too, there also are beneficial insects like the lady beetle which eats aphids and the assassin bug that walks on plants in slow motion looking for injurious bugs which play havoc with our gardens.

And by all means get some of the excellent booklets listed at the end of this book for specific and continued care of your garden.

If you really aspire to become a first-rate gardener, then by all means read the Garden section of *The New York Sunday Times, The Cleveland Plain Dealer,* or other locally available newspapers in which highly expert specialists give you seasonal advice as do specific garden and horticultural publications.

But perhaps, above all, do what Nancy Cook did, whose garden, eight years after her passing, is still the glorious thing it was during her life: keep a looseleaf diary of every plant, vegetable, tree, or shrub that you plant, with specific notes on care, failure, and success.

Nancy Cook's diary still serves a friend who has survived her and who also shares the diary's information with the gardener who worked on the place during Nancy's lifetime. This way, they keep on learning by direct experience—which, in gardening as everywhere else, is by far the best guide and teacher.

Lady beetles are not only attractive but welcome because they eat other harmful insects. (T. Lawrence Starke)

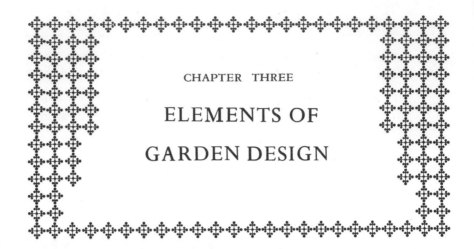

CHAPTER THREE

ELEMENTS OF
GARDEN DESIGN

DESIGNING a garden is like painting on canvas or illuminating a manuscript—perhaps most it is like the planning of a large piece of embroidery, a tapestry, a prayer rug. The designer must know what he wants to "say," what meaning or feeling he wishes to convey, and what response or reaction he desires. Although a garden is not like an advertisement, or a package, or even a living room, the overall concept, the "big idea," the "general theme," must be established. Elements of space and size must stand in the most expressive relationship to one another.

The designer must decide what colors to use (or not to use) so that the palette he creates is in harmony with his idea. He must attempt to reach a *whole,* a completeness, soft and modest, or harsh and drastic, with dramatic contrasts. The total effect must be an expression of himself as interpreted by plants.

And if you are a person who likes to take chances and doesn't mind learning by mishaps and mistakes; has the courage to fail and fail again until success is finally in sight; loves to create, experiment, and build; has the impatience of a child but the tenacity of a scientist; is willing to admit that you cannot create a whole world in bloom the very first year—and perhaps not the second or even the third; is ready to discover that gardening is among the "arts of the possible" with the impossible constantly staring you in the face, time after time, and place after place— then by all means go and lay out your garden. Dig and plant, sweat and swear, and then discover, when the first seed you have planted comes into bloom, that you have wrought a miracle with your own hands.

Before you begin there are many questions: On what kind of land will you start your garden? Is it an even stretch of bare earth, or is it strewn with rocks and promontories, up and down, hill and dale? Is there nothing at all growing on it, or are there already trees and shrubs and woods and meadows? Must you start from scratch, or do you have to deal with a garden that was there before—and how can you rebuild it to suit yourself?

At your command are nature's hundreds and perhaps thousands of variegated riches. Nature has given you sun and shade, and provided soil, rain, and wind. Nature shows an untold number of examples how she does her work. Although your ideas must follow hers and the prevailing conditions on your property you can nevertheless add your own style, adapting as much as necessary, or possible, to the realities at hand.

Then there are still other, artificial considerations. Do you like the view from the house, and, if not, do you wish to plant it out, as the saying goes? How would you prefer to get from one place to another . . . on a piece of lawn, on walks of stone or brick or gravel? And how would you proceed to create the most practical and agreeable pattern for traffic? Do you need a place for your children to play, or do they prefer to roam freely over your land?

Also, what is your style of living? What does your family like and want; will you need some outdoor space for entertaining, or just for using your barbecue? Do you agree with the contemporary concept that "less is more," that simplicity is in better taste than overdoing? Do you wish to make a status symbol of your garden, or do you just want to enjoy and have fun with it?

43

Let us assume that you have just built or bought a house and you are ready to begin filling your landscape with all the plants you need and want. Before pitching in, it's best to sketch out a plan of your grounds—where you can record your hopes and expectations, make notes on existing plants, and try out various solutions. "Artist's rendition" sketches are good too, but it is far easier to distort space when you are working on a picture of how it all should look from the ground.

You could also change trees and shrubs to other places than those indicated, or incorporate any planting that now exists on your property. Just take pieces of translucent paper and colored crayons or pencils and see what you can do to transform your land. I do hope that you have a weeping willow over your brook, shade trees around which you can plant flowers, or enough water to make a lily pool. But if herbs mean nothing to you, scratch herb gardens. If you don't want the labor and expense of building a wall and garden, use fences instead of stones; and if you are not eager to try gardens in one color—not the easiest thing in the world to do even though the results can be most rewarding—substitute mixtures of colors of your own choosing.

Reduce or enlarge the gardens in your plan; change the fences, the walls, the approaches, the type of garage. Determine how you want to reach your garden from various places of your new house. But if there is woodland on your property, and meadows, a brook or pond, or a swamp, don't insist on making them over. Leave them. Learn how to live with—and enrich—the pieces of wilderness which man has left, and enjoy their countless gifts.

The following table explains the various components—textures, types of plants, fences, walks, and so on,—which you will want to consider in your plans.

1. House.
2. Garage with garden, and other tools (sawhorses, cement-mixing buckets, etc.); storage of fertilizers, flowerpots, and so on.

44

3. Driveway.
4. Planting along driveways; evergreen shrubs such as mountain laurel and rhododendron, azaleas, underplanted with evergreen and other decorative ferns.
5. Lawn—this area could be allowed to grow into meadow.
6. Shade trees with underplanting of bulbs (tulips?) in two colors, or any other flowers or ground covers which bloom in spring and with foliage that remains green and pleasant-looking. Trees should have high crown so not to take away sun from plants and lawn.
7. Clipped hedge of two kinds of honeysuckle or two kinds of evergreen shrubs, or privet in some topiary design.
8. A symmetrical flower garden divided by paths. Four sections could be planted identically or with different plants. Tall plants in center, for example, delphinium; front planted with low annuals, or pink and red impatiens.
9. Herb Garden. (See chart in Chapter Seven.)
10. Meadow with wildflowers and native trees—maples, nut trees, and so on.
11. Brooks—planted with marsh marigolds, wild forget-me-nots alongside and a variety of primulas. (See Chapters Five and Eight.)
12. Terrace with potted plants. (See Chapter Nine.)
13. A porte cochère, an old European idea, is eminently practical to get people and things into the house dry.
14. Rock garden with low-growing junipers, and variety of rock and alpine plants. (See Chapter Six.)
15. Lily pond with water lilies and pickerelweed. (See Chapter Eight.)
16. Terrace around lily pond, with potted plants, if you wish. (See Chapter Nine.)
17. Rose garden; try colors, alternating from dark-red to lightest pink.
18. Cutting garden; cosmos, dahlias, anything you like to bring indoors for bouquets.
19. Porch and greenhouse.

20. Walled gardens, each with flowers of one color. For example; blue delphinium in several shades, bachelor's button, veronica, forget-me-nots, annual lobelia, ageratum, and so on. Choose only plants with good foliage. In a red color garden go from deepest red to light pink; in a white garden, from dead white to cream; in a yellow garden from orange to light golden yellow. (See Chapter Five.) Against wall, espalier fruit trees. (See Chapter Four.)

21. Foundation planting with espalier trees and vines against house, ornamental grasses and groundcovers. (See PART IV of this chapter.)

22. Groundcover planting on driveway to afford good view all around. (See PART IV of this chapter.)

23. Small orchard—apple, pear, peach, etc.: (See Chapter Four.)

24. Vines against house and groundcovers; stone terrace that goes on three sides of house and leads into utility gardens.

25. Woodlands with ferns, wildflowers. (See Chapter Eight.) Also native trees. (See Chapters Four and Eight.)

*This "woven" fence will never need paint —
just occasional creosote.*

I. FENCES

The border of a garden marks an important line of demarcation between the inner and outer world. In the early days of small farms, fences were important to keep cattle from grazing on a neighbor's land. Stone walls also served to delineate property lines, or parts of bigger holdings, and to set off areas such as orchards, barnyards, or gardens.

As landowners became more prosperous, particularly in the Victorian era, the elegant and fancy iron fences appeared, especially in the South. They are still copied today, and cost a great deal of money.

Perhaps the most prevalent regular fence design of all was the picket fence, which became important in the small villages and towns as a status symbol of the owner's stand in the community or of his own skill and taste.

Even today a do-it-yourselfer can have much fun designing and building his own fence, picket or otherwise, which is not so difficult if he observes a few basic principles. First, the posts must be set down deeply enough into the ground so as not to heave out when frost comes in winter. They may also be set in cement. Posts should be painted with creosote, or any other wood preservative to prevent rotting. Then the crosspieces and pickets are added (some of these are available in lumberyards).

Another version (I built a fence in front of my house, but did away with digging holes): I simply bought six foot lengths of iron pipe, hammered them into the ground, and boxed them in with one by three's—a fairly good trick for lazy or busy people.

So long as you have a framework for a fence, the interior can be "filled in" with practically anything: horizontal slats, wire or nylon washline, in a diamond pattern, a combination of wooden slats and rope tied loosely around the lower part of a post top, or

47

rope only. There are hundreds of ways to build this kind of fence; others are commercially available, but are not nearly as much fun to put up as the one you have designed and built yourself. Entirely different possibilities: use of cement or cinder block which can be decorated with flowerpots; or, somewhat on the order of the prehistoric megalithic buildings but not nearly so difficult, flagstones, one by three or four feet and one inch or one and one half inches thick, set vertically in cement into the ground, make extremely unusual and interesting effects.

Redwood slats may be woven into interesting and intricate patterns as shown in the nineteenth-century fences earlier illustrated, but similar fences are available here in lumberyards. And round wooden spheres for the top of fence posts are also available in lumberyards. The "Northern wide cedar pickets, machine-molded" and "Hand-peeled cedar pickets" really look as though the owners were trying to "fence you out" except when used with plants at the edge of a pool for privacy in swimming or sunbathing. On the other hand, few fences are more charming and welcoming than rails on which climbing roses grow, or a clipped hedge of evergreen mixed with viburnum, making it a pleasure to just go by.

II. WALKS AND WALLS

Just as contemporary houses are characterized by what is in the language of architecture called "a good traffic pattern," so a garden that is not only beautiful but also makes sense for the owner needs carefully planned ways of getting from one part of it to another, and, of course, from the house into the various parts of the garden.

Old or new bricks are one of the most desirable materials, and

To show what amazing imagination went into the building of fences in earlier times, reproduced here are illustrations from an encyclopedia published in the late eighteenth or early nineteenth century.

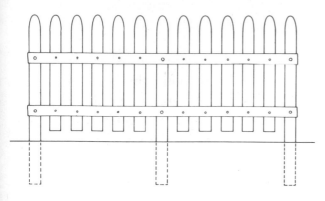

The simple picket-fence design, not at all difficult to make. The drawing is based on a six-foot section, but could, of course, be designed in other convenient units. (Lisa Federico)

A charming and elegant iron fence, painted white, is a good example of how the entrance or the demarcation of a property can be made pleasant and inviting. Although a fence can be a barrier, it can also serve as a welcoming decoration. (T. Lawrence Starke)

Small (one or one-and-a-half-foot square) flagstones make excellent stepping stones among plants. When you need them, they also make a fine substitute for a missing plant.

Pebbles make a good walk too, and interesting patterns can be created with them—as in this old English garden spot where they were cleverly combined with flagstones.

The use of very small white or black pebbles, to fill the spaces between stones is another way to make a walk interesting. Marble chips also work well.

If you have a carefully trimmed lawn, square flagstones make an elegant walk.

were used very early in architectural history. And just last year, the owners of an old very elegant house laid a matching walk around it made of mellow old brick. Nor is brick difficult to work with. The simplest way is to lay it atop sand and add more sand between the brick. It is, of course, also possible to use cement under and between bricks; but the underlayer should go down to frost level—which, in our northeast and other parts of the country with cold winters, is roughly 3 feet.

The combination of brick and large black pebbles is so good-looking that it could be used between flower gardens, different types of plantings, or even along the edges of walks or driveways.

Pebbles or small round stones are particularly useful on an incline when held with logs. The most popular material for walks today are flagstones, available in regular and irregular sizes and thickness from one to two inches. The thicker they are, the less they tend to break; but cost is usually a function of thickness. Flagstones too are best laid in sand and not with cement between them so that winter heaving is avoided.

To walks uphill, even sizes of flagstones separated by large pebbles will help; and so will uneven sizes, laid in larger stones, get you around the house. My favorite walk of all is one in a London townhouse garden, most precisely laid between areas of lawn with a variety of sizes of regular flagstones.

Irregular flagstone—which is quite a bit less expensive than regular square and oblong—can also make interesting surfaces to walk or sit on. They may lead to a small greenhouse at the side of the main building, or cover a large area with coarse sand between them. Even quarry stone, with its most even surface up, makes a good walk. And if you should be the lucky owner of an old millstone, or can find one in an antique shop, you can create still another interesting effect. But the latest fashion is round flagstone or slate which looks elegant indeed when laid on red gravel.

Walls, too, either on the outside or inside of a garden can help give full rein to a gardener's imagination. The texture of stone with the texture of green or the color of flowering plants can create a wide range of stunning effects. This is particularly apparent in the English countryside where a great many cottage gardens are enclosed by high stone walls inset with all sorts of growing things. High or low, old or new, any dry wall has cracks and fissures which can be filled with soil and then planted with many kinds of small specimens. Often, if you are lucky, it looks as though a wall had planted itself. Moss will appear; a fern, a piece of ground cover which you planted quite some time ago in quite a different place.

On the inside of a high wall, its weathered stone telling of its great age, I saw a planting of iris which could be easily and effectively done against any other kind of wall, high or low, over here. And if some earlier builder left you an outcropping of rock, connect it with a beautifully curved stone wall and have great fun with all sorts of planting at the base.

III. PATIOS AND TERRACES

A patio is a Spanish idea, probably of Moorish origin which today is a byword of architectural language. It refers to a space totally or partially enclosed by a house, and is open to the sky. Thanks to our unfortunate habit of squeezing the life out of a good idea the term "patio" gets mixed up with the word "terrace," even though historically and architecturally they embody different concepts.

Terraces are places for outdoor living. As we know, terraces were built thousands of years ago to add outdoor living to castles, mansions, and houses. Usually they are raised areas from which one can see the garden. They are usually furnished with outdoor furniture of which there are many kinds—metal, wood, rattan, all covered with water resistant or repellent fabrics or mats. One terrace I've seen is furnished with accents of red, which is the owner's favorite color. A large iron pot holds red salvia which in combination with the interestingly laid flagstone, and the

Brick need not be laid down in only one pattern; here the builder has created "paths" within a larger terrace.

In many Japanese gardens, slices of a tree trunk are set into the ground as stepping stones.

Hexagonal flagstones in a London park. The shape is repeated in containers made of cement. Not the easiest thing in the world, but quite feasible for someone who knows how to build forms for cement (inexpensive lumber will do).

white and red metal furniture looks very grand. But in reality it is a pleasant and quite simple place to sit or eat, since it is close to the kitchen and meals are easily served.

All sorts of other kinds of plantings are possible on terraces. I have removed one of the larger flagstones on one side of my small terrace and planted into it a lavender Hosta (plantain lily). The leaves look pleasant against the grayness of the stone and give me color when much else has already faded and the autumn flowers have not yet begun to bloom.

Terraces are fine for potted plants and borders. I have admired a mixture of Johnny-jump-ups and pinks bordering a terrace made of flat granite rock which Providence had conveniently placed in the path of the owners. And part of a tarred driveway in New England serves as a playground for small children; it could be called a miniature terrace, for it is richly bordered with pinks held back by a gray log.

A grass terrace (for a change) has an elevated rail of cement

This contemporary patio in California features low-growing rhododendrons and a potted chrysanthemum in a pleasant round container. Note use of high, solid fence for privacy. (T. Lawrence Starke)

blocks capped by flagstones and planted inside between grass and the rail. Another made of a combination of bricks and flagstones is edged with potted plants against the house and, further back, a bed of plants.

IV. LAWNS AND GROUNDCOVERS

A lawn can be the bane of a gardener—or his greatest pride. Few parts of a garden seem to evoke so much conversation, care, and curses. Indeed there is little more restful and pleasant than a well-manicured, closely cropped, weed-free lawn, or more distressing, inelegant, or downright ugly than a lawn, full of crabgrass and brown or bare spots. On a summer evening there are few sounds more pleasant than the whirring of a lawn mower (from someone else's garden). And yet, lawns are worth having; they cover a good deal of ground which could not be covered by everyday garden shrubbery or trees; they provide clean, open space for children to play; they smell sweet and are cool and restful to the eye.

If you *must* have a lawn, then by all means make or maintain one. Whether it will be easy depends on the part of the country in which you live. If your home was built where heavy forests or prairies once stood, leaving deep, rich layers of topsoil, you may have a restful expanse of lovely green areas all around your house. If, on the other hand, you live in any of the rocky parts of the country where the topsoil has leached away, or the subsoil is full of stone, or most of your property is actually on top of bedrock—I wish you luck.

Over the years you will spend thousands of dollars to keep your green space really green, and probably also thousands of man-hours (or woman-hours) of labor which could more profitably be devoted to the care of your trees, shrubs, and flowering plants.

If you *are* hipped on a lawn, this is what you can do: Clear

56

the desired area of all old weeds, grass, plants, rock, and stone. Get topsoil to cover. Rake. Add peat moss, work it in to about four inches, mix thoroughly with topsoil and rake until soil is even and fine.

The kind of seed you sow will have a great deal to do with your having a good lawn or not. Since the best seed mixtures vary with locality, consult with your local farm or garden store. The packages will also tell you how much seed you need for a given area. (I assume that you will measure it before you begin.) Sow grass seed either by hand or seeder (available in farm stores for rent) in *two* opposite directions. Thus the chances are better for an even lawn. Water carefully, gently, and thoroughly—then wait.

Once the grass is grown, cut frequently to a height of about two inches. This varies with location and kind of grass seed you have used. The proper way of mowing a lawn is in two directions. An edger is a good thing to have if you want to prevent grass from invading your flowerbeds. Leave cut grass on the lawn, unless you hate the look of it. Mow once a week in summer, and stop in October or so, again depending on where you live. If the grass gets quite high—which it may—do what a friend of mine does: instead of mowing, he keeps on raking his lawn in one direction which, as he says, looks like well-combed hair.

Weed if you hate dandelion and crabgrass. You can use a weedkiller if necessary. But for my money, some plants which others consider weeds are charming: buttercups and daisies, for example.

Chances are that you might have to renew parts of your lawn here and there each autumn, and sometimes in spring. But to make a lawn, autumn is the best time, say late September. The roots will then have a chance to establish themselves. In addition, you won't have to look at bare earth in spring. Just remember, a lawn requires constant care and attention.

57

In any case, don't overdo it when you design your garden. No matter how much you love the velvety green, it can take too much of your time. A lawn does not have to cover a large area but can provide an interlude between shapes, forms, and building materials. If bordered by a closely cropped boxwood hedge, and allowed to grow a bit taller than usual, which will give it resiliency and body, a small piece of lawn can be a happy and beautiful corner of your garden. If there is a great deal of bare ground around your house, you can cover much of it with flagstones, brick, or even gravel.

I have had only three comparatively small patches of lawn around my house at the beginning, but I found myself expanding the flagstone walks around it until the day finally came when I ripped out all the grass, releveled the ground, and covered everything with flagstones. Now I am surrounded by nothing but lovely tones of gray bordered by a few small flowerbeds, foundation plantings against the walls of my house, and pieces of green gardens and ferns. But even though all this happened at least fifteen years ago, I still battle tufts of the old grass which insists on coming up in the spaces between the stones.

I also keep on planting some of the several kinds of thyme which grow low and smell sweetly wherever there is room between the stones. And since the area in which I live has moist, rich woodland soil, tufts of moss keep growing in the cracks and spaces which give me small but eminently satisfactory patches of a deep and lovely green.

Another way to avoid grass and still have a good deal of restful green around you is to plant groundcovers wherever there is empty space, and also under trees where there is a good deal of shade, which does not help lawn anyway. Ajuga, myrtle, euonymus, ivy, and several sedums, and the beautiful wild ginger, bearberry and partridge berry will give you variegated masses of leaves, some all year round, and most of them with tiny flowers in spring and colorful berries in autumn—which is more than we can say about grass.

58

But lawn or flowers, trees or shrubs, walks or meadows, every garden still has problem spots. Always there are bare places in which nothing will grow, and are hard on the eyes and particularly on a gardener's self-esteem. This is again where the groundcovers come in—small, low-growing plants, most of which have tiny flowers in the summer and small leaves in the most pleasant shades of green. Also most of them will grow and spread, and in a year or two there are enough to transplant and cover more places.

A great many people favor pachysandra which in a short time will make a dense cover either under evergreen shrubs and trees, or in the open, and has white flowers in late spring. In the fall, dead leaves from trees fall in among pachysandra's six-inch stalks and quietly disappear. Weeds come out second best in any competition, too.

Other groundcovers include snow-in-summer (*Cerastium tomentosum*) which has small woolly leaves and will grow even in sand. Another popular "subshrub," as some of these plants are called is santolina, an evergreen plant that should be cut into shape. One variety is called lavender cotton. Ajuga will spread and spread and come up in the most unexpected places—flagstones and fieldstones, in hot sun and cool shade, and quite simply naturalizes itself wherever it likes. Bearberry (*Arctostaphylos uva-ursi*) is a wild groundcover which I have found on Cape Cod and elsewhere in New England. It has tiny white blossoms in spring, and is easily transplanted. And so is partridge berry (mitchella repeus) which grows in our woods.

There is also myrtle (*Vinca minor*) with the lovely blue flowers in spring and, of course, Ivy, which grows up the side of your house and clings. Another popular groundcover which spreads rapidly and fills in all sorts of spaces is wintercreeper (*Euonymus radicans*) which is evergreen and does well in sun or shade.

And then there are the sedums—five hundred species of them, and they make one of the best extralow groundcovers of all.

They bloom prettily in white, pink, yellow, or purple, with tiny evergreen leaves, and one would have to really have the blackest of thumbs to kill them. One variety in my garden is *Sedum acre* or wall pepper, also called mossy stonecrop, golden Moss, gold dust, or love-entangle.

V. BEDS, BORDERS, AND FOUNDATION PLANTING

After you have decided where and how you want your fences, walks, terraces, lawns, and groundcovers you should see whether there is still something missing. A garden is not determined by wood, stone, brick, or even grass; but by its trees and flowers and other plants which give color, form, and the essential part of garden design. If your builders have left you enough trees to start with—as they will, if you insist on it—and place your house so that not everything in the path of trucks and other heavy equipment has been mowed down; and if everything you need for living has been planned or built, then it is time to think of flowers to grace the spaces around your house. They will be in beds and borders, except for that part of the wilderness (woodlands or meadows) which has remained untouched.

Like so many other factors of garden design, the idea of putting plants inside a form or a frame is very old. But how else could a gardener take care of a mass of flowers; how else could they decorate an expanse of land? There have been flowerbeds in all shapes and manner, complicated or simple, easy to take care of or almost impossible without the help of professionals, since the earliest days of gardening.

But easy maintenance is certainly not the only consideration in making flowerbeds. Their location, that is, whether in sun or shade, semishade or "filtered light," the predominant direction of the wind, the contour of the land, the available soil (natural or enriched by the gardener himself); the view from the house, the accessibility and decorative value of flowers in one spot or another, and even the desire to share the beauty of one's plants and one's labors . . . all these considerations will play an important and sometimes an essential part in the design of one's flowerbeds.

The shape of a flowerbed is, of course, an entirely individual decision. Should it be square, oblong, straight, curved, or of a free-flowing shape that is more in keeping with contemporary design than the tightly formed and rigidly formal beds of earlier eras?

Many people believe that the simplest way to have beds of flowers is to plant annuals which bloom all summer and take less knowing or care than do perennials. Too, they can easily be raised from seed indoors and in cold frames and then planted outdoors when the time comes. One such example is a pansy garden on the French Riviera. Although I do not advocate such grandeur for the type of gardens discussed here, the idea of a square bed with a low-clipped (perennial) boxwood hedge is certainly practical and good-looking. In front of an outcropping of rock, a bed can be in the shape of a quartermoon.

But there is no law that a flowerbed needs to have any specific shape at all. A shrub geranium, planted between small rocks, makes as good-looking a bed as any we have seen.

These clean, square lines are softened by a small bed of perennial shrubs underplanted with marigolds.

If for any reason, decorative or practical, there are two low parallel walks of stone or cement on your property then make a bed of lantana, a plant not too hardy in our northeast but which can, however, be grown in pots indoors and then set out for the summer. It has profuse blooms and a pleasant variety of colors. But beds are not only those which are made of flowers. Have you ever seen beds of azaleas, in single or any of their different possible colors?

In contrast to beds, borders have been traditionally planted against (so as to soften) a background—a fence, a wall, or even a stand of shrubs and trees. The ubiquitous "perennial border," the pride and joy of "real" gardeners, has its probable origin in England where no respectable garden is without one. It has become another form of gardening art. The multitude of plants is grown so that something is in flower all season long, stands in direct relation to the gardener's skill. A border can be straight or curved, serpentine or round—if planted against an old well, for example, but in all instances it must be *full*. Very low borders can be made of violets. The leaves grow mightily all summer long and make a restful accent. I have done this very same thing with common blue and wild white violets, and where they grow thick and plump there needs to be very little weeding.

Very few house foundations are things of great interest or beauty, and there are many ways of covering them up. Usually there is a planting of evergreen shrubs, and sometimes a border in front of the shrubs. Here are a few unusual ways:

A great big healthy *Yucca* (or Adam's needle from the American Southwest) now well adapted to our northeastern climate, guards the door of a studio building I've seen. A contemporary designer who bought an old house and redesigned it placed cone-shaped evergreens into gravel and held in place by granite curbstones coming up from a flagstone walk leading into the house. Once more, no more weeding!

A house in California has a sunken bed as foundation planting at the base of the building, but the plants reach up the same level as the walk leading inside—an excellent example of contemporary planning in which the outside and inside flow together.

The foundations of another house are greatly enhanced in spring with plantings of naturalized narcissi with an "underplanting" of primulas against a background of evergreens. Naturalizing spring flowers is a wonderful idea, for the plants increase year after year and reward the gardener after the very first effort one has made.

One of the most charming sights I have ever encountered was a lawn with a mass of naturalized crocus in several colors. Before spring really arrives, and the grass needs endless cutting, a carpet of color is at your feet to cheer passers by and invite friends and neighbors to share the glory.

VI. COLOR, TEXTURE, AND ART IN THE GARDEN

The combinations of color in a garden can make it either into a thing of joy, or an indifferent, uncreative piece of land which shows little taste or imagination. It may be silly to say, "This flower is ugly, and I don't like it," because the word "ugly" tells more about a gardener and how he uses a plant than it

A delightful combination of garden elements: flagstone, grass, low borders, trees, fences, garden furniture, and ironwork all form a distinctive whole.

tells about any tree, shrub, herb, or flower. But is certainly is true that everyone has a favorite among plants. It may be a chemical attraction, or the harmony of same or of opposites; but all this is subtle, and we are rarely conscious of it. At any rate, one can learn a great deal about others when visiting and studying their gardens. And, too, tastes change with age and circumstances, with our state of health of mind and body. But it has never failed to enchant me when a gardener planted one single solitary yellow tulip in a garden that was otherwise all blue with forget-me-nots and columbine, or deep purple pansies among forget-me-nots, or as the British do, planted yellow and orange wallflowers in the same bed; or when spring spurge (*Euphorbia*) has mixed with *Ajuga,* bright yellow and deeply blue; or when someone has been clever enough to plant a violet clematis next to a yellow shutter.

Plant a bed of alyssum—with the multicolored leaves of *Coleus,* both of which may be treated as annuals. The alyssum is sown outdoors or bought in pots and planted; *Coleus* grows well in hothouses from seed and is transplanted outdoors (and then often abandoned and replaced the following year).

Experiment! Although a light-blue delphinium may turn out to be almost purple, these are among the chances you take and the surprises that are in store for you.

Textures, like colors, can make a garden either interesting or drab. Almost each flowering plant has leaves of a different design and "feel"; every fern in the woods of the wildflower or green garden, a different kind of bravura, and charisma. You can plant trees in rows so that shadows march throughout the day. As the sun plays among the plants, creating spots of shadow; or as a shady place allows the subtle differences between plants to appear, the pure pleasures of seeing and feeling them will have made all the hard labor a thousand times worthwhile. Take, for example, the shiny heads of garlic against the background of gravel in which they are planted, or iris seen behind a rock wall. They sing.

In Greek and Roman gardens, in the palatial gardens of the Italian Renaissance, the splendor of the vast parterres of the kings of France, among the baroque grandeur of the gardens around Austrian palaces—almost wherever a culture has reached its height, the landscape was adorned with works of art . . . perhaps to rest the eyes from the abundance of nature; perhaps because it seemed right and fitting to combine the arts of nature with the arts of men. . . .

Sculpture in stone or metal, or even in some of the new weatherproofed woods and plastics, may be fitted into almost any kind of garden. A Greek statue, next to a baroque lamp post and an early American fire bucket filled with hens and chickens greets the visitor to one large terrace. A contemporary sculptor has set one of his statues into a large bed of impatiens, and a loving husband the metal portrait of his wife among chrysanthemum.

The animal kingdom too may be represented in a garden. An ancient but sprightly cast-iron dog watches the entrance to his master's terrace; early American weathervanes on high poles can decorate the top of another garden wall. Try a sundial to tell time, or a delicately fashioned stone stand holding an iron flowerpot in the same shape (an idea I saw on the lawn of a London town house).

A clever young friend of mine made a copper fountain for his mother's garden. It looks like a beautiful exotic flower.

Outdoor garden furniture, to be really appealing, should be permanent—not simply a plastic deck chair, but a sturdy bench or table that can take weatherbeating and eventually grow to become a part of the landscape—at the very best it should resemble the nearby plantings in texture or color.

65

A piece of decoration from a Victorian house in New York now stands in front of a large rock in the middle of a meadow.

A clever gardener can make decorative designs with trained vines.

An old Korean votary set into a bed of ferns to guard the entrance to the house.

Two views, and two different positionings of a small Mexican statuette, showing how light and surrounding plants change the character of garden sculpture.

A contemporary statue (by Zoltan Medvecky) echoes the texture of the foliage behind it.

Probably of Mediterranean origin, a strawberry jar is only rarely planted with strawberries —more often with trailing plants. But it can also stand alone on a path or in a flowerbed, a striking shape in itself.

From France have come most of the innumerable designs of cast-iron garden decorations and furniture.

Chairs and benches made of oak will withstand many years and changes of the weather, as will those of board held in cement.

These picnic tables with matching benches were made for me by two young friends. The legs are frames made of one by four inch boards screwed into the underside of tables and benches, attached also with corner irons to prevent wobble, and painted to prevent rust.

Cast-iron benches which fit around large trees, for instance, add a highly decorative motif to a woodland garden. They are cast in two pieces, and easily fitted together. Besides acting as sculpture, these pieces allow you and your guests to slow down, sit, and meditate long enough to enjoy a particular vista or an especially alluring arrangement of plants.

As the poet Thomas E. Browne (1830–1897) so rightly said:

> A *Garden is a lovesome thing, God wot!*
> *Rose plot,*
> *Fringed pool*
> *Of peace; and yet the fool*
> *Contends that God is not—*
> *Not God! in gardens! when the eve is cool!*
> *Nay, but I have a sign:*
> *'This very sure God walks in mine.'*

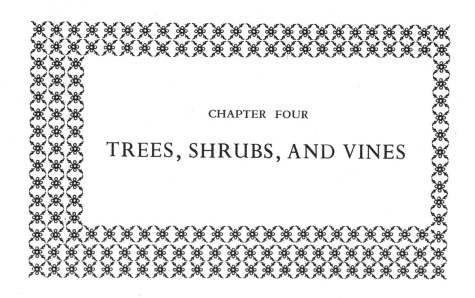

CHAPTER FOUR

TREES, SHRUBS, AND VINES

I love thee when thy swelling buds appear,
And one by one their tender leaves unfold,
As if they knew that warmer suns were near,
Nor longer sought to hide from winter's cold;
And then with darker growth thy leaves are seen
To veil from view the early robin's nest;
I love to lie beneath thy waving screen,
With limbs by summer's heat and toil oppress'd;
And when the autumn winds have stripped thee bare,
And round thee lies the smooth, untrodden snow,
When naught is thine that made thee once so fair,
I love to watch thy shadowy form below
And through thy leafless arms to look above
On stars that brighter beam when most we need their love.

"THE TREE," JONES VERY (1813–1880)

IN THE third century B.C., Celacilius Status wrote: "He plants trees to benefit another generation."

Trees are not the oldest plants on Earth, for mosses, ferns, and horsetails preceeded them in the long way to creating a blooming world. Nevertheless, they are three hundred million years old. The majestic grandeur of the forest inspired early man with fear, but also gave protection; it created shelter and food; and it aroused awe and worship.

Thus in the earliest tales and legends of reverence for the God-head, trees stand supreme. They not only meant strength, but also survival. To early man, a tree that had attained its height generations before and which would continue to grow long after his passing meant eternity. Trees were sacred; signs of a supreme power, unknowable knowledge, life itself. And if a tree that shed its color at one time of the year regained it in another was a wondrous thing to behold, how much more miraculous was another that never shed its leaves!

Tammuz in Mesopotamia, Osiris in Egypt, and Adonis in

Iranian metal plaque (eighth century B.C.) showing stylized tree with what appears to be buds or cones. (The Metropolitan Museum of Art)

Greece were all gods who vanished in autumn to return again in spring with the sun and the new leaves. Countless sacrifices and prayers were made to assure their return.

One of the earliest legends of Sumer tells of the man Sukallitida who had tried hard to plant a garden but had failed again and again. He looked once more at the heavens and studied their portents and the divine laws. When he had new learning he planted a tree in the garden, a tree whose shade lasted all day. Ever after that the garden blossomed with green. When Poseidon and Athena competed to decide who was the more important god, Poseidon invented the horse. But Athena smote the Earth and up came the olive tree, which was destined to bring riches and fame to the mainland and islands of Greece.

Perhaps even more significantly, in the countries of the Germanic North, sacred woods were kept into which people went to ask for favors from the god Thor. It was believed that trees were the homes of spirits who must not be hurt or sinned against. People who hurt trees were severely punished; if a tree had to be felled, it was asked for forgiveness. To be cured, an ill person was dragged through a hollow tree.

Today, by contrast, we have thriving towns and villages in the east, great industries, marvelous turnpikes, but few if any great forests remain. When heavy rains come, more of the soil washes away. Thus man's needs for arable land can be filled less and less, but his greed remains.

Today when it is late for the preserving of the forests, we talk about conservation. But in a small town like the one in which I live, the water table is sinking. New people move in, and ever more houses replace our trees. Several towns have tried to pass laws that would prevent developers from cutting down the remaining woodlands and forbid the destruction of trees of a certain diameter. But these laws are not being passed, and the bulldozers have no eyes. Thus only the rich can save their woods.

When you build or buy a small house on a small parcel of land, you must often *buy* trees and start all over. What has happened to man's worship of the tree?

In the year 1781, Thomas Jefferson in his notes on the State of Virginia, in answer to questions by a member of the French Legation, wrote: "A complete catalogue of the trees, plants, fruits, etc., is probably not desired. I will sketch out those which would principally attract notice as being 1. Medicinal, 2. Esculent, 3. Ornamental, or 4. Useful for fabrication."

For our purposes, we need only consider the "Esculent," or edible (i.e., peach, cherry, pear, apple, raspberry) and ornamental categories. But perhaps the word "ornamental" is misleading. Nowadays it usually refers to a tree whose foliage or flowers are a delight, but whose shape or habits may make it far less welcome.

Strictly speaking, trees are the architectural elements of garden design. Look at any landscape painting of any century and see how the trees are used to make large, bold, definitive statements. Lacy foliage of locusts becomes a backdrop; the white trunks of birches appear as a colonnade; a large, gnarled, age-heavy oak becomes a centerpiece, a focus for attention.

Lucky indeed is the gardener who has such aged, established specimens already on his land. Obviously decades, or even centuries, of growth produce overall effects that cannot be duplicated in a few months' or even a few years' time. Thus before you plant new trees it is wise to consider whether you are planting for "future generations" or for yourself, here and now.

A friend of mine tells with amusement about his own tortoise-and-the-hare experience with two species of trees with different growth habits. He had long admired a weeping beech on a neighbor's property—a great fountain of thick, deep green foliage that shot up at least thirty feet and "wept" down again. In winter, the leaves fell to reveal whorls and twists that seemed to

mirror the meanderings of candle wax. You can imagine my
friend's enchantment to discover a small, inexpensive weeping
beech for sale at a nearby nursery. He bought it, immediately
planted it, and mulched the roots over as one must do with
beeches to keep the roots cool. And he waited.

But beeches, even the run-of-the-mill American beech of our
native forests, do not take kindly to transplanting. This weeping
breed languished, eagerly weeping down, but not going *up*. Dis-
gusted, my friend took the branches which trailed on the ground
and wired them up again on thin bamboo poles.

Meanwhile he sought out faster-growing trees. He had long
been interested in the graceful columnar shape of the Lombardy
poplars depicted in Monet's impressionist landscapes, and so
he readily sent away for Lombardies, by mail, from a nursery
offering twenty-five trees for less than two dollars. No sluggards,

Black willow

these trees, they quickly shot up two feet the first year he planted them; and they increased an awesome ten feet the year after that. Their trunks thickened, their foliage fluttered in even the slightest breeze, their roots made a pleasant crisscrossing pattern along the top of the soil.

And then the kitchen sink backed up. A poplar root had entered through a crack in the pipe, and expanded into a mane of rootlets eight feet long. My friend's lawn began sprouting with thousands of baby poplars as the far-reaching roots of the parent trees hit "pay dirt" and decided to spread. And lastly one of the poplars, which had grown not wisely but too well, gave way in an autumn gale and toppled over—taking all the telephone wires with it as it fell. The roots, in their frantic, single-minded search for water, had never really managed to provide adequate support for the tree!

My friend has since dispensed with his poplars; the adults have fallen under the axe, and their water sprouts have all been pulled up one by one. But his beech tree grows on, getting a little better—but always better—each year. "It took a bit of imagination," he confessed, "but now I can begin to see how it's going to look ten or twenty years from now. And watching it get there, appreciating the ground it's already covered, is as satisfying in its own way as that poplar grove in its heyday. But as a compromise between the temporal and the eternal, I'm going ahead and planting a flowering crab apple right in front of the beech as you look out the window. It'll grow pretty fast, and when the beech gets really respectable we can always cut the crab down."

This is one idea I'd recommend to anyone who prefers to plant for long-term grandeur *and* enjoy the quick fruits of his labors. Remember, a small tree planted under a larger one is likely to become stunted and unsightly; but if two trees are planted *together,* they will go upward and develop straight long trunks. If you have a yen for Japanese maples, with exotic foliage and delicate bark that make them such ideal ornamentals, but which have growth habits that are inscrutably slow, it makes sense to plant them with albizzias, American red maples, even poplars.

These trees will swiftly outgrow the Japanese maples, but their foliage is not dense enough to keep the Japanese maples from developing underneath them. When the Japanese maples are sizable enough, cut down the competing plants, and your maples will surge upward—but atop slender, graceful trunks that they would not have if you had allowed them to develop in the open.

Again, it is always much easier to have nature on your side, to make "the nature of the beast" agree with your long- or short-range plans. And for this reason, especially because a tree is always a more or less permanent investment, it is necessary that you decide what overall *effect* you want from your trees before you actually begin planting. Do you want flowers, fruit, but not necessarily a large ungainly tree? Miniature apples, cherries, and pears will offer decoration and "esculent" fruit without ruining the view. It isn't hard to reproduce the feeling of natural vistas in your own backyard. Cut off the branches of trees that lie below the horizon on your lines of sight, and plant many small trees together so that they grow up rather than out.

If you want privacy, however, choose an evergreen for your hedge, a tree or shrub that won't drop its leaves or needles in the fall and leave you exposed all winter. If you can say what you want the tree or shrub to *do,* your nurseryman or botanical friends can almost always offer several good suggestions. This really makes much better sense than falling in love with a small blue spruce and planting it right in front of your porch where it will overspread the porch itself and seem out of place for most of its natural life.

Bark of yellow birch, black willow, gingko, black birch.

On the other hand, you can certainly orchestrate the trees of
your garden so that they contrast or match with one another.
For example, the rough back of pines against the smooth bark
of beeches or the delicate sprays of locust against the forthright
palmate leaves of sycamore. Every tree has a few subtle aspects

78

that you should recognize if you expect your trees to be permanent guests.

We cannot usually see the roots of our trees, unless they have become exposed by erosion and sometimes by forceful growth. We *can* see the bark of trees, each different from another, and even different on trees of the same species. Each forms a different pattern of texture and color as it protects the inner growing and expanding core of the tree.

Trees also have enemies that leave their "handwriting" on the bark: Nuthatches leave a fine tracery in the bark which is fascinating to look at but does not do the tree any good, and woodpeckers are particularly forward on the bark of a weakening birch. And as soon as a tree dies, fungi will appear on the bark and make interesting patterns which are, however, no more and no less than the writing on a gravestone. By this time the most you can do is cut the tree down—or use it as a trellis for some quick-growing vine such as wisteria, which may support the tree and engulf it before it rots away.

Then there are the beautiful leaves, each different in shape and color and in the tracery of its veins: Fig (among the oldest pieces of clothing known, and indigenous to the Near East), maple, sassafras (which seems to be the only tree that sports different shapes of leaves on its branches); oak, the mighty one, as grand now as it was when it was revered in the earliest days of the European North; and the curiously shaped leaf of the ginkgo tree, one of the oldest species known. Apple trees also have beautifully textured leaves; and my favorite tree of all, the tulip tree (Jefferson called it white poplar) has the most interestingly shaped leaves of all.

And then the blossoms! As though they were embroidered in the air, shimmering dots of color which make you feel grateful you are alive!

Mark how the green-growing bud is unfolded when
springtide approaches,
Leaf by leaf is developed, and, warmed by the radiant
sunshine,
Blushes with purple and gold, till at last a perfect blossom
Opens it's odorous chalice, and rocks with its crown in
the breezes.

"GROWTH," HENRY WADSWORTH LONGFELLOW
(1807–1882)

First, when the shad are beginning to run in the rivers, appears the shadbush (*Amelanchier*) snowcapped with white blossoms, and transplantable when small! Then soon the dogwood (*Cornus*) white or pink, arching over your head and blinding in its rich beauty. (My white dogwood was here when I came, so I literally planted a corner of my house under it. And I leave it alone, except for the suckers which take away some of the strength of the tree. Some of the branches have grown so low that I now have to bend my head way down to go under them. Perhaps I was just lucky, but I can't help feeling that more of our beautiful and ancient trees could be saved if more people had the courage to build their houses around the trees on their land instead of *over* the dead roots. Dogwoods are not too difficult to transplant; but get them small, and be sure they have good rich earth under their new roots. Water them plenty when first they grow. After a while you can leave them alone.)

Then come the cherry blossoms (*Prunus* of the rose family) which soon after they have come will shed their petals like a storm of snowflakes. But these will fast fade into the ground. Nor have I ever had one single cherry from my large tree, since the birds always get there first. And what a gaudy and lovable sight the apple blossoms make! But perhaps the most spectacular bud of all (and few people seem to ever know that it *is* a bud) is that of the hickory (*Carya*) tree as it slowly unfolds its pink splendor and then retreats to begin to form the fruit. Then, in the middle of spring, there is the sourwood, (*Oxydendrum arboreum*) with red leaves and white blossoms. Friends of mine have planted one of these in the middle of a patch of lawn circled by their driveway. Their house is on a hilltop, and as you approach it you see this tree glimmering through the nearby evergreens and maples. And then, of course, there are the horse chestnuts, with white candles of fragrance on their long limbs.

Earlier still are the magnolias, about fifty species in all, known to be among the very first blooming trees ever to evolve. Our own indigenous species can be transplanted, but be careful. Get a small specimen and water it daily all summer long. I got one

Magnolia

for a birthday present three years ago and I did everything according to the book, but it is still spindly and poverty stricken.

And then there is the incredible tulip of the tulip tree (*Liriodendron tulipifera*). So very special is this flower that I must copy a passage from *The North American Sylva, A Description of the Forest Trees of the United States, Canada, and Nova Scotia,* by F. Andrew Michaux, printed in Paris in 1818: "In the Atlantic States, especially at a considerable distance from the sea, Tulip Trees are often seen 70, 80, and 100 feet in height, with a diameter from 18 inches to 3 feet. But the Western States appear to be the natural soil of this magnificent tree, and here it displays its most powerful vegetation. It is commonly found mingled with other trees such as the hickories, the black walnut, the butternut, the coffee tree, and the wild cherry tree; but it sometimes constitutes alone pretty large tracts of the forest as my father observed in Kentucky. . . ."

In my part of the country, which is less than fifty miles from New York, there are many tulip trees still growing and new seedlings are constantly coming out of the ground. If you don't like their location, you can transplant them—when they are very small, for they have a taproot instead of a wide system of roots, and I wouldn't want to find out how deep that taproot goes when the tree has matured.

To continue with flowering trees, there are perhaps one thousand species of hawthorn (*Crataegus*) in the world. The pink one called English hawthorn is incredible when in bloom. A small tree I found in Virginia, called beauty bush (*Kolkwitzia,* also known as french mulberry) impressed me with its beautiful racemes of flowers. It should be more often used further north because it is said to be hardy in New England. Even the ordinary ash (*Fraxinus*) has lovely pendants of seed pods in early spring. The mountain ash (*Pyrus americana*), on the other hand, has lots of deep orange fruit which birds always get before we really see them.

As the seasons turn the fruit is formed on the trees, bursting with the seeds which will fall and, if they find welcoming ground, make new saplings, new trees. The winged seeds of the maples (*Acer*) glide gently down to earth; the long, fat pods of the honey locust burst and the seeds explode; and the brown chestnut breaks its shell. But our wild horse chestnut (*Aesculus*) is not the kind vendors on city streets roast on wintery days. In the meantime the fruit of the tulip tree has fallen down as graceful in design as the flower and chuck-full of seeds. Will they germinate in some of the places where they come to rest? Chances are that a few of them will.

Other trees are evergreen, the conifers' needles remain thin and straight and green summer and winter, spring and autumn, almost without change. The pines (*Pinus*) and spruces (*Picea*), the hemlocks (*Tsuga*), firs (*Abies*), and arborvitae, northern white cedar, make a garden stay green all year long. The pines smell sweetly in the woods as though they were meant to clear your lungs and freshen your spirit. If there are pines on your land, keep them growing; they will shed some of their needles each autumn and help prepare the ground beneath for ferns and wildflowers.

Ash

The white and the red pine are among our most common and most welcome conifers; they grow tall and straight, and, if not too crowded, they can become beautiful specimen trees in the middle of a lawn, wildflower garden, or at the edges of driveways and walks. Their blossoms are as striking as flowers, and the new growth is aptly termed "candles." Both trees grow fast, sometimes eighteen inches per year, and you must remember this when planting small seedlings found in woods or bought from nurseries.

Pitch pine, also called Virginia pine (*Pinus rigida*), is a smaller and denser tree but tough and determined to resist salt spray from the ocean (it grows abundantly on our East Coast) as well as the severest storms of the winter. I have seen pitch pine planted in gardens, close to houses and trimmed if necessary, along driveways, or even as a hedge to form the boundary line of a piece of property.

Two of my very favorites are the blue spruce and the larch. One spruce was given me many years ago as a very small Christmas tree. Now it is at least fifteen feet high, and so wide at the base that it is beginning to crowd out some other plants—another very good reminder to leave plenty of room around a healthy and desirable specimen. Larches, also called tamarack (*Larix laricina*), fascinate me with the tracery of their branches which are not, however, evergreen. Cypresses (*Taxodium distichum*), on the other hand, are among the toughest trees on Earth. Their branches twist and turn as though they were constantly defending themselves against the wind. They are good trees to have on a hillock, perhaps even the top of a slanting rock garden, for theirs is a rude kind of grandeur which few other trees can equal.

Many other trees, both deciduous and evergreen, are very decorative in gardens.

84

A full-grown cypress. (T. Lawrence Starke)

Ailanthus, "the tree of heaven," was imported from China; although it is not very long-lived, its roots have so many sprouts that it reproduces itself many times over. It does not like very cold winters, but is otherwise not particular where it grows.

Basswood, of the linden family, is a good lawn tree with many blossoms; it needs good soil, and should definitely be treated as an "ornamental," and not planted too close to the house.

The copper and purple beeches (*Fagus*), of European origin, have graceful hanging branches, and need good soil and ample water. A drought will kill them; some of the species have snow-white bark and are therefore much prized if grown among evergreens.

When planted on a good site, the buckthorn (*Rhamnus*) will grow into a small roundheaded tree, and its branches make interesting contorted patterns. If you don't mind a great deal of cleaning up after the flowers, fruit, and leaves have fallen, then a catalpa (*Catalpa*) is a fascinating tree for you. From China, it may even be grown from seed.

There are thirty species of cottonwood (*Populus*). Their symmetrically balanced leaves move constantly even in the lightest breeze. One of the best known of this group is the quaking aspen, which I have seen growing in Colorado at an elevation of over 9000 feet. This tree has a beautiful white trunk, but is short-lived and delicate—so delicate, in fact, that the slightest injury to the bark will kill it. Friends of mine have nevertheless successfully transplanted a few of these very young trees into their garden in lower Connecticut.

Crab apple trees (*Pyrus coronaria*) are highly desirable for their color in spring, and their fruit in autumn. The hardiest species come from Asia. I have already mentioned the dogwood, which needs no recommendation. Elms would be beautiful in any garden if they were not subject to a beetle-borne disease which spraying does not seem to stop.

Euonymus, also called spindle tree, can attain great height; one species, *Yeddo euonymus,* produces two colors of foliage in the autumn. The very ancient ginkgo tree or maidenhair tree has two species: one grows very tall, and the other insists on spreading. I have seen both in the Japanese Stroll Garden of the Hammond Museum in North Salem, New York, where they get the proper pruning and soil maintenance. If they were not so difficult to transplant, the two species of gum tree, sweet or sour, could be seen in more gardens. I love all the hickories— shagbark and others with their pink buds and upright growing habits.

Horse chestnut is another of my all-time favorites, as I have already indicated. In the center of Vienna, where I lived as a child, there is a great plaza completely surrounded on one side by white and purple lilacs backed up by an enormous row of white and pink chestnuts. Every day during May we stopped there on our way home from school, never tiring of the sight. Those shrubs and trees were planted during the heyday of the Habsburgs, something like one hundred and fifty years ago. Even in the great replanting schemes of Washington, there will never be anything like this; for no matter how rich and power-

The hickory bud resembles an iris when it has just opened in early spring.

ful America becomes, there never will be such total abandon to the beauty of trees and shrubs.

As I am writing this, I look up at a fairly small tree in the middle of my fern field—an ironwood tree (*Carpinus carollana*), its twisted branches stark and black against the sky now that the leaves are gone. I must say that in its way, and in my totally ungrandiose way of life, I am not at all sure that I have not made an excellent and admirable exchange.

It seems to be difficult to find locust trees (which belong of all things to the pea family) in nurseries, but if you are lucky you may find some growing in the wild. They too are tall and strong, don't mind growing between rocks, and some species have lovely leaves and fruit of flat pods.

Many species of maples (*Acer*) are grand for shade and for their fall coloring. You must remember that they are among the few trees under which you cannot plant flowers or even ground-covers. Norway maple, perhaps one of the most popular trees for city planting, almost completely desiccates the soil in which it grows; its deep shade drowns all but the hardiest plants. The much-heralded crimson king maple is another variety of Norway; but for the connoisseur, there are fantastically lovely, more delicate species available. I have already cited the Japanese varieties which show a constantly expanding range of colors, growth, habits, and foliage. The Orient also offers the trident and amur maples, which grow small and shrublike, respectively. But, too, there are the box elder, also called ashleaf maple, the only form of maple with a compound leaf; the mountain maple with erect, shrubby habits; and the literally striped maple with bark that is decorated with stripes of bright green, white, and brown. All these are American species.

The oaks (*Quercus*) are among our mightiest trees, and perhaps the most dramatic and useful. Almost all of them—white, black, pin, post, and shingle oak grow to tremendous heights.

Their acorns, like the nuts of the hickories, feed the squirrels and chipmunks, which is not necessarily a great advantage for the gardener because these small animals insist on burying acorns throughout the lawn. And then there are the plum and cherry trees, and wild and cultivated apple trees (*Pyrus inalus*) of which you can make an orchard if you have the time and the ambition. But if you don't, a specimen here and there will make your garden happier.

I am not sure that it pays to transplant a sassafras or buy one, for they don't last long. But if they grow wild on your place, cherish them and show your children the different leaves— a matter of astonishment to all comers. For a good shade tree you might get a walnut (*Juglans*); it comes into leaf late, allows grass to grow under it, sheds its leaves early in the fall, and then allows the grass to complete its cycle.

Willows (*Salix*) can be a garden designer's dream, for some of them have the most graceful tumbling branches which set off a space with elegance and grace. These are the weeping willows, of course, which are the first to spring into leaf as soon as the sun gets higher and the days grow longer. The only problem with these trees is that they need a great deal of water the first year of their planting, and sometimes even thereafter, and therefore it is best to put them very close to a pond or a brook. Another of this group is the fascinating black willow, with the most amazing twists and turns in its trunk. None of us who used to drive into New York on one of the Parkways will ever forget the long rows of black willows which grew along the sides for several miles and gave us joy every time we passed them. Then, one day, another intersection had to be built. All the black willows are now dead and gone.

You may well want to plant only saplings and watch them grow; but if you buy large trees, you must have professionals to transplant them. They need enormous balls of earth intact around their roots, and wires put into the ground to hold them up for the first couple of years. I just hope that you will not be among the people who have built a new house and torn out all the trees around the property, only to find that now the house is built, you need trees to cover up the torn-up naked earth for solace, for beauty, and for shade.

The wise designer and owner will mix deciduous trees with evergreens wherever possible for the ever-changing concert of color and shape. True, most evergreens prefer acid soil, and leaf-bearing trees more neutral ground, but if one knows how to plant them and where and in what proportion all will be happy.

Learn about your land, its contours, the consistency of your soil, the rocks, the fences, and the placement of your house as well as the direction of the prevailing winds. Think about lining your driveways with trees and shrubs—perhaps using the white trunk of a birch instead of a glass reflector to mark your driveway (try the European white birch; it's hardier and stronger than our native variety). Plant them around your house to help delineate its shape (or to cover it up); think before you transplant trees from the woods or plant cultivated varieties around your piece of land.

Remember that it is the trees which will shape and condition the life of your house and your garden. They will dictate the flowers and groundcovers you can use, and sometimes even the plants you can grow within a hundred-foot radius! Black walnut, for instance, emits a toxin from its roots that is detrimental to tomato plants, but only if tomatoes are grown in close proximity of the tree roots.

Although I certainly suggest that you leave plenty of room for your prize trees to grow and spread, I also suggest that you try the technique of a "copse"—particularly if you're pressed for space. Plant a number of smallish trees together, almost as if they were a flower arrangement, and plant groundcovers around their roots to bind the whole group together. These natural-looking "islands" can be kept carefully pruned and clipped back, and will provide a cool refuge for the eye in the midst of a green sweep of lawn.

A Westchester County tree surgeon has suggested that for one of the most unusual hedges to be ever seen one might take seedlings from the woods and plant them as a hedge—then clip. The result, I am told, can be a fantastically lovely marbled effect, with one type of foliage contrasting with another. A European tree, popularly called the hedge maple, is used for a more homogeneous hedge; and I have heard of pine, spruce, beech, and even oak hedges.

But how to distinguish which trees should be properly grown as "ornamentals"—free-standing, in the center of an open space, an object of attention—and which should be relegated to backdrop or hedge use? "Basically," my friend who played poplar against beech tells me, "you should look at the mature shape of the tree. Any species can be used to its fullest potential. An oak, for instance, will branch out sideways if given enough light, and make a wide thick crown which is quite attractive. But that same oak, if grown in partial shade, will still look okay although taking on a different and taller shape. In other words, an oak can grow in a number of different environments without compromising itself.

"But take a flowering crab apple, blue spruce, or a weeping willow. These trees always maintain approximately the same shape—a sphere, a cone, and a weeping mound. Plant them with other trees, and they lose the shape that's part of their charm. They can't adapt to squeezing, like an oak, and therefore it makes sense to me to put them in the open where they can do their best."

As you drive through the countryside, for instance, notice

the difference between a spruce that has grown under a shade tree and one that has been allowed the middle of a lawn. The first tree will be spindly, with many dead branches toward the base. The second will be full and vigorous, with a skirt of branches sweeping the ground. The same, of course, goes for flowering trees and willows. Unless planted with others of their kind (the hedge principle, where competition is minimized) they tend to disappear from sight.

The subject of hedges brings me to the shrubs: if trees are the beams, walls, and rafters of your garden, then shrubs are the furniture often deliberately placed to define space and to cut a "room" in two.

Shrubs are also woody plants but, in contrast to trees, have several stems instead of a single trunk. As we've seen in the case of maples, it's not always clear where shrub ends and tree begins. Usually shrubs are lower and better suited for foundation planting, the edging of terraces, driveways, ponds, swimming pools, and so on.

Think of every shrub as a partial hedge—if only one plant wide—and you will begin to see other relationships of size and space that may have escaped you before. The eye follows any series of objects laid out in a line, and thus the mountain laurels around my house form as much of a hedge—although a round-about and free-form one—as that of my neighbors who preen their privet in imitation of a stone wall.

You may not care to use shrubs as deliberate transition between tall trees and smaller flowers, but always remember that because of their medium size these plants are always leading your vision to the larger or to the smaller. Here too are the same distinctions between deciduous plants and those that are ever-green. However, most evergreen shrubs belong into the "broad-leaf" group since few shrubs (except the junipers) bear cones or needles.

There is an almost infinite variety of shrubs which you can plant; it depends entirely on the effect you want, the colors and textures you like, and, believe or not, the sympathy and empathy you have for a plant. I know people who hate forsythia; I happen to love it. I know people who don't care about lilac; I do. I have yet to find anyone who didn't love laurel and azalea and rhododendron, but one can always argue about the color of the blossoms. If you wish to populate your garden and haven't as yet decided on the plants you'd like, the best bet is to talk to your garden designers or nurserymen and to look at the seed and garden catalogues that carry the plants best suited for your neighborhood.

You can also return to the wilderness and find some of your favorites. One of these might be Scotch broom (*Cytisus*) of which there are several varieties according to geographical location. The broom on Big Sur in California, for example, won't do well if you live in Connecticut or New York. But a lovely variety of broom grows near the shores of Rhode Island and Massachusetts, and can be planted in a rock garden or at the edge of your driveway. I have never tried to transplant one of the wild beach plums (*Prinus maritima*) which grow so abundantly on Cape Cod because it is too far from home. But if you live in that neighborhood, why not try to enhance a spot in your garden with the shimmering white bloom?

One of the first sweet-smelling shrubs to show its color is spicebush (*Pindera*); I have several among the ferns and I hugely enjoy them. Friends of mine have transplanted a few and they come up year after year, showing their delicate blossoms among the still-brown woods and patches of earth. And there is the sweet fern (*Comptonia peregrina*), a single variety of fernlike shrubs, bushy and not growing very tall but very aromatic and with beautifully designed branches and leaves. It needs sandy soil, so the chances are that wherever you have a bare spot with no loam at all it might do well, perhaps even in a rock garden. And if, by chance, you should find a small witch hazel, by all means get it to your place; its greatest advantage is that it blooms in the autumn when almost every other flower has disappeared.

There are many kinds of lilac (*Syringa*): white, purple, and the so-called double French species so well known and so fragrant that little has to be said about them. Sometimes they get stringy, and if so cut them back down. It may take two or even three years to get new bloom, but you will be rewarded with much thicker and more abundantly-blooming bushes. Another favorite is weigela which is an extremely sturdy and easily grown shrub even from cuttings rooted in sand; it is one of the most abundantly flowering plant known in nature. It should be pruned after it has bloomed to give even more flowers the following year. Weigela is an Asiatic plant named after the German physician Weigel; it needs ordinary garden soil. I also admire daphne, usually a small shrub; its flowers come out before the leaves. It comes from somewhere in Eurasia, and its name is misleading because daphne is what the Greeks called the laurel.

Another enormously popular group of shrubs (and small trees) is the viburnums which bear profuse flower clusters of various shapes and designs. I saw *Viburnum tomentosum* forming a long ridge along the back of a canal on an Irish estate. Hundred and fifty species of viburnum are now in cultivation, and every gardener could do worse than to plant one or the other against a wall, a fence, or freestanding on his lawn. If I had the room and the proper soil I would plant along my driveway the species I saw in Ireland. The viburnums have lovely, showy berries in the autumn.

A shrub that I have promised myself for a long time is one introduced by the Wayside Gardens in Ohio, called coral beauty

(*Cornus alba atrosnguinea*). Its stems are red in winter, and what a sight that must be when snow covers the ground. There are so many other beautiful flowering shrubs that it is impossible to name them all. Get a catalogue from a first-rate nursery, or one of the many available books on flowering shrubs, and you'll spend a happy evening dreaming and planning. Then take a walk along roadsides where viburnum, alders, and other seedlings grow in abundance—and don't forget your shovel and pail!

The broad-leaved evergreen shrubs serve a similar purpose as evergreen trees, with the addition of a fabulous assortment of possible bloom. First among these, at least to my way of thinking, is the American native mountain laurel, also called calico bush (*Kalmia*). It grows wild in the woods from Northern New England to Florida, among the greatest blessings of our wilderness. The flowers range from white to pink, sometimes turning white as they mature. Laurel is easy to transplant with just a few precautions. (See Chapter Seven.) I have at least thirty all around my house, in foundation plantings, in the back of a terrace, and in the middle of the field of ferns in back. All of them were dug up in the woods when they were small; some are now well over ten feet high. Each blooms in profusion every other year. In the in-between years they have fewer blossoms, but it seems as though the branches which had no bloom in the spectacular year were now trying to make up. Sometimes a branch dies as though it had done its job. But then new seedlings appear around the old plants. If for one reason or another one shrub must be cut back, it will come up again from the bottom. You can buy mountain laurel in almost every good nursery all along the East Coast; but wherever they come from, they must be planted in the same acid woodland soil from which they germinated.

Another great favorite is the native pinxter or wild azalea, probably the ancestor of many of the cultivated many-colored azaleas. Botanically speaking, they all belong to the rhododen-dron family; but in garden parlance, the rhododendron has come to mean another evergreen shrub which is wild in some of our Southern states but cultivated everywhere else. The Arnold Ar-boretum of Harvard University at Jamaica Plains in Boston has an incredible display of rhododendrons and azaleas in almost all colors of the rainbow and every shade in between.

Pyracantha, or firethorn, is an immensely popular evergreen plant that will grow up and down your house; its colorful deep orange berries will make it look like an early Christmas decor. This is an Asiatic plant that grows in ordinary soil, and in sun or shade. Cotoneaster, of the same family, on the other hand, with *its* lovely red berries in the autumn, can be made to grow very low, against a driveway or over a stepped terrace. And then there are the hollies (*Ilex*) of which there are around 400 species, mostly evergreens. They are easily transplanted when small, but need careful watering the first year. Another thing to remember is that you must plant a male plant with a female for cross pollination—and ultimately berries. They are slow growers, quite expensive, and highly decorative; they may fit into your foundation planting, perhaps next to laurel or azaleas which would give you an interplay of green colors and shapes. There are other evergreen shrubs, but these mentioned here are among the best.

Another important and extremely decorative group of plants for the garden and around the house are the vines—by definition, deciduous or evergreen plants which need support for growing. There are literally hundreds of them, some grown for flowers, others for fruit (grapes, for example); some grow in the open, some rapidly, others mature slowly; twining, clinging, good for banks, for groundcovers, in the sun, in the shade, liking moist or preferring dry soil. . . . My own favorites are wisteria, either purple or white, which is great over doors, breezeways, and porches; clematis, in many different colors and sizes, pink honey-

A climbing vine that forms a kind of portico, defining a doorway opening.

Wisteria readily covers an arbor or trellis.

Close-up of clematis blossom.

suckle (*Lonisera*), and trumpet vine, also called trumpet creeper with astounding orange flowers. All these are fairly easy to grow and quite spectacular in their bloom. You can train them almost any way you want, as you can many other vines (see the last chapter) but I for one prefer to leave all plants pretty much to their own devices. Who am I to make them obey my whims?

Since time immemorial, however, gardeners have tried to improve on nature or to bend her to their will. The Egyptians clipped their trees into spheres and columns; this was perhaps just another expression of their love for stiff formality, but it also started the art of topiary. The Greeks took it up and gave it to the Romans who were, as the saying goes, the first to go to town with it. The clipping and shaping of shrubs and trees reached a high degree of sophistication in France and England, where one can still encounter animals, birds, and all sorts of geometric figures dotting the landscape in gardens and parks. They are carved not from marble but usually from yew (*Taxus*), ilex, or boxwood.

Richardson Wright, the first great editor of *House and Garden* called topiary "nonsense." But when I drove to a nearby town some time ago, I saw several forsythias trimmed to form perfect spheres and I didn't mind them a bit. They looked like golden balls suspended in mid-air and were rather graceful. But then forsythia has no real shape of its own, and probably benefits from a little discipline.

Another old art is that of training fruit trees against a wall. A pear or apple tree, and, for that matter, any other tree can be so espaliered as to form beautiful patterns and greatly enhance a building. This means attaching a young tree to a wall or a support, trellis or such, and by constantly pruning this branch and that, forcing it to grow flat against its background in two dimensions. The idea also has a practical side: it allows light to reach all the branches and ripens the fruit evenly. The art of espaliering has been greatly developed in France, where

The opening flower of clematis.

1
uatre belles branche
uec quelques foi=
bles venües dans
la premiere
année.

2
taille pour la I.re
année
Je laisse les branche
plus longues parce
qu'il est fort vigou-
reux.

3
Effet de la I.re taille
d'un Arbre qui la
I.re année a poussé
4 belles branches

4
+
branche laissée lon
gue pour y faire pe
dre une partie de l
seue qui ne donner
que de grosses bra
ches et jamais de
branches a fruit
+

5
uatre belles branche
uec quelques foibles
venües dans la
I.re année.

6
taille de la premiere
année de ce mesme
arbre

7
Effet de la I.re taille
de ce mesme arbre

8
deuxieme taille
+ branches coupées
en forme de croche
pour y laisser perd
de la seue
+

branches coupée
en forme de moignon

9
x belles branches
poussées dans
la I.re année.
auec trois
foibles

10
taille de la premier
année.
J'ay laissé les bran=
ches longues acause
de la grande vigueur
de l'arbre

11
8 belles branches
poussées dans
la I.re année
auec trois
foibles.

12
taille de la I.re
année.
branches longues
acause de la grande
vigueur de l'arbre

12
77

Pag 77.

the director of the gardens of Louis XIV, Mr. De la Quintinye, gave the most explicit directions in his book *Instruction pour les Jardins Fruitiers et Potagers,* printed in Paris in 1700. Of course many other trees and vines can be espaliered too, one of the most successful being *Euonymus.*

To keep trees, shrubs, and vines healthy and often enhance their shape (without going to the length of topiary work) they must be carefully pruned. It is not only necessary to cut out very weak or dead growth, but also to trim back new growth to encourage side branches and thus better bloom. And though I haven't seen any mountain laurels doing poorly in the woods, where nobody comes around with a pair of shears, I have certainly had to cut off the lower branches of my white pines and hemlocks; they were dying and interfering with other plants. Hedges must be pruned and trimmed to be neat; dead growth occurs in almost all plants and must be removed. Pruning also gives plants more air, and more room to expand, and all this quite aside from the fact that your garden *looks* better and neater if you do just the minimum essential pruning and cutting out.

If you do have to cut branches, for example, some which were broken in a storm, be sure to use tree paint to cover the wound and protect it from rot. Any real, heavy pruning, shaping, and cleaning, however, should be left to experts. Sometimes a heavy branch has to be tied back with a cable, and I wouldn't want any amateur to do that. Trim your forsythias, your privet hedges, and your small shrubbery in any way you want; but call in a tree man to preserve and protect your beautiful ornamentals which make the smallest piece of land into an empire. And, with good care, they will still be here long after we are gone.

The Art of Espalier, a page from Instruction Pour Les Jardins Fruitiers et Potagers, *by Louis XIV's gardener.*

An espaliered flowering pear. (Sue Koch)

I appreciate the rewards of open sun and exclusive flowerbeds. But I would rather keep the sun-dappled road, lined with the trees which have been left standing by wind and weather and the whim of my fellow men; I would rather plant a new dogwood against an old pine tree so I could gorge my eyes in their different colors; and I would rather plant young birches to make a new small forest where before there was only dust.

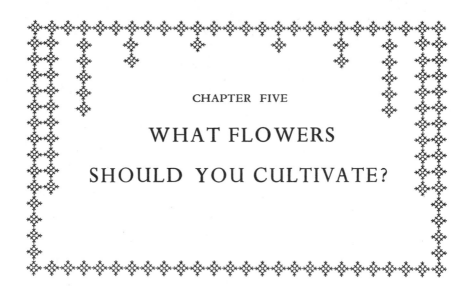

CHAPTER FIVE

WHAT FLOWERS

SHOULD YOU CULTIVATE?

Shed no tear—O shed no tear
The flowers will bloom another year.
Weep no more—O weep no more!
Young buds sleep in the root's white core.
JOHN KEATS (1795–1821)

FLOWERS have been said to be an unbroken link between the past and the future. Every year they come, every year they go: tentatively at first they put out their stems and leaves and ecstatic blossoms, then they fade and disappear until it is time for another awakening.

Most species of flowers in our gardens have existed since time immemorial; longer than the lifetime of a man, a generation, a civilization. They have given birth to others: cross-bred by nature, by the accident of pollination, the seed of one kind mixing with another, hybridized and frequently enhanced and glorified in the workshops of thousands of botanists and breeders, growers, and often gardeners. Thus have come about almost one hundred lilies from the first one in Iran, and 30,000 varieties of roses from the modest wild variety.

Seeds and plants have been exchanged along the old trade routes ever since men began to travel, by cart, by wagon, and by ship; on horseback, on mules, and on foot; by couriers and diplomats, by adventurers and businessmen—and three kings who came from the East to bring myrrh and frankincense, the plants second only to gold.

There is a seed catalogue that comes from England, and which I read as though it were poetry; and how I wish I had the time and space to plant all the seeds! And when winter nears its end, how beguilingly the nursery catalogues, with their fairy-like colors and shapes, tug at our imaginations no less than at our pocketbooks! And though I greatly admire the skill and patience of those who have made new flowers out of old, stronger strains from the weak, more glorious color from the less distinguished, and more strength, better health, and more abundant bloom, I still wish I knew more how each variety originated: what is the modest flower of the wilderness that now greets me in royal robes; when and where and why it got its name; and who were the first people to cherish it. Although we know the history of many flowers, we don't know them all.

The origin of the word "flower" itself explains part of the question, although we don't know what came first: the word itself, or the Roman goddess Flora who took care of all the growing things. Flora had a Greek counterpart called Hera, and there had been other mistresses of fertility before her in Egypt, in Mesopotamia, in the Far East, all over the world. From Flora came *fleur* and flower. In the ancient Germanic North the word was *bhlo,* hence blow, by puffs of wind, and blossom. The German word for flower today is *blume.* An early alternate spelling, it is said, was *flour,* the blooming part of wheat.

At first specific plants derived their names from whatever medicinal value people thought they had. The word peony, for example, from the Greek *Paion,* healer of the gods. Dianthus, the flower of Zeus, means *dios,* god, and *anthos* is the Greek word for flower. The Greek word for gold is *chrysos,* and *anthos,* combine in chrysanthemum, the golden flower. The Anglo-Saxons have given us daisy, derived from *daegesaeage,* day's eye. And although the Greeks gave this name to a different flower, our ageratum stems from *a,* meaning "not," and *geras,* "old age"—a rather perfect designation for an annual plant.

Our own hepatica stems from the Greek *hepaticos,* meaning liver, and thus the common name liverwort. Other plants were named after their discoverers: *Kalmia,* for example, is the Latin name for mountain laurel, which was discovered by the Swedish botanist Peter Kalm. Others were dedicated to other botanists, and even to distinguished diplomats and other important persons. Poinsettia was named after an American Secretary of War, Joel Robert Poinsett, of South Carolina; the beautiful yellow alpine flower clintonia for DeWitt Clinton, several times governor of New York.

In addition to names, flowers have *meanings.* Much superstition, astrology, and black and white magic seem to have had a hand in the naming of flowers. Many lists of floral significance and symbolism have been compiled over the years; the following list is from Laura Greenwood's *The Rural Wreath of Life among the Flowers,* published in Boston in 1845.

FLOWERS	INTERPRETATION
Acacia, Rose	*Elegance*
Almond, Flowering	*Hope*
Alyssum, Sweet	*Worth beyond Beauty*
Aloe	*Grief*
Amaranth	*Immortality*
Anemone	*Forsaken*
Arbor Vitae	*Unchanging Affection*

FLOWERS	INTERPRETATION
Aspen Tree	*Excessive Sensibility*
Auricula, Scarlet	*Pride*
Bachelor's Button	*Celibacy*
Balm	*Sympathy*
Balsomine	*Impatience*
Basil	*Hatred of the other Sex*
Bay Leaf	*I Change but in Dying*
Bay Wreath	*Glory*
Bayberry	*Sourness, or Sharpness*
Bell Flower	*Constancy*
Bindweed	*Humility*
Box	*Stoicism*
Bramble	*Weariness*
Buttercup—Kingcup	*Riches*
Camomile	*Energy in Adversity*
Carnation	*Disdain*
Catchfly	*Artifice, or a Snare*
Cedar Tree	*Strength*
Cherry Blossom	*Spiritual Beauty*
Cinquefoil	*The Dead*
Clematis	*Mental Beauty*
Coreopsis	*Always cheerful*
Cowslip	*Native Grace*
Crocus	*I Am His*
Crown, Imperial	*Aristocracy*
Cypress	*Disappointed Hopes*
Daisy	*Innocence*
Dandelion	*Coquetry*
Eglantine, or Sweetbrier	*Poetry*
Evergreen	*Poverty and Worth*
Everlasting	*Always Remembered*
Fir	*Time*
Flax	*Domestic Industry*

FLOWERS	INTERPRETATION
Flower-de-Luce	*I Am Burning with Love*
Flower of an Hour	*Delicate Beauty*
Flowering Reed	*Confidence in Heaven*
Forget-Me-Not	*True Love*
Foxglove	*Ambition*
Geranium	*Gentility*
Geranium, Dark	*Despondency*
Geranium, Rose	*Preference*
Geranium, Scarlet	*Consolation*
Geranium, Silver-leafed	*Recall*
Hawthorn	*Hope*
Heliotrope	*Devotion*
Hellebore	*Calumny*
Hibiscus	*Short-lived Beauty*
Honeysuckle	*Fidelity*
Honeysuckle, Wild	*Inconstancy*
Hydrangea	*Heartlessness*
Ice Plant	*Frigidity*
Ivy	*Friendship*
Japonica	*Excellence*
Jasmine	*Amiability*
Jonquil	*Is My Affection Returned*
Laburnum	*Pensiveness*
Ladies' Delight	*Forget Me Not*
Ladies' Slipper	*Capriciousness*
Larkspur	*Fickleness*
Laurel	*Fame*
Lavender	*Acknowledgment*
Lilac	*First Emotions of Love*
Lily of the Valley	*Unnoticed Affection*
Lily, White	*Purity and Modesty*
Locust	*Affection beyond the Grave*
Lotus	*Estrangement*

FLOWERS	INTERPRETATION
Love in a Mist	*Perplexity*
Love Lies Bleeding	*Hopeless, not Heartless*
Mignonette	*Moral Worth*
Mimosa	*Sensitiveness*
Mistletoe	*Not Discouraged*
Moss	*Maternal Affection*
Mulberry Tree	*Wisdom*
Myrtle	*Love in Absence*
Narcissus	*Egotism, or Self-love*
Nasturtium	*Patriotism*
Nightshade	*Dark Thoughts*
Oleander	*Warning, or Beware*
Olive	*Peace*
Orange Blossom	*Woman's Worth*
Oxeye	*Patience*
Pea, Everlasting	*Wilt Thou Go*
Pea, Sweet	*Departure*
Periwinkle	*Early Friendship*
Petunia	*Elegance without Pride*
Phlox	*Our Souls Are United*
Pink, China	*Aversion*
Pink, Red	*Woman's Love*
Pink, White	*Fair and Fascinating*
Poppy, Red	*Evanescence*
Poppy, White	*Oblivion in Sleep*
Primrose	*Modest Worth*
Primrose, Evening	*Inconstancy*
Rose, Burgundy	*Simplicity*
Rose, Bridal	*Happy Love*
Rose, Carolina	*Love Is Dangerous*
Rose, Multiflora	*Grace*
Rose, Versicolor	*Mirthfulness*
Rose, Musk	*Charming*

FLOWERS	INTERPRETATION
Rose, Moss	*Superior Merit*
Rose, Yellow	*We Will be Strangers*
Rosebud, Moss	*Confession of Love*
Rosebud, White	*Too Young to Love*
Rosemary	*Affectionate Remembrance*
Saffron	*Marriage*
Snapdragon	*Dazzling, but Dangerous*
Snowball	*Thoughts of Heaven*
Star of Bethlehem	*Reconciliation*
Sweet William	*Hollowness, or Treachery*
Syringa	*Memory*
Tansy	*Courage*
Thistle	*Never Forget*
Tulip, Red	*Declaration of Love*
Tulip	*Beautiful Eyes*
Venus' Looking Glass	*Flattery, or Vanity*
Violet Blue	*Faithfulness*
Violet, White	*Modesty*
Wall Flower	*Fidelity in Misfortune*
Walnut, Black	*Intellect*
Water Lily	*Eloquence*
Weeping Willow	*Forsaken Lover*
Woodbine	*Fraternal Love*
Yarrow	*Cure for the Heartache*
Yew	*Sorrow*
Zinnia	*Absence*

Some plants are grand and formal: roses, lilies, delphiniums, lupines, some primulas, tulips (if grown *en masse*); the tall irises, fritillaria imperialis, carnations, dragonheads, dahlias, peonies, and sunflowers. Others are humble in appearance and countenance: violets, snowdrops, crocuses, scillas, pinks, other primulas; Johnny jump-ups, bluebells, alyssum, marigolds, and most other annuals. And some are in between: salvia, wall-flowers, rockroses, bachelor's buttons, daisies, yarrow, polygonum, and many more. In some fashion, flowers have created their own social order: aristocrats and plebians, and the vast mass of bourgeois creatures in between.

A mass of color in a garden is the usual feature. A range of one color is much more difficult to obtain and keep, because sometimes flowers change their color as they grow more mature. But if you go over the charts at the end of this chapter, you will soon find out that you could have a garden of yellow and orange flowers, or blue to purple, growing through the entire season. It will depend on the shape of your garden, and whether you want tall plants in the background and low-growing species in the front (wall gardens, for example) or tall varieties in the middle of a bed, and graduating sizes all around it in a round, oval, or free-form bed.

There are other themes for gardens. For example, a scented garden of violets, nicotiana, roses, some lilies, carnations, hyacinths, and other fragrant bulbs; scented geraniums, perhaps mixed, with fragrant herbs, heliotrope, lavender, wormwood and rosemary and planted with a honeysuckle in the background and a wild sweet pepperbush nearby which perfumes the air in later summer days.

If you are interested in history, you could have an Early American garden by mixing imported plants with the native bloodroot and bouncing Bet, viper's-bugloss with dianthus, star-of-Bethlehem with old-fashioned roses, rue and sweet rocket with bee balm, hepatica, trillium and lady's-slippers, and some ancient peonies with native ferns. You might have some problems mixing cultivated plants with the wild, but some ferns like sweet soil and some cultivated plants are not too particular about the soil in which they grow. And if you want to put some may-apple in your garden, remember it is *not* the mandrake of ill repute.

You could also (depending on where you live) recreate old English gardens as was done with outstanding success in Williamsburg. I have before me *Plants of Colonial Days,* by Raymond L. Taylor, which was printed for Colonial Williamsburg. This book lists some of the flowers, both imported and native, such as:

Althea, also called hollyhock; autumn crocus, bee balm, scilla, black-eyed Susan, blue iris, phlox (*Phlox divaricata,* wild); bouncing bet, calendula, canterbury bells, carnation, cattail, China aster, coralberry, columbine, coreoplis, cornflower (bachelor's button), crocus (spring and autumn blooming); daffodil, English daisy, primrose, foamflower, foxglove, marigold, germander, golden ragwort, grape hyacinth, grass pink, hydrangea, jonquil, larkspur (*Delphinium*); lemon day lily, lily of the valley, lizard's tail, mimosa (not hardy north of Washington, D.C.); moneywort, nasturtium, Oriental poppy, pansy, peony, pickerelweed, narcissus, rose mallow, Saint-John's-wort, scotch rose, scilla, snowdrop, spearmint, Stokes' aster, summer phlox, swamp rose, sweet william, tawny day lily, tulip, turtlehead; valerian, veronica, violet, yarrow, yellow iris, and yucca.

All of which goes to show that the seventeenth-century American gardeners knew how to mix cultivated and wildflowers —and how well they did it!

In some public parks (Central Park in New York, for example) there are Shakespeare Gardens. It would not be very difficult to design a Shakespeare garden around a country house, where wildflowers—pinks, daisies, buttercups, hemlock or parsnip, ragged robin, cowslip, wild roses (eglantine) and common blue violets, columbine, and harebell—are planted together with cultivated flowers such as carnations, primulas, pansies, several colors of iris, cabbage roses, marigold, daffodils, narcissus, and madonna lily (which although a descendant of the first lily known is now widely cultivated) together with several herbs: rue, rosemary (which has to be taken into the house in the winter) and marjoram, lavender, and thyme. It could be an appealing pastime to keep a diary, with verses from the plays and sonnets that refer to the plants. There could be other literary gardens, for many of the poets of all times have written about the flowers they had loved.

Friends have told me that there is a garden in Israel in which are cultivated many of the plants mentioned in the Bible. A good gardener with a bend for history and research could create wonders with any of the plants which have been known since time immemorial and which are just as appreciated today as when they were first discovered. The Persians, it is said, loved their gardens so much that they could not bear to live without the flowers indoors, and that is why they came to make their beautiful rugs with a thousand blooming plants.

And, of course, there are specific collections possible in gardens. I, for one, love the delicate columbine, one species an

Cowslip. (Lisa Federico)

American native which, however, also grows in somewhat different forms in China and in other parts of the world. It has been hybridized and cultivated for centuries. Our own species, *Aquilegia canadensis,* was popular among the American Indians who boiled the roots for a tea for intestinal disorders and for cough. An English variety was used for speedy delivery of babies (but with what success, nobody seems to know).

Roses must have grown in Oregon and Montana perhaps thirty-five million years ago, for fossil specimens have been found there. Today many of the original varieties, with five petals, are still represented in the *Rosa virginica* which grows wild in the eastern part of the United States, and *Rosa setigera* which blooms on the prairies. Others grow wild in most other parts of the world. Then came the semidouble rose, and finally the many-petaled rose cultivated by growers and gardeners. But how the transition occurred, and whether people before the Egyptians and Romans (who went mad over them) cultivated roses, is not known.

We do know that their first representation in art occurred in Crete, and that roses were so abundant on the Aegean islands that the flower gave one island their name: Rhodes. Ever since, at all times and in all forms of art—pagan, Christian, Mohammedan, Buddhist—the rose has been the symbol of love, of holiness, and of grandeur. In war, the red rose of Lancaster fought against the white rose of York; and in peace, since the 15th century the Pope gave first a single golden rose and then a whole bouquet of golden roses on the fourth Sunday of Lent to the most pious and deserving lady in Europe.

Basically there are still three kinds of roses. From the wild single-petaled flowers, the "old-fashioned" roses were cultivated in Europe until about the year 1800. These were beautiful specimens, but blossomed only once a year. Then the China rose was brought to England and France, and as it was crossed with the older roses it began to bloom almost the entire season.

From these come our garden roses—white, yellow, pink and red, in great profusion, also hybrids and crossbreeds, tiny and enormous, stately even when they climb over a country fence. Only specialists and rose growers know them all; and if you have decided on a rose garden, go to the best nursery in your neighborhood and choose your favorite colors and kinds.

Roses are aristocratic and exclusive plants. Perhaps because their ancestry goes back so far and they have been dedicated to the gods of Greece and Rome and Christian saints; they like to grow among themselves, and despise having to share a piece of ground with other lesser plants. If you love roses, as so many people do, by all means give them their own plot be it ever so small. Better half a dozen of the beauties in their very own place than mixing them (as I have done to my sorrow) with other flowers. And it is much easier to take care of a garden patch in which only roses bloom rather than at the same time try to take care of several kinds of flowers mixed in with roses. There are special rose fertilizers and rose dusts available that will help to bring out their full glory from the first small bud in May to the "last rose of summer"—usually a November blossom.

By all means reserve a sunny and well-drained spot with good garden soil, and spread peat moss or pine bark among your plants. Cut the plants down before frost to about one foot, and hill up the soil around the stems about four inches high. In cold climates, surround the roses with salt hay. When cleanup time comes in the spring, straighten up the bed and trim the stems some more. And then watch how bit by bit they become green again, leaflets and thorns and leaves appear, and before you know it, the delicate flower buds will come to grow and blossom into their majestic blooms.

Nor is the rose meant only for elegance and beauty. American Indians used its leaves and petals for a great variety of ills, and a concoction of "rose hips" (the rose fruit) has its merits. Gerard says of the eglantine: "The faculties of these wilde Roses are referred to the manured Rose, but not used in Physicke where the other may be had: notwithstanding, Pliny affirmeth that the root of the Briar Bush is a singular remedy found out by Oracle, against the biting of a mad dog, which he sets forth in his eight booke, Chap. 41."

Even today we find rose-hip jelly, rosewater, and, of course, perfumes, even vitamin C made of rose hips.

> *But earthlier happy is the rose distill'd*
> *Than that which withering upon the virgin thorn*
> *Grows, lives, and dies in single blessedness.*
> WILLIAM SHAKESPEARE, "A MIDSUMMER
> NIGHT'S DREAM," ACT I, SCENE I.

From the first white lilies around the Iranian city of Susa came countless others. But for a long time the stately pure white flower remained one of the dominant motifs in Cretan art. It may even have grown in Crete in Neolithic times. Botanists, and Bible historians, are still not quite agreed whether the biblical "lilies of the field" were really lilies; rather it is thought that they may have been narcissi, anemones, or even mountain tulips. We do know that the Romans were as enthusiastic about lilies as they were about roses, and no wonder. When the Roman roses were fading, the lilies came into bloom with their beautiful petals and sweet perfume. And there is the tale of Roman legions who took their lily bulbs to plant wherever they were encamped, so as not to be without their favorite bloom during long campaigns. Some were even left behind in Britain where in spite of war and weather, their descendants have survived to our very own day. Dioscorides recommended a concoction made of lilies and other herbs for snakebite. Later, medieval herbals suggested lily bulbs for the curing of burns. Gerard has an interesting—and silly—horticultural comment: "If colors were injected into the bulb of white lilies, all manner of colored lilies could be grown."

The white lily (*Lilium candidum*) of the lily family was not, of course, the only lily known. Other colors of lilies were seen in the Middle and Far East, soon imported into Europe (and later in America); lilies such as the Turk's-cap lily, which today grows wild in our woods and roadsides in addition to our own wild lily, the beautiful wood or Philadelphia lily. (See Chapter Eight.)

Today there are at least 80 species of lilies known. White Flower Farm, a famous nursery in Litchfield, Connecticut, has 58 species growing in its gardens. And what a sight when they are in bloom during late summer days! There is an announcement that a new group is to come soon from the workshop of the Hollander Jan de Graaf who has literally invented new forms and colors.

The lily has been much used in heraldry for many centuries and in many places. It has emblazoned the crests of kings and princes, and even some elegant old schools in England.

Lilies are not difficult to grow. The bulbs are best planted in good garden soil in the fall; and since they blossom late in the summer, some growers recommend overplanting the bulbs with low-growing annuals and perennials. Choose your favorites from the many bulb and general flower catalogues, or buy them from your local nurseries or garden stores. They will grace your garden no matter which ones you choose.

Faith is like a lily lifted high and white

CHRISTINA GEORGINA ROSSETTI (1830–1894), FROM HER POEM "HOPE IS LIKE A HAREBELL"

Turk's-cap lily. (Lisa Federico)

For many thousands of years the iris has been a cure for many ailments, an additive and fixative for perfumes—under the name of orris root—a symbol of the kings of France, and simply an extraordinarily beautiful flower that has grown wild in damp places since time immemorial on much of the earth and is now cultivated in many forms and colors.

The Greeks believed that iris was the rainbow personified, a messenger of the gods. Modern Egyptologists no longer believe that the figure on the forehead of the Sphinx is a representation of a wreath of iris—which was first mentioned, it seems, by Napoleonic discoverers who must have imagined in it the famed fleur-de-lis of France. But the iris is represented in Egyptian and Minoan carvings and paintings, and it is believed that this flower is also seen in some Etruscan forms of art. Clovis, first Merovingion king of the Franks (481–511) had his empire threatened by Germanic tribes; he promised his Christian wife that he would change his religion, and the insignia on his banner to an iris if he won the battle. Win he did, and, for the first time, the iris was embroidered on the banner of what was later to become France. Then, Louis VII (1137–1180) of France had a dream about the iris before he went on his crusade, and from then on the iris was known as the fleur-de-Louis, or de Lys. Although at first Louis used many fleurs-de-Lys on his banner, he reduced the number to three to signify the Holy Trinity. The French Revolution tried to obliterate all signs of the kingly symbol, but it has remained in high esteem among the decorative arts.

However, already Dioscorides knew that iris roots helped coughs and colds, and later herbalists added their own ideas. Gerard wrote of the "Dalmatian" variety of what he called floure-de-luce (flower of light): "The juice of these Floure-de-luces doth not only mightily and vehemently draw forth choler, but essentially waterie humors, & is a singular good purgation for them that haue the dropsie, if it be drunke in sweet wort or whay. The same are good for them that haue euill spleens, or that are troubled with cramps or convulsions, and for such as are bit with serpents. It profiteth also those that haue Gonorrhea, or running of the reins, being drunke with vinegar, as [Dioscorides] saith; and drunke with wine they bring downe the monethly termes."

In Gerard's *On the Historie of Plants* there are no less than twenty illustrations of diverse iris species, ranging from the blue and yellow flags which grow wild in our wet places, and German, Austrian, Dalmatian, Florentine, Turkish, Byzantine, variegated, dwarf and giant, white, red, and blue as well as narrow-leaved and grasslike. Therefore it is not surprising that today we find 150 species growing, to which virtually untold thousands of additional horticultural varieties must be added which are grown by fanciers and hybridizers. Recently I almost

Bee balm does well in sunny woodlands, and is easily grown in gardens.

Pl. 61.

Bessa del.

Gabriel sc.

Poplar *or* Tulip Tree.
Lyriodendrum tulipifera.

Poplar or tulip tree (from The North American Sylva)

Pl. 70.

Bessa del.   Gabriel sculp.

Common European White Birch.
Betula alba.

Common European white birch (from The North American
Sylva) has more attractive leaves and a thicker, sturdier trunk
than our American variety.

A border planned to perfection. Alyssum, scilla and forget-me-nots
are in full bloom; the iris have passed, but the leaves stand
straight and beautiful behind the bloom and will last all summer.

A clipped hedge of differing species of evergreens in Irela..

A London town-house water garden, with violets, grasses and
iris. Outside the flagstone are planted mint and other herbs.

A water garden in London

The beautiful pistils of a golden splendor

Clumps of blue fescue, with mulch in between to add contrast

My own fern garden

believed a friend when she told me: "All you have to do is to shake two kinds of iris together, and next year you have a new species."

Irises grow from rhizomes which can be partially exposed above ground. They should be planted in good, well-drained soil, in sun, and not too close to other plants. Small or large, there are two main groups—beardless and bearded, which are distinguished by the lack or the presence of a beardlike growth in the center of the haft of the petals. Some grow well in rock gardens; others like to be near water; their range of color is immense, their swordlike leaves are decorative at any time of the growing season; they lend themselves well to collections in special places of almost any garden. From Japan, where they have been grown for many centuries, come enormous, ruffled, double-flowered varieties. Thus when you begin to talk to a specialist, or just iris fancier, you might as well prepare to stay the night.

The following are brief definitions of other favorite garden flowers, some ancient and others not so old, which have evolved throughout the years and give gardens the multitudinous colors and scents that are among the reasons why we love a garden.

BACHELOR'S BUTTON, also called cornflower (*Centaurea cyanus*) of the composite family, has for a very long time grown abundantly in the fields of Europe including England. Over here it grows wild in fields and at roadsides, and is somewhat more purple than the cultivated variety. But there also are different colors in cultivation, ranging from white to deep blue. A highly decorative plant for borders, it is not particular about soil but needs full sun.

BUTTERCUP (*Ranunculus*) of the buttercup family belongs to a large group of herbs which we know well from our meadows; but the cultivated variety makes a good accent plant in a bed or border. Since it is low-growing, it is best put in front of taller plants. There are varieties for the rock garden, and others like to grow near water.

CARNATION (*Dianthus caryophyllus*) of the pink family is not only
the plant we see in florist shops, but a hardy perennial in warmer
parts of the country and widely grown in English gardens where
it came into popularity in the time of Elizabeth I. It is just as
much a Dianthus as the rock garden pinks, but of a cultivated
variety. Many species and names of carnations have survived
from as far back as the sixteenth century; pinks from the thirteenth. Gerard calls both varieties "gilloflowers," others "gylli-
flowers," and all species were beloved for their color and their

*Dianthus, a capricious and amus-
ing plant. (Lisa Federico)*

pungent clove-like fragrance. Even Gerard says that there are too many "kinds" to describe in detail.

Suffice it to say that in addition to many colors, the gardener has a choice between the "picotee" carnation, which has an edge of color different from the rest of the flower, the *bizarres* which have stripes of contrasting colors in the petals, and the *flakes* with one-color stripes. All these and many more can be raised in the greenhouse without much trouble, and set out in the spring; but where winters are not severe, they will live in a sunny garden spot all year.

CHRYSANTHEMUM of the composite family is another important genus for the garden with an enormous number of species, some annuals, some biennials, shasta daisy, for example; but most are perennials and quite easily grown in well-drained soil with sun most of the day. They come from the Old World, but have been grown in China and in Japan for over three thousand years.

DAHLIA of the composite family comes from Mexico and South America, but was named after Andreas Dahl, Swedish pupil of Linné. Dahlias are spectacular flowers. They bloom in late summer and early autumn, and are mostly grown for cutting. There are now something like 14,000 varieties. Although they dislike "wet feet," they do need watering and good garden loam for success.

DRAGONHEAD (*Dracocephalum*) of the mint family is a flower not seen often enough in gardens. I saw it for the first time among other plants in England, and was struck by its color and form. There are annuals and perennials of this species, the latter grow well in partial shade and in fairly moist ground. The plants can be easily divided in spring or autumn to make more plants. If you are lucky you can find dragonheads growing wild in open ground and waste places, and can then transplant them into your garden.

EVENING PRIMROSE (*Oenothera*) of the evening-primrose family is another plant that still grows wild in many places of North

America, where it originated. But many species are also cultivated in gardens where they make a very good show. Some plants
bloom at night or on dark days, others bloom in daylight. They
are easy to grow in sandy loam but sometimes get weedy, which
means they should be cut back.

FLAX (*Linum*) of the flax family is one of the oldest plants known,
for it was the source of linen, which was used in Egypt and to
which there are many biblical references. Gerard, quoting both
Dioscorides and Galen, tells of wondrous qualities of the wild
as well as the cultivated varieties. Another story has it that flax
is a lucky plant, for a bride in Thuringia puts it in her shoes
as a charm against poverty. Cultivated flaxes are annuals; they
can grow in gravel and could be planted here in a rock garden.
The small flowers are lovely.

GARDEN LOOSESTRIFE (*Lysimachia vulgaris*), of the primula family
is all too seldom seen in our gardens. It is a truly spectacular
plant, and originally came from Asia Minor. It can also be
found at some of our roadsides and waste places, where it has
escaped and been naturalized. It is related to our own wild
loosestrifes, although it is also of European origin. Its name was
coined by Lysimachus (c. 355–281), a Macedonian general
and bodyguard of Alexander the Great who was the first to
discover that if put under the yoke, this plant appeased the
unruliness of oxen. Gerard reports that loosestrife was used in
stopping nosebleeding, and, furthermore, "that the fume or
smoke of the herbe burned, doth drive away flies and gnats, and
all manner of venemous beasts."

Garden loosestrife grows well in somewhat moist soil with
an open exposure, blooms through much of the summer, seems
to have neat and tidy habits, and deserves at least as much attention as it enjoys from the English.

HOLLYHOCK (*Althea rosea*) of the mallow family is a very old plant
that originated in China. It was brought to England in 1573.

122

But evidently it also grew wild in high mountain canyons, for the Indians of the Rocky Mountains are said to have made a richly nourishing flour from the roots of this plant. Few early settlers lived without hollyhocks. Now it is seen in old-fashioned gardens, where it grows high and proud and with flowers budding from the bottom of the stalk and up. It may be grown as an annual or a biennial in ordinary garden soil and a sunny location.

JOHNNY-JUMP-UP (*Viola tricolor*) of the viola family is, in fact, a low growing perennial kind of pansy with much smaller flowers, and best grown at the edge of gardens or even walks and driveways. It needs sun or semi-shade, but cool and moist soil. The best I have ever seen it grow year after year was at the edge of a driveway and in gravel. Pansies and their relatives were "invented" in this country. They can be grown from seed, if these are merchandised by reputable firms; otherwise it is best to buy plants from good nurseries.

LARKSPUR (*Delphinium*) of the buttercup family is one of the most dramatic and desirable as well as hardy garden plants. Its origin is uncertain. John Parkinson has this to say about it: ". . . but whether it be the true *Delphinium* of Dioscorides, or the Poet's Hyacinth, or the flower of Ajax, another place is fitter to discuss than this. We call them in English Larkes heeles, Larkes spurres. . . . The last or Spanish kinde came to mee vunder the name

Hollyhock should not be planted with other flowers, for its striking habits demand to be admired alone.

of *Delphinium latifolium trigonum,* so stiled eyther from the diuision of the leaues, or from the pods, which come vsually three together."

Few early American gardens were without delphinium. John Bartram, the American botanist who worked with so many other native and foreign flowers, is said to have been the first to hybridize delphinium. Today we have "old-fashioned" strains as well as newer ones, and since some grow to a height of seven feet they must be staked to keep upright. Some bloom again in late autumn. They are easy to grow in sun and in ordinary garden soil. There is an annual variety which, at least so far as I am concerned—rightly or wrongly, isn't quite worth the trouble.

LUPINE (*Lupinus*) of the pea family is another "universal flower" of great beauty and usefulness. This plant was known to Theophrastus and Dioscorides, and has been used and eaten ever since it was discovered. It still grows around the Mediterranean. I have also found an enormous stand of wild lupine in New Hampshire. (See Chapter Eight.) The Indians of the Rocky Mountains used to steam the leaves and flowers and eat them with soup.

One species has been hybridized to grow up like a tree; but most others are beautiful garden flowers with gorgeous leaves. In fact the leaves alone are so exciting in design and color that I, for one, would be happy to have them cover a good part of my garden. One could not have a more appealing ground cover. I have a few of them in front of my south window and enjoy them hugely all summer long. Plant lupine in spring, in full sun and with lots of moisture, but protect them from strong winds.

PEONY (*Paeonia*) of the buttercup family is another ancient plant that has become immensely popular in gardens all over the world. A very long time ago, the Chinese found a wild species and began to cultivate it for their gardens. Early Greek legends tell

124

that it was the peony with which Paeon healed wounds in the Trojan War. In fact "paean" was the word for Greek physician. There was an old country called Paeonia, somewhere in the north of Greece; it is mentioned several times in Homer's *Iliad*.

During medieval times the peony was still used for many medicinal purposes, all going back to Theophrastus, Dioscorides, Pliny and Galen, and recounted by Gerard and Parkinson: the root was recommended for the cleansing of women after delivery of a child; for jaundice; to be hung around the neck of children against epilepsy, and even against the diseases of the mind. The "berries" or seeds made a good wine for what seems to have been kidney or gallstones—and so forth. And so on. Who can be sure that some of this did not work?

Peonies are easily grown from seed, sown in early autumn in well prepared soil. Bloom may not appear for two or three years. Of course good nurseries have more advanced plants. If you don't wish to wait, it might pay you to buy a few specimens. There are single and double peonies, both are worth having. A friend of mine has planted a whole long row in front of her house, and what a delightful sight it is when the flowers begin to bloom!

PETUNIA, of the potato family, is a popular annual that originated in Argentina; is useful to cover empty spots in a garden, or can be grown in pots to brighten a terrace. It comes in many colors, single and double flowers; and though it can be grown from seeds in hothouses, it is so inexpensive that it is simpler to buy young plants in the spring. They may self-sow, but they won't do much the next year and are best discarded when cleaning up the garden in the autumn.

POPPY (*Papaver*) of the poppy family is another very old plant that was used by Egyptian physicians for the opium they already knew how to extract from it. There are annual and perennial species of poppies grown in gardens, single and double, ranging from

125

the most delicate pink to a deep blood-red; all flower until mid-summer. They make beautiful patches of color in a perennial border. But no matter how lucky you are in growing them, you haven't seen poppies at all if you haven't driven down the main road of the Pelopennesus, flanked on both sides by glittering weaving fields of wild poppies—probably still descendants from those that grew in Greece in Neolithic times.

Iceland poppies from the Far North now grow wild in California and in Arizona, and have been habituated to our gardens; others are from Eurasia, Syria, and Iran, and some of these are annuals. Most need light or gravelly soil and sun. There is also an Alpine poppy for rock gardens.

PRIMROSE (*Primula*) of the primula family is an English flower; so much so, it is said, that when an Englishman has to live in a foreign country where, being the good gardener he usually is, he tries to learn all about the local garden flora and will almost always also try to grow some primroses.

There are five hundred species of primulas today. Many are cultivated, most grow in damp and shady places. Some tolerate some sun, but all need moisture. The most spectacular of all are those growing in large whorled tiers, which according to their color are called Primula beesania, pulverulenta, japonica, purple, pink, rose and white. I saw an enormous bed of these growing against a wall in Mount Usher Gardens near Dublin in Ireland. Another species, *Primula polyanthus,* comes now in many colors from white to deep purple and makes another spectacular showing when planted en masse. Some of the primulas come from West China, others from the Himalayas, and some among all these are highly desirable rock garden plants.

In addition to their beauty, herbalists (even before Gerard and Parkinson) recommended leaves, flowers, and roots for a variety of diseases. To this day several native species grow in the Rocky Mountains, and were highly prized by Indians who boiled the roots for their nutritive value.

126

ROCKET, also called dame's rocket (*Hesperis matronalis*) of the mustard family, is a lovely European annual which grows well alongside pinks in the rock garden and also makes an excellent edging plant for driveways and borders. It grows easily in ordinary garden soil, sometimes turning out to be a biennial. In addition to its lovely and striking color, one of the greatest virtues of this plant is the sweet scent that it emits at night.

ROCKROSE (*Cistus*) of the rockrose family, is a low-growing Mediterranean shrub which does not like hard winters. It does well in Florida and in California, and can be used in the north if wintered in a hothouse. It requires open and well-drained sweet soil and sunlight. The low-growing species are excellent border and even rock-garden plants.

"SHRUB" GERANIUM (*Geranium ibericum*) of the geranium family is an especially beautiful species of geranium, but the word "shrub" is not used in proper horticulture. It is merely used in garden parlance to describe the unusual height and growing habit of this plant. This is a perennial flower that looks beautiful in a rock garden as well as in the middle of a flowerbed, and can easily be divided. It comes from Asia.

SNAKEWEED (*Polygonum bistorta superbum*) of the polygonum family is a special cultivated strain with a fancy name of a very usual flower which grows wild and very pretty in many of our wet places and, in fact, all over the world. We call it knotweed, and it is also called smartweed. It is easily grown in full sun and good soil, and makes a showy plant for a border.

STONECROP (*Sedum*) of the stonecrop family, is usually a low-growing and rapidly expanding ground cover. *Sedum spectabile,* one of about five hundred species, all growing in the northern part of the world, is worthy of your attention for it grows in any kind of soil and in late summer or early autumn when other blossoms begin to fade; it flowers in tight bundles of pink which enliven the landscape.

SUNFLOWER (*Helianthus*) is of the sunflower family and is found mostly in North America. The seeds make delicate eating for birds, and health-food enthusiasts and children glory in the enormous height of the plant. Sunflowers are usually grown in vegetable gardens, mostly for fun; in spite of their enormous size (to twelve feet). They are annuals.

Some species of Helianthus grow in swamps. Indians ground the seeds for gruel and cakes; and crushed and roasted seeds are supposed to have tasted like coffee. Many of the early American explorers commented on the bright-yellow plants which dotted the countryside. And today the sunflower is still of great value: the seeds contain a high-grade oil used in paints and margarine. (The Indians used it for greasing their hair.)

TOBACCO PLANT (*Nicotiana*) is of the potato family. In times when smoking has become one of the more dangerous habits, it is still among the sweetest-smelling of garden plants and easily grown from seed (and *not* for smoking).

TULIP (*Tulipa*) of the lily family is among the widest known and best beloved garden flowers. There are now perhaps 100 species, and more than 1,000 hybrids, in addition to a few wild varieties in Asia Minor, Spain, China, and one species that grows in the meadows of Pennsylvania—probably a European escape. Tulips may also have grown in Crete; for among the many jars excavated in Knossos, one is decorated with a beautiful rendering of a tulip. Mountain tulips were also known in biblical lands, but how the tulips arrived in the gardens of Europe is among the most curious and fascinating stories in the world of flowers.

Ogier Ghiselin de Busbecq, the Austrian ambassador from the court of Ferdinand to the court of Suleiman the Magnificent of Turkey, found not only the first known copy of the work of Dioscorides but also a new flower that had not been seen on the European continent before and was called Tulipan by the Turks, meaning turban. He had bulbs and seed sent to Vienna.

Sunflowers grow up to twelve feet.

A page from John Parkinson's PARADISI IN SOLE, PARADISUS TERRESTRIS, *published in London in 1626.*

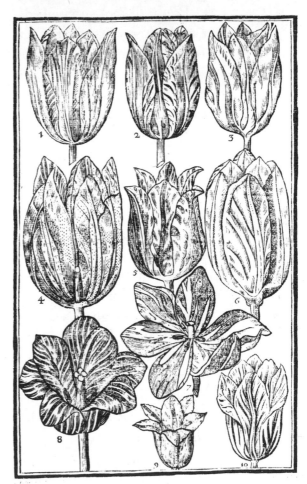

This was in 1556. By the end of the century the tulip had become a sensation, and fantastic sums of money changed hands for a single bulb.

Between 1634 and 1637 "tulipomania" came to Holland; fortunes were made and lost, and so great was the staid Hollanders' lust for tulips that when they tired of their fad the whole country was in deep economic trouble. And still, to our very own day, the best bulbs come from Holland. To see a grower's field in full bloom is an astounding sight.

England too succumbed. John Parkinson devoted almost twenty pages to "greater" and "lesser" early and late flowering tulips, with minute instructions and descriptions of their colors, habits, and values. He reports that several people, thinking they were onions, boiled the roots and ate them in soup and never found cause to dislike them.

Even in Turkey, where they originated, tulipomania took hold after the European fashion. New designs in turbans appeared, and the tulips became the main motif in many decorations. At the same time the great European flower painters, everywhere, included the stunning new plant in their bouquets.

In the meantime German settlers arrived in Pennsylvania and began to work on their "fractures," birth and marriage certificates, countless pieces of furniture, dishes, earthware and so on. And in nearly all of them the tulip appears in one way or another, almost as though it were the settlers' special signature. However, Frances Lichten, one of the greatest authorities on rural art in Pennsylvania, has made out an excellent case for believing that the famed tulip was not a tulip at all but a lily—the flower of faith and purity, which the settlers had seen for so long in their religious art of the Old World, but which was difficult to draw and paint.

Tulips are easy to grow. Plant the bulbs three or four inches deep in the fall, and in the spring overplant them with some low-growing flower or groundcover. The tulips will grow right through them. When they are through blooming, take up the bulbs and store them in a dark place until the next autumn. And don't be disappointed if your gorgeous tulips get smaller and paler with the years. If you don't have to mass them by the thousand, but just plant a few here or there, it might pay you to replace them with fresh bulbs after the second year. Local nurseries and garden stores have many of the best Dutch varieties, all displayed with a picture of the species you may wish to buy.

VIOLET (*Viola*) of the Violaceae family of which many species grow wild in woods and meadows is another ancient plant, once sacred to Io and Venus. Persephone was sent into the underworld while picking violets. This tale may be the reason why, in many countries, violets were set on graves. Among the first and favorite flowers cultivated in Greece, violets grew everywhere in Europe and were beloved for their scent and their colors from white to the deepest blue.

Gerard recommends the use of the flowers for "the sides and lung," and many other uses which seem to be similar to those our Indians put the many lovely violets of the mountains to. They ate the leaves like salad greens, and made syrup which they added to their gruel.

Including the pansy (of the same family) there are 500 species of known violets, many still are wild. The confederate violet (*Viola priceana*) grows wild in our southern states but has been brought into cultivation for northern gardens.

I have transplanted both the common blue and the wild white violet into a flowerbed in front of my south windows, and the plants grow bigger and healthier with each year in full sun (although the wild white violet is supposed to grow only in shady woods). After the flowers are gone, the leaves make their own thick carpet—the best groundcover anyone could ask for.

English gardeners have been able to hybridize many species from the Pyrenees as well as from other parts of the world. Although some professionals recommend dividing and transplanting, and growing from seed, I somehow feel that they are best left where first put for year after year of enchantment. If I had the room, I would make a collection of all known violets because each species has a different leaf and it is great fun to guess what is coming up next. Incidentally, my common blue violets like it so much where I live that each year more pop up between the flagstones!

WALLFLOWER (*Cheiranthus cheiri*) of the mustard family is a European wildflower naturalized in Britain. In fact there is hardly a garden on the British Isles anywhere which does not have yellow and orange wallflowers against a wall, around a tree, or in a bed or border. And how right they are! The brightness of the plants brings sunshine to a foggy day.

Although it appears that Dioscorides might have already known it, the wallflower did not seem to have been popular until troubadours wore it on their caps to express "constancy to the feminine ideal." The name itself has a romantic origin: A prince had fallen in love with the daughter of another clan. The lovers decided to elope, and the young swain attached a rope to the window of his beloved on which she was to glide down into his waiting arms. But the rope gave way, and she fell and died in front of the wall. White magic changed her body into a wallflower so that, as the author tells it, "a new form of beauty appeared where one more prized had been."

WINDFLOWER (*Anemone*) is of the buttercup family (which we encounter again in Chapter Eight). It includes the beautiful pasque flower (see Chapter Seven) and a number of species well suited to rock gardens. It is most widely known, however, in forms cultivated for indoor decorative use. (See Chapter Nine.) European, Japanese, and American species are easily grown in rich well-drained soil and partial sun. The "poppy anemone," the most spectacular species, will give you great pleasure for many weeks.

The idea of the name Windflower came from England, where it had been observed that the tiny flowers opened at the first breeze of spring. For once Gerard seems to know nothing about its special uses, for he ends his dissertation about many of the species by saying: "There is nothing extant in writing among Authors of any peculiar vertue, but they serve onely for the adorning of gardens and garlands, being flowers of great beautie."

When you are making your choice of flowering plants for your garden, try to remember that perennials make self-perpetuating gardens and that annuals have to be replaced year after year. Perennials will increase in size, by themselves and by division; annuals, unless they self-seed, turn into weeds in the autumn. All they are really good for is to fill empty spaces, or give you additional lines of borders, as for instance marigolds and zinnias do. Also, mix ferns with your flowers; they will give you a kind of green texture which nothing else will. All this applies to *all* kinds of gardens—open, rock, and alpine, and even vegetable gardens. Keep the higher-growing annuals—cosmos, nasturtium, annual poppies, and coreopsis, for example—in your cutting garden where they won't interfere with your perennials.

But all the colors of the rainbow by themselves don't make a garden. The leaves of the plants form the background against which the colors shine, setting them off against a foil as many-hued and variegated as the flowers themselves. And at times you might even get tired of all the blaze, were it not growing against the coolness of the green in the leaves, the grasses, the groundcovers, and the trailing vines. There are plants whose leaves alone are as interesting in texture and design as the blooms. I have already mentioned the leaves of violets and lupines, but a bed of geranium leaves (before the plants are fully grown) makes lush carpeting.

Equally beautiful are the leaves of the foamflower (*Tiarella cordifolia*) of the saxifrage family, a woodland plant of great beauty which is now often cultivated in gardens; leaves of primulas, also prunella of the mint family of which the heal-all or self-heal (see Chapter Eight) is a member and which makes a particularly dense and interesting textured filler for bare spots and empty places.

CASTOR-OIL PLANT (*Ricinus communis*) of the spurge family is a decorative annual native to Africa. Its fruit has well known medicinal value, and its leaves make an interesting show among flowering plants.

COLEUS, of the mint family, often just called the foliage plant, must be started indoors and cannot be set out in the garden until all danger of frost is passed. The surprising shades of its leaves—brown, red, crimson, with frilled or plain edges, make it a good plant which children can grow.

On the following pages you will find three charts, one for perennials, one for annuals and biennials, and a third for bulbs, from which you will be able to choose the flowers you wish in your garden. The first two charts are arranged by color; all you have to do is to follow the shape of your beds and borders, check on the sizes to which the plant will usually grow, and then make your plants. It is a good rule of thumb to allow one to one and a half feet of space between the larger plants, and six to ten inches between the smaller ones.

The growth of any plant is not entirely predictable; of course you will learn about spacing by trial and error.

Following the charts is a list of the most popular bulbs, corms, and rhizomes which require planting spaces different from perennials and annuals, although you can, of course, use many of them with the rooted plants.

PERENNIALS—WHITE TO CREAM
Sun = ○   Shade = ●   Partial Sun = *

COMMON NAME *Botanical Name*	Season	Height In Inches	Location
ACONITE *Aconitum napellus*	June	24	*
ALPINE ROCK CRESS *Arabis alpina*	April	12	○
ARCTIC DAISY *Chrysanthemum articum*	Sept.	6	○
ARTEMISIA *Artemisia lactiflora*	Aug. to Sept.	48–72	○
BABY'S BREATH *Gypsophila paniculata*	June to July	30	○
BALLOONFLOWER *Platycodon grandiflorum*	May to Oct.	24	○
BALLOONFLOWER *Platycodon Mariesii*	May to Oct.	12	○
CANYON POPPY *Romneya Coulteri*	June	48	○
CARPATHIAN BELLFLOWER *Campanula carpatica*	June to Oct.	8	○
CHRISTMAS ROSE *Helleborus niger*	Winter	12	*
CLETHRA LOOSESTRIFE *Lysimachia clethroides*	July to Aug.	24	*

COMMON NAME *Botanical Name*	Season	Height In Inches	Location
CULVER'S PHYSIC *Veronica virginica*	July	48–60	○
DROPWORT *Filipendula hexapetala*	June to July	12–24	○
EVERGREEN CANDYTUFT *Iberis sempervirens*	Mar. to Apr.	9–12	○
GAS PLANT *Dictamnus albus*	May	36	○
GIANT DAISY *Chrysanthemum uliginosum*	Sept.	60	○
GREAT ASTILBE *Astilbe grandis*	June to July	60	○
GROUND CLEMATIS *Clematis recta*	June to July	48	○
IBERIAN GERANIUM *Geranium ibericum*	June	12	○
ICELAND POPPY *Papaver nudicaule*	June to Oct.	12	○
JAPANESE PRIMROSE *Primula japonica*	June	24	●
JUPITER'S BEARD *Centranthus ruber*	June to Aug.	18	○
MILKY BELLFLOWER *Campanula lactiflora*	June to Sept.	36–74	○
MUNSTEAD COLUMBINE *Aquilegia vul.nivea*	April	18	○

What Flowers Should You Cultivate?

COMMON NAME *Botanical Name*	Season	Height In Inches	Location
PEACHLEAF BELLFLOWER *Campanula persicifolia*	June to July	24–36	○
PEONY *Paenoia*	May to June	18–48	○
PLUME POPPY *Bocconia cordata*	July	72–96	○
PRIMROSE *Primula Sieboldii*	May	10–12	●
SCABIOSA *Scabiosa caucasica*	June to Sept.	24	○
SHASTA DAISY *Chrysanthemum maximum*	June to Sept.	24	○
SIBERIAN LARKSPUR *Delphinium grandiflorum*	July to Sept.	18	○
SILVER KING *Artemisia albula*	Summer	24–36	○
SNOW-IN-SUMMER *Cerastium tomentosum*	June	6	○
SPOTTED BELLFLOWER *Campanula punctata*	June	18	○
STOKES' ASTER *Stokesia laevis*	July to Aug.	12–24	○
TAURUS CERASTIUM *Cerastium biebersteinii*	June	8	○
TUNIC FLOWER *Tunica saxifraga*	July to Oct.	6	○

COMMON NAME *Botanical Name*	Season	Height In Inches	Location
VIOLET BOLTONIA *Boltonia latisquama*	Sept.	48–72	○
WALLCRESS *Arabis albida*	April	12	○
WHITE BOLTONIA *Boltonia asteroides*	Sept.	60–72	○

PERENNIALS–YELLOW

Sun = ○   Shade = ●   Partial Sun = *

COMMON NAME *Botanical Name*	Season	Height In Inches	Location
ALYSSUM *Alyssum montanum*	May	15	○
AMUR ADONIS *Adonis amurensis*	April	12	○
AMUR DAY LILY *Hemerocallis Middendorffii*	June	24	○
AUTUMN SUN *Rudbeckia nitida*	Aug. to Oct.	60	○
AVENS *Geum Lady Stratheden*	July to Sept.	24	○
COWSLIP PRIMROSE *Primula veris*	April to May	9	●
CUSHION SPURGE *Euphorbia epithymoides*	May	24	○
DUSTY MEADOW RUE *Thalictrum glaucum*	June to July	24	○

What Flowers Should You Cultivate?

COMMON NAME *Botanical Name*	Season	Height In Inches	Location
DWARF GOLDENTUFT *Alyssum saxatile*	May	8–10	O
EARLY TORCH LILY *Kniphofia rufa*	June	18	O
FERNLEAF YARROW *Achillea filipendulina*	June to Aug.	36	O
GLOBE CENTAUREA *Centaurea macrocephala*	July	18	O
GLOBEFLOWER *Trollius europaeus*	April to June	24	O
GLOBEFLOWER *Trollius Ledebouri*	June	36	O
GOLDEN COLUMBINE *Aquilegia chrysantha*	May to Aug.	24	O
GOLDEN FLAX *Linum flavum*	June to Aug.	12	O
GOLDEN TUFT *Alyssum saxatile*	May	18	O
GOLDWINGS *Solidago virgaurea*	Sept.	60	O
ICELAND POPPY *Papaver nudicaule*	June to Oct.	12	O
JAPANESE DAY LILY *Hemerocallis thunbergii*	July	48	O
LEOPARD'S BANE *Doronicum caucasicum*	May to June	24	O

COMMON NAME *Botanical Name*	Season	Height In Inches	Location
LEOPARD'S BANE *Doronicum plantagineum*	June	24	○
MACEDONIAN LINARIA *Linaria macedonica*	June	36	○
MAXIMILIAN SUNFLOWER *Helianthus Maximiliani*	Oct.	84	○
MAXIMILIAN SUNFLOWER *Helianthus orgyalis*	Oct.	84	○
MEXICAN COLUMBINE *Aquilegia Skinneri*	April	12	○
NEPAL CINQUEFOIL *Potentilla Warrensii*	June to Aug.	24	○
PRAIRIE SUNFLOWER *Helianthus scaberrimus*	Sept. to Oct.	48	○
SILVER ALYSSUM *Alyssum argenteum*	June to Aug.	15	○
SPRING ADONIS *Adonis vernalis*	April	8–12	○
SUNFLOWER *Helianthus atrorubens*	Sept.	36–72	○
SYRIAN CENTAUREA *Centaurea babylonica*	June to Aug.	36	○
THINLEAF SUNFLOWER *Helianthus decapetalus*	Aug.	72	○
WELSH POPPY *Meconopsis cambrica*	June	12	○

COMMON NAME Botanical Name	Season	Height In Inches	Location
WOLFBANE *Aconitum lycoctonum*	July	36	*
YELLOW CEPHALARIA *Cephalaria alpina*	June to Aug.	72	○
YELLOW LARKSPUR *Delphinium zalil*	June to July	12–24	○

PERENNIALS–ORANGE

Sun = ○   Shade = ●   Partial Sun = *

COMMON NAME Botanical Name	Season	Height In Inches	Location
BLANKETFLOWER *Gaillardia aristata*	May to Oct.	12–15	○
BONFIRE TORCH LILY *Kniphofia Uvaria var. Pfitzeriana*	Sept.	36	○
GLOBEFLOWER *Trollius asiaticus*	May to June	24	○
GLOBEFLOWER *Trollius sinensis*	July	24	○
ICELAND POPPY *Papaver nudicaule*	June to Oct.	12	○
OLYMPIC POPPY *Papaver pilosum*	June to Oct.	24	○
ORANGE DAY LILY *Hemerocallis aurantiaca*	June	36	○

COMMON NAME *Botanical Name*	Season	Height In Inches	Location
ORANGE DAY LILY *Hemerocallis dumortierii*	June	18	○
ORANGE LARKSPUR *Delphinium nudicaule*	July	18	○
PITCHER HELIOPSIS *Heliopsis pitcheriana*	July to Aug.	36	○
TORCH LILY *Kniphofia Uvaria*	Aug. to Sept.	36–48	○

PERENNIALS–PINK

Sun = ○   Shade = ●   Partial Sun = *

COMMON NAME *Botanical Name*	Season	Height In Inches	Location
ASTILBE *Astilbe japonica*	June to July	24	○
DWARF PINK RAY BOLTONIA *Boltonia nana*	Sept.	24	○
FALSE DRAGONHEAD *Physostegia virginiana*	July to Sept.	36–60	*
FALSE DRAGONHEAD *Physostegia var. vivid*	July to Oct.	18	*
LEBANON STONE CRESS *Aethionema coririfolium*	April	9	*
MEADOWSWEET *Filipendula palmata*	July	24–36	○
PEONY *Paeonia*	May to June	18–48	○

COMMON NAME *Botanical Name*	Season	Height In Inches	Location
PERSIAN STONE CRESS *Aethionema grandiflorum*	May	12	*
ROCK CRESS *Arabis aubrietioides*	April	12	O
ROSALIE THRIFT *Statice montana* (Alpina)	June	8	O
ROSALIE THRIFT *Statice plantaginea* (Dianthoides)	June	18	O
THRIFT *Statice armeria*	June to July	6	O

PERENNIALS–ROSE

COMMON NAME *Botanical Name*	Season	Height In Inches	Location
ANEMONE *Anemone hupehensis*	Aug. to Sept.	12	*
BEAR'S BREECH *Acanthus millis*	July to Aug.	36	O
CATTAIL GAYFEATHER *Liatris pycnostachya*	Aug. to Sept.	48	O
CHECKERBLOOM *Sidalcea malvaeflora*	June to July		O
CHEDDAR PINK *Dianthus caesius*	June to July	8–12	O
DAVID'S ASTILBE *Astilbe Davidii*	June to July	60	O

COMMON NAME *Botanical Name*	Season	Height In Inches	Location
FLOWER OF JOVE *Lychnis Flos Jovis*	June	18	○
GAS PLANT *Dictamnus albus*	May	36	○
GRASSLEAF GAYFEATHER *Liatris graminifolia*	Aug.	24	○
NEPAL CINQUEFOIL *Potentilla nepalensis*	June to Aug.	18	
PRIMROSE *Primula Sieboldii*	May	10–12	●
ROCKY MOUNTAIN CRANESBILL *Geranium Fremontii*	June	12	○
ROSALIE THRIFT *Statice Laucheana*	June to July	9	○
SATIN CHECKERBLOOM *Sidalcea malvaeflora Listeri*	June to July	12–60	○
SILVERDUST PRIMROSE *Primula pulverulenta*	June	30	●
TUNIC FLOWER *Tunica saxifraga*	July to Oct.	6	○

PERENNIALS–RED

COMMON NAME *Botanical Name*	Season	Height In Inches	Location
AVENS *Geum chiloense florepleno*	July to Sept.	24	○

COMMON NAME *Botanical Name*	Season	Height In Inches	Location
AVENS *Geum Mrs. Bradshaw*	July to Sept.	24	○
BLANKETFLOWER *Gaillardia aristata*	May to Oct.	12–15	○
BLOOD PINK *Dianthus cruentus*	July	4–5	○
CARDINAL LARKSPUR *Delphinium cardinale*	Aug.	36	○
CORAL BELLS *Heuchera sanguinea*	July	12–24	*
DOUBLE CLUSTER PINK *Dianthus latifolius*	July to Oct.	12–18	○
JUPITER'S BEARD *Centranthus ruber*	June to Aug.	18	○
PEONY *Paeonia*	May to June	18–48	○
PINK BEAUTY *Penstemon barbatus*	June to July	36	○
TORREY PENSTEMON *Penstemon Torrei*	June to July	36	○
VERBENA *Verbena canadensis*	June to Sept.	9–12	○

PERENNIALS–BLUE

COMMON NAME *Botanical Name*	Season	Height In Inches	Location
ACONITE *Aconitum napellus*	June	24	*

COMMON NAME *Botanical Name*	Season	Height In Inches	Location
ASTER *Aster subcaeruleus*	June to July	15	○
AUTUMN MONKSHOOD *Aconitum autumnale*	Sept. to Oct.	36	*
AZURE MONKSHOOD *Aconitum Fischeri*	Sept. to Oct.	36	*
AZURE SAGE *Salvia azurea grandiflora*	Aug. to Sept.	48	○
BAIKAL SKULLCAP *Scutellaria baicalensis*	July	12	○
BOG SALIVA *Salvia uliginosa*	Aug. to Sept.	36	○
CARPATHIAN BELLFLOWER *Campanula carpatica*	June to Oct.	8	○
CLEMATIS *Clematis integrifolia*	June to Oct.	18–24	○
COLUMBINE *Aquilegia glandulosa*	May to June	12	○
COLUMBINE *Aquilegia sibirica*	May to June	12	○
CUPID'S DART *Catananche caerulea*	Sept.	18	○
DROPMORE BUGLOSS *Anchusa Italica*	June to July	36–60	○
EARLY BUGLOSS *Anchusa Barrelieri*	May	24	○

COMMON NAME *Botanical Name*	Season	Height In Inches	Location
FUNKIA, PLANTAIN LILY *Hosta caerulea*	July to Aug.	24–36	*
IBERIAN GERANIUM *Geranium ibericum*	June	12	○
LARKSPUR *Delphinium belladonna*	June to Sept.	24	○
LARKSPUR *Delphinium bellamosum*	June to Sept.	24	○
LOW GLOBE THISTLE *Echinops humilis*	July	12	○
MEADOW SAGE *Salvia pratensis*	June to Aug.	24	○
MEALYCUP SAGE *Salvia farinacea*	Aug. to Sept.	48	○
MILKY BELLFLOWER *Campanula lactiflora*	June to Sept.	36–74	○
NARBONNE FLAX *Linum narbonense*	May	24	○
PEACHLEAF BELLFLOWER *Campanula persicifolia*	June to July	24–36	○
PERENNIAL FLAX *Linum perenne*	June to Aug.	18	○
PITCHER SAGE *Salvia Pitcheri*	Aug. to Sept.	48	○
SEA HOLLY *Eryngium maritimum*	July to Sept.	12	○

COMMON NAME *Botanical Name*	Season	Height In Inches	Location
SEA HOLLY *Eryngium Oliverianum*	July to Aug.	36	○
SEA HOLLY *Eryngium planum*	July to Aug.	24	○
SIBERIAN BUGLOSS *Anchusa myosotidiflora* *(Brunnera)*	May to June	12–18	○
SIBERIAN LARKSPUR *Delphinium grandiflorum*	July to Sept.	18	○
STEEL GLOBE THISTLE *Echinops Ritro*	July	36	○
SWISS FORGET-ME-NOT *Myosotis dissitiflora*	May	9	*
VIOLET MONKSHOOD *Aconitum Wilsonii*	Sept.	48	*

PERENNIALS–LAVENDER

COMMON NAME *Botanical Name*	Season	Height In Inches	Location
BALLOONFLOWER *Platycodon grandiflorum*	May to Oct.	24	○
BALLOONFLOWER *Platycodon Mariesii*	May to Oct.	12	○
BASTARD SPEEDWELL *Veronica spuria*	June to July	18	○
BEAR'S BREECH *Acanthus nollis*	July to Aug.	36	○

What Flowers Should You Cultivate?

COMMON NAME *Botanical Name*	Season	Height In Inches	Location
BIGLEAF STATICE *Limonium latifolium*	Aug.	20	○
BLUEBEARD *Caryopteris incana*	Sept.	36	○
CLUMP SPEEDWELL *Veronica maritima*	Aug.	24	○
DANE'S BLOOD *Campanula glomerata*	July to Aug.	18	○
EUROPEAN COLUMBINE *Aquilegia vulgaris*	April	18	○
FUNKIA, PLANTAIN LILY *Hosta japonica*	July to Aug.	12–24	*
HIMALAYAN PRIMROSE *Primula denticulata*	May	10	●
JAPANESE SCABIOSA *Scabiosa japonica*	June to Sept.	24	○
LILAC GERANIUM *Geranium grandiflorum*	June	12	○
MOUNTAIN BLUET *Centaurea montana*	June to July	48	○
MUSSIN CATMINT *Nepeta Mussini*	May to Sept.	12	○
SCABIOSA *Scabiosa caucasica*	June to Sept.	24	○
STATICE *Limonium Gmelini*	Aug.	20	○

COMMON NAME *Botanical Name*	Season	Height In Inches	Location
STOKES'S ASTER *Stokesia laevis*	July to Aug.	12–24	O
TATARIAN STATICE *Limonium tataricum*	Aug.	20	O
TUBE CLEMATIS *Clematis heracleaefolia*	Aug.	36–48	O
YUNNAN MEADOW RUE *Thalictrum dipterocarpum*	Aug.	48	O

PERENNIALS–PURPLE

COMMON NAME *Botanical Name*	Season	Height In Inches	Location
AMETHYST ERYNGIUM *Eryngium amethystinum*	July to Aug.	24	O
ARMENIAN CRANESBILL *Geranium armenum*	May to July	24	O
ASTER *Aster Amellus*	July to Aug.	18	O
BETHLEHEM SAGE *Pulmonaria saccharata*	April to May	6–18	O
BETONY *Stachys Betonica grandiflora*	June	12–36	O
BLUETOP ERYNGO *Eryngium alpinum*	July to Aug.	24	O
CATTAIL GAYFEATHER *Liatris scariosa*	Aug.	24	O

What Flowers Should You Cultivate?

COMMON NAME *Botanical Name*	Season	Height In Inches	Location
CLAMMY CAMPION *Lychnis viscaria*	June	12	○
COLUMBINE MEADOW RUE *Thalictrum aquilegifolium*	May to June	12–36	○
DRAGONHEAD *Dracocephalum Ruyschiana*	June to July	24	*
FUNKIA, PLANTAIN LILY *Sieboldiana*	June to July	30	*
PRIMROSE *Primula Sieboldii*	May	10–12	●
ROCKET *Hesperis matronalis*	June to July	36	○
SPIKE SPEEDWELL *Veronica spicata*	June to July	12	○
VELVET CENTAUREA *Centaurea gymnocarpa*	June	18	○
WOOLLY BETONY *Stachys Betonica lanata*	July	12	○
WOOLLY SPEEDWELL *Veronica incana*	July to Aug.	12	○

PERENNIALS–VARIOUS

COMMON NAME *Botanical Name*	Season	Height In Inches	Location
ALLWOOD'S PINK *Dianthus Allwoodii*	June to July	12–18	○

COMMON NAME *Botanical Name*	Season	Height In Inches	Location
ARENDS PHLOX *Phlox Arendsii*	May to June	24	○
ENGLISH PRIMROSE *Primula acaulis*	April to May	6	●
ENGLISH PRIMROSE *Primula auricula*	June	12	●
JAPANESE PRIMROSE *Primula polyantha*	April to May	6–10	●
JAPANESE WINDFLOWER *Anemone japonica*	Sept. to Oct.	36	*
ORIENTAL POPPY *Papaver orientale*	June	36	○
PAINTED LADY (PYRETHRUM) *Chrysanthemum coccineum*	June	24	○
SIBERIAN LARKSPUR *Delphinium hybrids*	June	60	○
SMOOTH PHLOX *Phlox suffruticosa (glaberrima)*	June to Sept.	24	○
SWEET WILLIAM *Dianthus barbatus*	June	18	○
TUFTED PANSY *Viola cornuta*	April to Oct.	6–10	*
WASHINGTON LUPINE *Lupinus polyphyllus*	June	36–48	○

MOST USEFUL ANNUALS–WHITE
Sowing date varies according to area. B = Biennial

COMMON NAME *Botanical Name*	Height In Inches	Remarks	Location
BABY'S BREATH *Gypsophila elegans*	10–18	Also pink	○
BUTTERFLY FLOWER *Schizanthus* *hybridus*	36–50	Various colors	○
CANDYTUFT *Iberis, Umbellata*	12	Also pink, violet	● or ○
CAPE MARIGOLD *African daisy* *Dimorphotheca* *annua*	8–14	Also orange and lemon	○
CHINA ASTER *Callistephus* *chinensis*	8–18	Also blue, lavender, pink and red	○
CHINA PINK *Dianthus chinensis*	12–18	Also red and lilac	○
Clarkia elegans	18–36	Rose to white and purple	○
COSMOS *Cosmos bipinnatus*	60–100	Crimson to white	○
DRUMMOND PHLOX *Phlox Drummondii*	9–18	Also magenta, rose, tawny and purple	○

COMMON NAME *Botanical Name*	Height In Inches	Remarks	Location
FAREWELL-TO- SPRING *Godetia amoena*	12–30	Rose to white	○
FOUR O'CLOCK *Mirabilis Jalapa*	14–30	Also pink and yellow, dark red	○
GARDEN BALSAM *Impatiens Balsamina*	18–30	Also pink, rose, purple and violet	○
GARDEN VERBENA *Verbena Hortensis*	low	All colors	○
Gilia Capitata	18–24	Also blue	○
HOLLYHOCK *Althaea rosea*	48–60	Various colors	○
HONESTY *Lunaria annua*	18–24		*
FLOWERING TOBACCO *Nicotiana alata*	24–60		○
LOVE-IN-A-MIST *Nigella damascena*	12–15	Also blue	○
MADAGASCAR PERIWINKLE *Vinca Rosea*	12–18	Also rose	●
NEMESIA *Nemesia strumosa*	8–18	Also orange and rose	○
PANSY *Viola*	10	Also yellow, blue, purple	○ or ●

COMMON NAME *Botanical Name*	Height In Inches	Remarks	Location
PETUNIA *Petunia hybrida*	7–12	White to bright rose and purple Red	○
PINCUSHION FLOWER *Scabiosa atropurpurea*	18–24	Also purple, blue, mahogany and rose	○
POPPY *Papaver, annual sp.*	12–20	All colors but blue	○
ROSE MOSS *Portulaca grandiflora*	low	Also purplish-crim- son, and yellow	○
Silene Pendula	6–10	Various colors	○
SNAPDRAGON *Antirrhinum*	6–36	Also orange, yellow, pink, red and purple shades	○
SNOW-ON-THE- MOUNTAIN *Euphorbia marginata*	8–12		○
SWAN RIVER DAISY *Brachycome iberidifolia*	8–18	Also blue and pink	○
SWEET ALYSSUM *Lobularia maritima*	6–12		○
SWEET PEA *Lathyrus odoratus*	24–60	Also pink, rose, purple, yellow, peach and orange	○
SWEET SULTAN *Centaurea moschata*	18–24	Also blue and pink	○

COMMON NAME *Botanical Name*	Height In Inches	Remarks	Location
STOCK *Mathiola incana*	12–20	Also in shades of pink to purple	O
ZINNIA	18–30	All Colors but blue	O

MOST USEFUL ANNUALS–YELLOW

COMMON NAME *Botanical Name*	Height In Inches	Remarks	Location
AFRICAN DAISY *Arctotis* *atoechadifolia*	30–48	Also blue	O
BLANKET FLOWER *Gaillardia pulchella*	12–20	Also red	O
CALIFORNIA POPPY *Eschscholtzia* *californica*	12–40	Also orange, pink, white	O
CONEFLOWER *Rudbeckia bicolor* *superba*	12–20		O
GOLDEN COREOPSIS *Coreopsis tinctoria*	12–36		O
GOLDENWAVE *Coreopsis* *drummondi*	12–24		O
MARIGOLD *Tagetes*	15–24	Also red, orange, brown	O
MIGNONETTE *Reseda*	low	Yellow-green	O

Botanical Name COMMON NAME	Height In Inches	Remarks	Location
NASTURTIUM *Tropaeolum majus*	7–15	Yellow-red	○
POT MARIGOLD *Calendula officinalis*	8–20	Also orange	● or ○
PRICKLE POPPY *Argemone grandiflora*	24–36		○
Salpiglossis sinuata	18–30	Yellows and purples variegated	○
SUNFLOWER *Helianthus*	48–120		○
SUMMER CYPRESS *Kochia scoparia*	20–36	Also red	○

MOST USEFUL ANNUALS–ORANGE and GOLDEN

COMMON NAME Botanical Name	Height In Inches	Remarks	Location
AFRICAN DAISY *Arctotis breviscapa*	low		○
MEXICAN TULIP POPPY *Hunnemannis fumariaefolia*	12–20		○
MONARCH OF THE VELDT *Venidium fastuosum*	18–30		○
STRAWFLOWER *Helichrysum bracteatum*	24–36	Also red, white	○

COMMON NAME *Botanical Name*	Height In Inches	Remarks	Location
TICKWEED *Coreopsis stillmani*	12–18		○
WALLFLOWER *Cheiranthus cheiri*	12–18	Also yellow, red	○
			.

MOST USEFUL ANNUALS–RED

COMMON NAME *Botanical Name*	Height In Inches	Remarks	Location
EVENING STOCK *Mathiola bicornis*	low	Purple-black	○
FLOWERING FLAX *Linum grandiflorum*	12–24		○
FOXGLOVE *Digitalis purpurea*	30–48	Also white, pink	*
GLOBE AMARANTH *Gomphrena globosa*	8–12	Magenta, amaranth, salmon-white	○
JOSEPH'S COAT *Amaranthus tricolor*	12–36		○
LOVE-LIES- BLEEDING *Amaranthus caudatus*	46–50		○
SCARLET SAGE *Salvia splendens*	18–30	Scarlet	○

MOST USEFUL ANNUALS–PURPLE and MAGENTA

COMMON NAME *Botanical Name*	Height In Inches	Remarks	Location
TICKWEED *Coreopsis atkinsonia*	24–48	Brown-purple	○
SPIDERFLOWER *Cleome spinosa*	48–60	Rose-purple	○
SWEET ROCKET *Hesperis matronalis*	24	Also white	*

MOST USEFUL ANNUALS–PINK

COMMON NAME *Botanical Name*	Height In Inches	Remarks	Location
CUSHION GYPSOPIIILA *Gypsophila muralis*	6–8		○
MALLOW *Lavatera trimestris*	24–40	Also white	○
ROSE OF HEAVEN *Lychnis Coeli-rosa*	12–15		○
SPIDERFLOWER *Cleome spinosa*	36–48	Also white	○
SWEET WILLIAM *Dianthus barbatus*	6–18	Also maroon, white	○

MOST USEFUL ANNUALS–BLUE

COMMON NAME *Botanical Name*	Height In Inches	Remarks	Location
AGERATUM *Ageratum*	4–9		* or ○
BABY BLUEEYES *Nemophila menzitsii*	6	Also white	*
BLUE LACEFLOWER *Didiscus* *Trachymene coerulea*	18–30		○
Browallia speciosa *major*	8–12		○
CHINESE FORGET- ME-NOT *Cynoglossum* *amabile*	18–24		○
CORNFLOWER *Centaurea Cyanus*	12–24	Also white, pink	*
EDGING LOBELIA *Lobelia Erinus*	low	Also white, wine	○
FORGET-ME-NOT *Myosotis, annual sp.*	6–9	Also pink, white	*
LARKSPUR *Delphinium ajacis* *and consolida*	12–24	Also pink, white, lilac	○
STATICE *Limonium sinuatum*	12–24	Also white, rose	○

BULBS, TUBERS, AND RHIZOMES
NOTE: All in sun

COMMON NAME *Botanical Name*	Season of Planting	Season of Bloom	Depth of Planting	Height of Flower
LILY FAMILY				
CROWN IMPERIAL *Fritillaria*	Autumn	April, May	7″ (on side)	10–12″
DOGTOOTH VIOLET *Erythronium*	Autumn	April	4″	4″
GRAPE HYACINTH *Muscari*	Autumn	Early spring	3″	4″
MADONNA LILY *Lilium candidum*	Autumn	Late summer	4″	12″ to 6′
ORNAMENTAL GARLIC *Allium*	Autumn	May to July	2″	Various
STAR OF BETHLEHEM *Orthnigalum*	Any time	May, June	3″	8″
TULIPS *Tulipa*	Autumn	Spring	4–5″	4″ to 3′
WOOD HYACINTH *Scilla*	Autumn	Early spring	Surface	4″
IRIS FAMILY CROCUS	Autumn & Spring *	Spring & autumn	2″	2–4″
GLADIOLAE	March to May	Late summer	4″	1–4′
IRIS (RACEME)	Autumn	Spring & summer **	5″	Various
AMARYLLIS FAMILY DAFFODIL & NARCISSUS	Autumn	Spring ***	8″	2–18″
SNOWDROP *Galanthus*	Autumn	Late winter, Early spring	3″	7–8″

* For next season's bloom.
** Some rhizomes, great variation of species.
*** Depending on species.

Whatever flowers you decide on, you must either grow them from seed or buy seedlings or grown plants from nurseries. There are thousands of nurseries in the United States, large and small, in all neighborhoods. One I know of—B. deJager & Sons, in South Hamilton, Mass.—carries only bulbs. The White Flower Farm in Litchfield, Conn., and the Wayside Gardens in Mentor, Ohio, 4460, have excellent catalogues with much useful information about every plant they sell. The G. W. Park Seed Co., Inc., in Greenwood, South Carolina 29646, will send you their seed catalogue. The seed catalogue to end all seed catalogues, however, comes from Thompson and Morgan, Ltd., Ipswich, England.

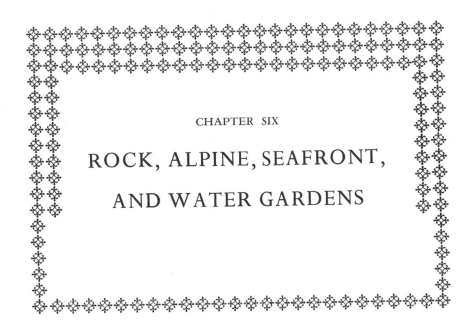

CHAPTER SIX

ROCK, ALPINE, SEAFRONT, AND WATER GARDENS

He builded better than he knew;
The conscious stone to beauty grew.
RALPH WALDO EMERSON, POEMS (1847)

ONE of the most rewarding ways of gardening is with rock and stone. Here you are free to let your fancy fly; your love of color, your feeling for design, your imagination and ingenuity are limited only by what nature has placed in your path. Perhaps making a blooming world among haphazard outcroppings of inert rock (though stone is by no means dead) is closer to an experiment in creation than almost any other kind of gardening.

In early spring, when not much else is yet in bloom, you can make magic with color where there are only cracks, fissures, rough planes, and crags. With seeds and seedlings, with bulbs and burgeoning plants, you can paint in rock. There are no two rock gardens alike; each is its Creator's own; each as singular and personal as the impression of a hand. For the gardener who

163

takes a moment to look, stones and rocks show surprising surfaces, depths, and elevations; they change in the light of day;
their texture and color vibrate and glisten under the moon and
the stars.

The idea of rock gardening came from England. Already
Francis Bacon wished they existed, using "hillocks" for strawberries, herbs, and other plants. It took another century for rock
gardens to be understood and become popular—mostly in the
English countryside and its innumerable "cottage gardens."
Gradually other and perhaps more sophisticated gardeners discovered the fun and the beauty of working with natural stone.
And all of a sudden, rock gardens became the fashion—almost
de rigueur, in the parks and enormous gardens of the noble and
the rich.

Travelers began to collect rock garden or "Alpine" specimens
from all over the world—from the Himalayas to the Alps. And,
of course, the mountain climbers of Austria and Switzerland
had long ago discovered that the most extravagantly beautiful
rock gardens of all were those which nature had planted in the
rugged wilderness just below the timberline. And is there anything more breathtaking than an Alp in bloom?

American gardeners followed the English; and today a rock
garden is part and parcel of many gardeners' lives . . . particularly where natural rock outcroppings abound, as in our
northeastern and northwestern states.

Such a natural outcropping, somehow almost always in proportion to the rest of the space around your house, and the
garden, makes the best and perhaps the most beautiful and
practical basis for a rock garden. More often than not, wind and
rain and the natural accumulation of humus have already done
some planting: lichens and mosses may have established themselves in the cracks and fissures, and at least part of your work

might have been done for you. Dam up an open fissure with a few matching rocks, add more earth here and there, and the new planting can begin. See if you can continue and perhaps embellish nature's work.

Whatever one decides to do, however, the basic idea was well expressed by H. S. Adams at the beginning of this century: "No rock garden worthy of the name has ever been created by man that did not depend on a study of those that nature has given the world in prodigal abundance. There were the where

An especially good rock garden planted in levels in front of a wall, showing how several kinds of plants can be grown in a harmonious whole.

and the why of it all, and man simply saw and made use of his observations.

"The advantages of a rock garden are primarily an element of picturesqueness that nothing else can provide, and the possession of a place in which can be grown some of the loveliest flowers on earth that, if they flourish at all, will never do as well in the ordinary garden as in conditions more or less approximating their natural habitat. Also it may be made a pleasance of extraordinary attractiveness. Occasionally—and here is one of the most important things to be learned about the rock garden— it is the veritable key to the garden situation; there are small places where no other kind is worthwhile, if, indeed, it is possible."

On the other hand, if you own a perfectly flat piece of land without a single natural rock or stone sticking out from the soil, it is not too difficult to have the pleasure and excitement of a rock garden anyway.

If you happen to have an old stone wall that serves no particular purpose and is made of assorted, fairly large, and usually flat fieldstone (dug up by the early settlers), and you have the energy and strength of a horse and the creative urge of a Michelangelo—or perhaps even some atavistic craving for moving boulders as though you were to build a temple to the gods of the earth, or say with Isaiah, "I will lay the stones with fair colors and lay the foundations with sapphires" (54:11)—then by all means, build yourself a cairn of rocks in which to grow the jewels for your piece of land.

Even if you don't have an old stone wall, there are companies which sell natural stone and will deliver to your garden as much as you need (or your purse permits). But before you do anything, several experts suggest that you put down pieces of newspaper in the shape of your planned rock garden to determine the best placement of rocks. There are two problems with using this method, however: a rock garden, like Rome, cannot be built in one day, and no flat pieces of paper will give you any idea how high you want to go. A better idea is to get empty grocery boxes in varying sizes (your supermarket is usually happy to get rid of them) and experiment with placement, and thus compose your rock garden plan. It will then be easier to determine what size of garden your property can accommodate, and how much work you really want to do.

Any stoneyard will be able to tell you how many rocks you need for a given area; and many companies will even advise you how best to go about building. Then, if you have any feeling for composition, you will have a great deal of fun and healthy exercise just doing it. As you place a stone here, and another one there, and then frame the view between cupped hands, you will get the "feel" of your design.

Walk around your work and view it from all directions. Just remember that you don't want your work to end up in a pyramid with four equal sides or some other geometrical form. Free and easy, are the words; when you are finished, and your rock garden begins to bloom, you want it to look as though the Creator Himself had strewn the plants and rocks at your feet.

There are a few other essentials to remember. Choose a piece of ground where an outcrop would *naturally* occur, dig into it about a foot deep, cover the area with gravel and small stones and some sand, and then lay the flattest and largest of your stones on top and not too close together. This will form the basis for the all-important drainage, almost like a dry well. In a natural rock assemblage, excessive water will find its own way. In a constructed rock garden, you have to help it.

Then add soil between the lowest stones, and, as you continue, add more soil between the rocks. The location of your new garden spot will determine what kind of soil to use. Most flowering alpines need full sun, but wildflowers and ferns will give you a more "natural" look and will tolerate some shade. Provide pockets of woodland soil for them wherever there is room. You may also wish to add low-growing evergreens which soon will give your garden a look of age and permanence.

In some places you may wish to add smaller pebbles such as the flat stones often found on the beaches and among which succulents will take hold and add their lovely gray-green and red to the other, more specific colors of your rock garden plants. At any rate, either sun or partial shade will allow you to grow a wide variety and diversity of plants.

If you have a single large boulder jutting out in the middle of nowhere—many people have, without quite knowing what to do with it short of blasting it to smithereens—it could be extended with other rocks and leave it, as perhaps, the high point of your "rockery." Or, the boulder can be extended with "scree" —that kind of small broken-up stone which forms the moraines of glaciers high up on the mountainsides, but can be duplicated artificially. A great many small rock plants will grow here and find their way in and around the stone; usually they will bloom or spread a year or two after they have been planted. Mosses and small evergreens will also do well; but the best plants for scree are Alpine flowers as we know them from the Rockies, the Alps, and the Himalayas. But growing Alpines is a difficult task for the average gardener, and we shall return to it.

One of the most stunning *natural* rock gardens I have ever encountered was made in an existing formation of ledge, with careful additions of pebbles, some scree and other stone found around the ledge and matching its color to perfection. Added to the flowering plants are now patches of sedum which grow over some of the stone and stay green until late into the season. Several kinds of *Dianthus,* or pinks of various shape and color grow side by side; some—of uncertain identity and provenance, some already known to Theophrastus. Gerard mentioned twenty-three different kinds including some of the wild ones which grow profusely over here; others are well known, such as sea pink or thrift (*Armeria*) with their whitish blossoms contrasting but also somehow blending with their neighbors. There is also *Dianthus alpinus,* or Alpine pink, with a deep red center.

With the years the plants have grown thicker in luscious tufts, and much of the ledge is now covered with the lovely plants. In late summer, when the seeds have dried in their pods, my friends simply touch them with a sweeping motion of their hands, and the seeds fall where they may, and next year, more sheets of pinks!

In other clefts of this ledge grow thick masses of "hens and chickens" (*Sempervivum tectorum*)—Old World succulents which are also known as "houseleeks" because they have been grown for many centuries on the thatched roofs in several European countries. They flourish in almost any soil, and fill in areas of rock gardens where little else would do as well; and, incidentally, in other spots of the garden they are useful as border plants —along walks, at edges of watery spots, and so on.

In thousands of rocky places along roadsides (where they have been planted by or escaped from the owners of adjoining gardens) as well as in an unbelievable number of rock gardens, grows the seemingly most popular pink of all—not even a dianthus, but rather *Phlox subulata*; in popular parlance, moss or ground pink. It owes its immense popularity to several factors. Its leaves are practically evergreen; it is a creeping perennial which needs no care and seems to like being left alone to spread, wander, and flourish. At times it outgrows everything else, and covers the earth like a lavender-pink and sometimes a white woolly blanket.

There are other plants ideally suited for rock gardening: the exquisite pasque flower (*Pulsatilla vulgaris*) now considered to be an anemone, in a variety of colors, among the early flowers of spring; but not as early as *Crocus tomasinianus,* purple, blue, yellow or white (one of the best is called "taplow ruby") one of the hybrids grown by specialists with infinite and pains-taking care. Although many other croci come up almost as early as the snowdrops and lend themselves to planting in rock gardens as well as beds, borders, and lawns, this particular kind is so stunning in combination with the colors of stone that it deserves to be seen more often.

Not specifically a rock garden plant, but used by some sophisticated gardeners is *Tulipa Kaufmaniana,* the water tulip, another early bloomer—red or yellow. It does exceedingly well in one rock garden I've seen planted among swamp buttercups (*Ranunculus septentrionalis*) and is a good example of how wild plants can coexist with cultivated flowers. Another favorite are the dwarf varieties of iris, such as *Iris lacustris*; and cypress spurge (*Euphorbia cyparissias*) is another wild plant that grows profusely almost anywhere, contrasting its golden color to the grayness of the stone. It is now also cultivated by several growers. And you should not forget saxifrage (see Chapter Eight) which is among the wild rock-loving plants and easily moved from its native locations. There are other wildflowers growing in acid and rocky soil, and if you can match the conditions in your garden, by all means experiment.

Another favorite wildflower in rock gardens is *Phlox divaricata,* often mistakenly called wild sweet william (it belongs in the pink family) with its soft blue, and its welcome habit of spreading. And there are many other early bloomers, wild and cultivated, well suited for the rock garden: primulas, *Scillas* (wood hyacinths); various kinds of potentilla (cinquefoils); alyssum, yellow and white; pentstemon (beardtongue) white or purplish, and many more. We should not omit low-growing evergreens such as juniper (*Juniperus communis*), with its lovely gray berries and far-reaching branches; it easily covers expanses of rock that would otherwise remain bare.

All sorts of ferns will also grow among rock; some prefer limestone to granite; among these are the "walking fern," which actually moves over stone, some of the spleenworts, even Christmas and maidenhair fern which will stay green all summer and thus replace some of the color that fades with the hot days.

Actually it is impossible to write a recipe for a rock garden because plants will have to be selected for available or created spots although it is not impossible to turn the whole idea around and build a rock garden for specific and favorite plants. And although this might require some professional help, it isn't quite as impossible as it sounds. What more fun could there be than to grow exactly what you want, and where you want it? At any rate, like every other part of a garden, a rock garden should in a very real way say something interesting about the owner.

Neither is it necessary to confine a rock garden somewhere in the inner parts of a piece of property. If the edge of a driveway happens to have outcroppings of rocks, or you wish to create them with a few pieces of stone, it can be made into a beautiful and welcoming stretch of Earth: here can grow spurge, candytuft, Virginia bluebells, and, small blue iris and scilla . . . another example of how a true lover of nature can improve on what civilization demands.

Heather is a fascinating plant of many colors and varieties; it grows jewel-like among rocks. Dioscorides knew about heather (or *Erica* as reported by Gerard) which has grown, evergreen and blooming, along the Mediterranean and in Africa for a very long time. Another species grows wild in the Scottish Highlands; others were imported to our country and have escaped into the wilderness. It is now going the way of the tulip, the rose, and the geranium as aficionados breed hybrids with new colors and habits. Some species need protection for the winter; but once you have learned the knack of working with heather, you will agree that there are few plants more worthy of your love and attention.

One friend of mine planted a whole heather garden among the rocks which border her lake; and another brought me photographs of a stunning white shrub from the south of France; and one of the newer varieties is a gorgeous purple-flowered plant from American nurseries.

The "truest" rock plants of all, of course, are those which grow through the scree or nestle against rocks in the pure air and brilliant mountain sunshine. And they are more ravishing than any plant grown anywhere else in the world. Mrs. Lydia Sigourney, an English poet born at the end of the eighteenth century knew this well:

> *Whence are ye? Did some white-winged messenger*
> *On mercy's missions, trust your timid germ*
> *To the cold cradle of eternal snows?*
>   *. . . There ye stand*
> *Leaning your cheek against the thick-ribbed ice,*
> *And looking up with radiant eyes to Him*
> *Who bids you bloom unblanched amid the waste*
> *Of desolation.*

If you live in a rocky country, preferably a bit above sea level; if you know how to gather seeds or where to buy them; if you have endless patience and realize that some seeds will take more than one season to germinate, and that some can be raised under artificial light and others in cold frames; if you are willing to read and listen, to talk and to correspond with other growers, and collect seeds and specimens on your own tours into the mountains—then, with love and luck and perseverance you too may be able to transform your rock garden or wall into an Alpine collector's pride and joy. Found wild and then transplanted, or grown from seed, collected or obtained from a catalogue, the often tiny but usually rounded and tufted plants produce many thousands of shimmering flowerheads.

There are Alpine buttercups and anemones, campanulae, gentians, lady's-slippers and yarrows, large lilies and tiny orchids, and some of the most delicate leaves and grasses in all the world. There is a very special, fat forget-me-not (*Myosotis alpinis*); a brilliant Alpine or mountain goldenrod (*Solidago cutleri*) which, according to the Appalachian Mountain Club, was discovered in 1784 by the Reverend Cutler on his first visit to Mount Washington. I have also seen the Lapland rosebay (*Rhododendron lapponicum*) up there, and the almost white but actually blue columbine of the Rockies at almost nine thousand feet, as well as the Indian paintbrush, also called painted brush, and Wyoming paintbrush (*Castilleja narviflora*) which, however, I have also encountered in the Bluemount Nurseries of Maryland, where it gaily bloomed in flats.

In many places all over the world, Alpine gardening is a cherished pursuit of botanists and gardeners alike. In the back of famed Belvedere Castle, in Vienna, for example, has been

Part of the Alpine section in Dublin Botanical Gardens.

established a large and luscious garden exclusively planted with the plants of the Alps. A breathtaking sight in May and June.

Similarly in the Botanical Gardens of Dublin, Ireland, a great deal of work is being done with Alpine plants. They are started in an "Alpine house," where they are carefully nurtured until they can be set outside. Here they then form the typical small mounts and hillocks, already hoped for by Sir Francis Bacon. A yellow mount is *Draba bryoides,* a good plant for scree, of the genus whitlow grass, suitable only for this kind of gardening; a plant with white flowers is *Anthemis,* still only little known in the United States—related to camomile and quite popular abroad. There are several kinds of saxifrage cultivated for rock and alpine gardens; they are all descendants of the white, wild saxifrage growing in many of our woodland rocks. A particularly handsome plant, in foliage and flower is *Celmisia* which originated in New Zealand; it is related to the daisy, and should do quite well over here. Finally, don't forget that any wall can be garnished with tiny succulent plants.

Instead of adding more names of the Alpine plants you can grow in your rock garden, I would suggest that you write to Alpenglow Gardens, Michaud & Company, 13328 King George Highway, North Surrey, B.C. Canada, since the more unusual Alpine plants can be grown in appropriate climates; and what will grow in British Columbia, certainly will grow in our northern and Alpine regions.

Blessed are ye that sow beside all waters
ISAIAH, 32:20

Perhaps nothing expresses the idea of a personal kind of gardening better and more completely than some of the things Margaret Cousins wrote in her foreword to *The Salty Thumb,*

174

an excellent small book published in 1967 by the Montauk Village Association, Montauk, Long Island: ". . . But when I got down to the sea I became a gardener. For one thing, there was nobody to stop me. I was able to engage in hand-to-hand combat with the indigenous flora of my sandy acres without anyone being able to tell the difference, including me. For another thing, those green outcroppings of tenacious nature, having withstood wind and wave, rain and snow, salt and spray, hot sun and dank fog, deer, rabbit, and chipmunk, were not about to give in before the onslaughts of an inept human being. They were growing there before I came, and they meant to be growing there after I had gone.

"If I hacked at the ancient sumac in an effort to eradicate it in one place or another, it returned with renewed luxuriance in the proper season. If I pruned the old sea roses back to their very roots in an effort to free the tangled path to the beach, they flung out three-foot branches in the spring, and strewed their profligate mauve petals and heady fragrance on every passerby. If I divided the enormous clotted clumps of hardy lilies, the original clumps not only doubled in size and blossomed with vengeance but bulbs I had dropped by mistake sprang up between the flagstones of the terrace and pushed them apart. The pines threw off their cones and produced progeny where I did not expect or really need them. The blackberry vines laced the driveway and caught in my hair, and the wild grape projected powerful tendrils which grabbed my ankles in the dark. . . . Stunned with success, I have invested in various nursery specimens which have entered in direct and aggressive competition with the bayberry and the beach plum and seem bent on outdoing the native product. . . .

"So if you have never achieved progress as a gardener, do not despair. The seaside garden may be a solution if you do not have dreams of a tame and orderly landscape with proper paths, neat hedgerows, and manicured beds of flowers, but are simply interested in growing things. As for myself, I have scarcely experienced such blazing happiness as in those moments when I have stood exhausted by my exertions, my black thumb rimmed with salt, my mouth crammed with blackberries hot from the sun, staring out at the sea over the expanse of green that I call my garden. Though all the while I am forced to suspect that it is something God alone has wrought."

Although the salty waters and the unexpected winds from the sea do not necessarily create the most ideal conditions for the growth of plants, nevertheless, more gardens, large and small, have sprung up along our coasts from the first day European settlers began to turn the American earth. Alice Lounsberry, an earlier writer on gardening, tells this tale:

"While riding last summer in a dusty train, through the full length of Long Island, I heard a man tell his little daughter to remain quietly in her seat while he went into another car to smoke a cigar.

"On his return he asked her if she were tired.

" 'Oh, no,' she answered, 'I have been counting the gardens. There is another! That makes one hundred and twenty.' "

The same thing happens when one drives along the coast of New England. I have never seen better climbing roses or more lush morning glories than at Martha's Vineyard or on Cape Cod.

Other flowering plants successful in seaside gardens are evergreen candytuft (*Iberis sempervirens*); columbines and lupines; Johnny-jump-ups, iris, day and tiger lilies, pinks, sedums and ajuga; most of the usual annuals, and groundcovers which help to hold the sand and native evergreens such as American holly

(*Ilex opaca*); pitch pine, white birch, crab apple, honey locust, willow, oak, and mountain ash. If you can bear to leave the native shrubs alone, beach plum and broom, and the grasses which keep on holding the sand, and perhaps even transplant some of the seaside goldenrod which is even richer and fuller than any of the other goldenrods, you will come up with quite a garden near the sea.

And if you have ever wondered what makes the wild roses in the dunes on the Cape so unbelievably beautiful in the middle of a world that looks all but dead or sleeping, just remember that salt water holds not only salt but also many other life-giving minerals, and that long, long ago it gave birth to life itself.

All other bodies of water—natural or manmade, or natural and man-improved, ponds and lakes, brooks and rivers, swamps and the tiniest pools one may have built with one's own hands—can and do sustain all sorts of life and plants which can be made into lovely garden spots. (Even a large shell filled with water makes a lovely birdbath that can be surrounded with *Phlox diranicata* and myrtle.) Water changes from moment to moment, and the reflections of trees, shrubs, ferns, and flowers create an ever-moving imagery all their own, uniting shapes and separating them, imperceptibly growing and receding as the water and the light move. One can stay by such water, quietly and in peace, musing and resting, forgetting the turmoil of the day.

> A *murmuring sound*
> Of *waters issued from a cave, and spread*
> Into *a liquid plain; then stood unmoved,*
> Pure *as th' expanse of heav'n.*
> JOHN MILTON, 1608–1674

A fern grows happily alongside a small round pool outside a London townhouse.

A round lily pool and a formal garden hedge of boxwood. A wet wall encloses the whole garden in gentle curves.

Often you will find many plants already growing in the wild wet places. If you wish to include them into the general scheme of your garden, all you have to do is to neaten up the edges here and there, thin out the jungle, single out the plants you like best and make room so that they can grow better. You can also transplant other waterflowers you may have found elsewhere: Pickerelweed, arrowhead, water and pond lilies (depending on the flow of the water); some of the stately cattails, and several kinds of iris which bloom in spring but give you their lovely leaves all summer long. And you should not forget to plant marsh marigold and wild forget-me-nots (see Chapter Eight). On the other hand, if you have arranged for a more formal pool within your garden you can edge it with flagstones and plant water lilies right into it, as was done in a London garden. You could add ferns to a place such as this, perhaps a few of the fat buttercups—which like water, and, at the edges, several kinds of primulas (see Chapter Five) echoing the emerald of the water.

CHAPTER SEVEN

BRINGING THE
WILDERNESS CLOSE

To thee a well of never-failing joy—
Hath the earth naught so blessed as the groves
Budding in spring, with choir of nightingales
Vocal in shadowy moonlight? Dost thou love
The glorious changes of the dappled sky,
Whether the circle of the golden sun
Shower the heavens with brightness, newly risen,
Scattering the morning frost, or glorify
The liquid clearness of the summer heaven,
Or the West fade in twilight, till the dark
Fall on the fields, and silence and sweet peace
Pass hand in hand along the dewy earth?
Desire and its fullfillment, side by side
Ranged ever, all along bright days of heaven—
These shall be thine, in that fair city of God
Dwelling, where ever through the blessed streets
Serene light vibrates, and the starry gulfs
Of ether lie above in perfect rest.
"TO THE EARTH", HENRY ALFORD, 1810–1871

THE wilderness is our last domain of freedom. No human laws govern the life of wild plants, the structure of their societies, the ways in which they must flourish or perish. They have been growing alone, wherever it has pleased nature to seed them down, unharried, unrushed, unchanged, over millions of years. They live quietly and grandly by their own tenets, willed only by the earth in which they grow, and the trees and rocks and bodies of water near which they bloom. Wild plants are close to an immortality we shall never know. Their coming is often a mystery, their bearing miraculous.

But men, in their greed for immediate happenings, can destroy the wilderness; and we are on the way to doing just that. Ever since the first settlers came to America we have decimated the land, the forest, and the waters in a rampage of waste such as the world has never known before. We continue to fell more trees and kill the shade in which the woodland flowers bloom. We dam up ponds and rivers and ruin the swamps which have created abundant soil and given life to rare and beautiful plants. We kill the healthy black earth and pour cement and asphalt over it, never again to allow the tiniest living thing to grow. But this is "progress," this is how we build the empires which shall parcel up the world.

Every flower, every ornamental grass, every herb, fern, and tree now growing in our gardens has come from the wilderness at one time or another. After laborious and painstaking experiment, we have learned to manipulate plants as though they were toys or intricate mathematical games; in fact we are justly proud: from the wild rose which grows so modestly at the edge of meadows and woods we have made the lush and pompous "American Beauties" we now find in the catalogues. We have created new varieties from the common blue violet to the sweet carnation. We have turned the wild irises which grew in Egypt and around the Mediterranean into the new thousand-hued and imperious irises which are bred and bred again until now few know how many there are, or how many more tricks are possible. Many are works of art. We have even taken the modest windflower and made large and lush hothouses and garden anemones by the hundreds.

But in the meantime we are obliterating the wilderness; and we call many of the plants of the meadows "weeds" and exterminate them. And yet, in the order of things as they were established long ago—as the stars are in heaven; as the sea is the breeding ground of life; and as the rain nourishes the earth, and wind distributes the semen of the blooming world—wildflowers and plants must have their place. They hold the earth and prevent erosion; they hold the water table at a steady level; they sustain each other and nourish life around them.

This is why the idea of conservation is so important today, why each of us must help to preserve whatever he can. And this is why almost every gardener can do his share in *his* place, no matter how small and seemingly unimportant.

To make wild plants at home amid cultivation is an exciting pursuit. For many of us it is a labor of love, and almost no other kind of gardening is so rewarding. But one must study the lay of one's own piece of land and then try to recreate—if they do not already exist—the exposure to the sun, the necessary amount of shade, the soil, and the general conditions which make life possible for our native plants. One must try to understand the needs of wild plants quite as well as we do our own preferred living conditions. We must look at a group of plants, an entire section of the wilderness as it lives and thrives, and the plants mutually dependent, mutually agreeable, and mutually loving and giving. And just as there is much that we can do to alleviate our own environments, so there is much a gardener can do to help preserve and recreate the fruitful conditions of the wilderness.

It is no more difficult to build a wildflower garden and tend it throughout the year than it is to do the same for any garden of cultivated plants. In many ways it is easier. Once found and planted in their proper places, wild plants need little care; once established, in fact, they seem to like being left alone, like children, to their own ways of growing up. And when you think of the endless labor a flower border or a bed needs—the planting, replanting, and fertilizing, the moving and dividing, the weeding and cultivating, the staking up and cutting back, the removal of finished bloom and the protecting for the winter—you may begin to wonder why anyone started the civilized and cultivated garden in the first place.

In the back of my house is a sweet-smelling, weaving field of ferns—a small sea of green that comes back year after year without my doing anything at all about it. It is bordered on three sides by the typical New England stone wall; I made small paths through it so that it's easier for me to contemplate its splendor. This field is only about two hundred feet on one side, and one hundred feet on the other, and some of my experienced and skillful gardening friends smile sweetly at my excitement.

Hay-scented ferns come up slowly in early spring; the tiny fronds are tightly curled as they grow out of the earth, a mass of the lightest shimmering green. As the ferns grow older and stronger, the color deepens, the curls straighten out, and before I know it the large but delicate fronds are back in full glory. My field of ferns needs little care: an occasional cutting back of bramble; destroying poison ivy—which keeps on returning although I have eradicated most of it through the years; ripping out nettles which are unsightly and have an amazing way of

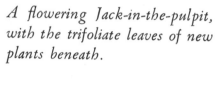

A wild garden, complete with swamp (good for skunk cabbage and cardinal flower).

A flowering Jack-in-the-pulpit, with the trifoliate leaves of new plants beneath.

The fiddleheads of various ferns suggest the tail of a wet monkey, the tongue of a hawkmoth, and a bishop's crozier swathed in gauze.

multiplying, and making small shrift of everything in their way.

In a swampy area to one side is a great mass of cinnamon fern, rich and aristocratic, taller than a man. Here and there are others: Christmas fern, wood and New York fern thriving happily among the others. Some of them I have transplanted closer to the house, some into my very special "Green garden," and others even among my shrubs and flowers. And too, year after year, there are ever more jacks-in-the-pulpit among the ferns, bigger and mightier every year; some are more than three feet tall. I love to see their flowers unfold under the bent leaf, and then the bright red fruit—if I can catch the gleaming sight before the birds do.

It was all there hundreds of years before I came. It grows better and fuller every year, because I love it and can leave it alone. Now there are even wildflowers among the ferns, such as daisies, whorled loosestrife, Queen Anne's lace, wild honeysuckle, deptford pink, and wild geranium, which now wander off up where my herbs and flowers are and between the flagstones, and it would not occur to me to rip out the delicate pink and lavender heads.

A few years ago I dug up a clump of black snakeroot and put it near a rock in front of the ferns; each year it grows taller and the glittering wands loom larger and stronger, weaving in the breeze. This year, without my knowing how it got there, suddenly there was another clump nearby; and though its flowers are small this year, they will grow to be as tall and beautiful as their parent. No doubt that a bird or a gust of wind dropped the seed and I had nothing whatever to do with the bounty.

The two baneberries I planted in another place, have grown tall and fat. The bergamot in back of the herbs grows taller and stronger each year, and the pink blossoms brighten the late summer days. Behind the mountain laurel I had brought from the woods—tiny shrubs then, and now huge—a small dog-

Mountain laurel

wood has begun to bloom this year. I had no idea it was there. And best of all, the giant tulip tree at the corner of my house has dropped seedlings. I have found half a dozen among the ferns, and can only hope that I shall live to see their first blossoms.

Perhaps this is the secret of wild plants. When you have made room for them, when they have come into your life or you have entered into theirs, there is a "thing" between them and you—a feeling, an understanding, a kinship. And though each of us can do only a little, this closeness with the wilderness, perhaps a revival of a very great need in the midst of the confusion of our time, can recapture much we have wantonly lost; a refinding and rebuilding of our lost wilderness.

If you have woods on your property, then your task is easy; you may already have trees, shrubs, ferns, and wildflowers right there. You can add to them, transplant more, make them fuller and richer. You can plant more ferns among the outcroppings of rock, more woodland flowers among those already there, and perhaps a mountain laurel or two.

If your property boasts nothing at all which faintly resembles woods, then these can be created if you have the patience and the time. Twenty years ago I arranged for a few white pines and hemlocks to be planted on a flat and totally indifferent place, next to a driveway. They were only saplings then, no more than a foot or two high. They are giants today. They have created their own bed of needles and their own acid soil. Now there are lady's-slippers among the trees, goldthread, trillium, and mayapple, and, of course, ferns. There is also a beginning carpet of Canada mayflower (false lily of the valley). I had nothing whatever to do with *that*. The carpet will spread, the flowers will bloom; and as time goes by there will be other wildflowers, planted by me or by that generous hand which sets out plants according to an unknown pattern and plan. One year I tried a trailing arbutus, which loves to grow among pine needles, but I failed. Some day I shall try again.

If you own a piece of meadow, *don't* make it into a lawn. Let it be. From spring to late fall there will be many flowers, and along the roadsides and in other meadows you can find many more you can transplant. Cut the meadow down in the autumn; rake up the hay when the grass is dry and add it to your compost heap—or give or sell it to a farmer.

And if there is a brook or a swamp on your place make the most of it. Put marsh marigold in your brook, and wild forget-me nots; they will multiply in no time. And while other flowers fade in the summer, the forget-me-nots will bloom almost to the end. Unless they already grow there, plant cardinal flower and blue lobelia in wet places. Plant water lilies and pickerelweed in a pond, and leave the swamp alone. Cattail and skunk cabbage will give you much pleasure.

Talking about transplanting—which is what the true wild-flower collector will have to do—remember a few things: Never go out without a pail of water and a small shovel or trowel. Be sure that you dig deeply and get all the roots of a plant whatever it may be—small shrub, fern or flower, and make notes mentally or on paper of the exact surroundings in which you dig. You must recreate them as closely as you can to make sure that your new plants will live and prosper. And though this is true of woodland and water plants, it is also true of meadow flowers. Most of them are tougher than the others, but they will not stay alive without your most tender and conscientious care.

Plant *all* varieties in the cool of the early morning, or in late afternoon, or on a dull day as you would any other plant. Keep the roots moist the first few days. And above all, make them welcome. Visit them, and admire them. They just might return the favor. Get together with other wildflower aficionados in your town or village, and arrange with the road crews to let you know in advance when they will open a new road through the woods and meadows, dig up a swamp, or widen existing roads. Whole banks of hepatica, bloodroot, coltsfoot, columbine, Turk's-cap lilies, and a host of other lovely wildflowers could be saved if roadbuilders and gardeners were willing to talk to each other and work together.

Thousands of flowers, shrubs, and ferns could be saved and transplanted into town parks, around public buildings, and into private gardens. Many years ago, the then Governor of Vermont, now Senator Aiken, did just that; and this was one way in which he truly became a wildflower pioneer.

A great many suburban and country roads have been cut through the wilderness long ago, and still woodland flowers come back at the sides of many roads. For instance, whole banks of bloodroot still appear early each spring in our town, and long stretches of columbine and ferns. But each year they become a little smaller; and as the roads are widened and more asphalt and tar are put down to fill the potholes left by winter snows and ice, and crumbling shoulders are repaired, the plants will eventually disappear altogether for want of nourishing soil. Wood lilies and Turk's-cap lilies and bee balm and many others are already gone.

The yearly cutting back of tall grass and "weeds" which obscure the corners is an almost imperative safety measure. But is it really necessary to cut everything back *six* feet deep just because the road crews have acquired lovely new power sicklebars and joyfully use them to their full depth? The old country sound of men with scythes cutting slowly and carefully, and making small and pleasant talk which could be heard from a distance on a quiet day has been replaced with the screech of gorgeous red or yellow machinery.

Nor is this all you can be concerned with if you are a "compleat" gardener. Some time ago, a friend with incredible legerdemain succeeded in growing a cardinal flower right next to a rose. Her secret was simple, and since she had the time and passion to do it, she had mixed a large number of fertilizers in dozens of small pails. Around the rose she made a small ring of rose food, and around the cardinal flower she crumbled acid peat and made sure that never the twain should meet. The plants grew and prospered, year after year, to the amazement of all comers.

In Great Britain, on the other hand, mixing wildflowers with garden flowers is nothing new or unusual. The following varieties, all at one time or another imported from the United States, may be seen not only in the cottage gardens of the countryside but in some of the most elegant townhouse and manor gardens:

Adder's-tongue, also called dogtooth violet (*Erythronium*); bee balm or Oswego tea (*Monarda didyma*); bergamot, also called horsemint (*Monarda fistulosa*); black snakeroot (*Cimicifuga racemosa*); blue lobelia (*Lobelia siphilitica*); cardinal flower (*Lobelia cardinalis*); celandine poppy (*Stylophorum diphyllum*); Dutchman's-breeches (*Dicentra canadensis*); goldenrod (*solidago*); several varieties of hepatica (*Hepatica nobilis*), joe-pye weed (*Eupatorium maculatum*); marsh marigold (*Caltha palustris*); New England aster (*Aster novae-angliae*); pickerelweed (*Pontederia cordata*); Solomon's-seal (*Polygonatum canaliculatum*) and false Solomon's-seal (*Smilacina racemosa*); spiderwort (*Tradescantia*); trillium in several species; turtlehead (*Chelone, glabra and obliqua*); Virginia cowslip (*Mertensia virginica*); wild iris, often falsely called wild sweet william (*Phlox divaricata*); and also yucca or Spanish bayonet which comes from our southwest and now grows even in England and in our own northeast.

And this is not all. Many other British and European wildflowers have been transplanted and domesticated in English, Scottish, and Irish gardens. And North American trees have also been made at home in Great Britain: the tulip tree, sequoia, American holly, black adler, and witch hazel among others.

The flowers grow in formal borders, walled gardens, foundation plantings, or wherever a gardener likes them to bloom among his cultivated plants. Over here, we seem to be more conventional and rigid: we seldom plant wild and cultivated violets together, and certainly no goldenrod; for many people still mistakenly think that the latter is a source of hayfever.

In the following, arranged by season and location, is a list of plants the average gardener can readily transplant. Because of the irregularity of the local seasons, they are here set down merely as a general guide for spring and early summer.

WOODLAND FLOWERS

COLTSFOOT (*Tussilago farfara*) is of the sunflower family, and comes up early in fairly damp soil. Its light-yellow rays brighten the landscape as well as many roadsides where it still grows. Sometimes it gets to be eighteen inches tall, but usually it is less high than that. It can be transplanted into well-drained, fairly acid damp soil, among rocks, in filtered light. Coltsfoot gets its name from the stem, which indeed looks like a young horse's foot. *Farfarus* is the Latin name for coltsfoot; it is a European import, and has been used for coughs. As Gerard describes it: "A decoction of the greene leaues and roots, or else a syrrup thereof, is good for the caugh that proceedeth of a thin rheume."

BLOODROOT (*Sanguinaria canadensis*) is of the poppy family. It is one of our best known and most easily recognized wildflowers. It has one large white flower; its common name seems to have come from the use some Indians have made of it. They cooked the rhizome for making dyes, some say, for war paint. It is an American original which was not discovered by white botanists until 1932. It grows about six inches to twelve inches tall in rich woodland soil.

192

HEPATICA (*Hepatica nobilis*) is of the buttercup family, and is also called liverwort for the shape of its leaves. It comes in shades of white, pink, blue, and purple; grows in rich acid woodland soil, and is only a few inches tall. It transplants well. It is native to our country, and seems to have no other use than its extraordinary delicacy and beauty. Be careful where you put it, for it can be crowded out by other plants.

SAXIFRAGE (*Saxifraga virginiensis*) of the saxifrage family belongs to a large group of perennials in North and South America and in Eurasia; its name literally means rock-breaking. This plant can be found in cracks it seems to have made itself. It grows from four inches to one foot. A wine made from boiled saxifrage roots seems to have been a diuretic, or so Gerard says.

TRAILING ARBUTUS (*Epigaea repens*) of the heath family, is now almost extinct because so many people have picked it for its lovely fragrance. The leaves remain green through the winter, but new leaves appear in the spring. If properly planted and cared for it could make an outstanding groundcover. It is also called Mayflower; or, in Quebec, fleur-de-mai. It comes in white and pink, grows in sandy soil, usually in the company of evergreens. This is an American form, but another species is said to grow in Japan.

WOOD ANEMONE (*Anemone canadensis*), of the buttercup family, is also called "windflower" because it is said that the petals open at the first spring breeze. Anemones grew in Greece and in Rome, and were dedicated to Aphrodite and Venus. They are lovely little flowers, white and delicate, and must be transplanted with care for their root system is widespread.

RUE ANEMONE (*Anemonella thalictroides*) is distinguished from the wood anemone by its six petals versus the four of the former, but grows in similar woodland conditions. The flowers are white or with a pink tinge, and grow only from six to eight inches.

TRILLIUM, also called wake-robin (*Trillium*) of the lily family, one of

193

our most popular woodland flowers, comes in several species, and most of them are easily transplanted from rich woods into the same kind of soil. Perhaps the most often seen are *Trillium erectum* with dark-red, brown, or purple flowers, and *Trillium grandiflorum* with large white flowerheads which turn pink with age. Another is *Trillium undulatum,* or painted trillium, perhaps the most charming of all trillium, although somewhat more rare; it has small white flowers with pink or purple lines or streaks. This is a North American and East Asian "herb." Many of its other species have become so rare that generally they are not found on simple woodland exploration walks.

COLUMBINE (*Aquilegia canadensis*) is of the buttercup family still commonly seen in our woods and even at roadsides, and is easily transplanted into the usual flower garden where it grows happily with its cultivated cousins. The wild columbine of the Rocky Mountains is of a heavenly blue. This is one wildflower which can be raised easily from seed.

LADY'S-SLIPPER, also called moccasin flower (*Cypripedium calceolus*) of the orchid family is one of the most striking of woodland flowers. The pink variety is *Cypripedium reginae,* most often found in wet woodlands or near bogs almost everywhere in North America.

As an example of what must never be done with lady's-slippers or *any other* woodland flower: In Massachusetts a gentleman who has a stunning wildflower garden one day heard a great deal of noise at one end of his property, and on investigation found a family *picking* his precious pink plants. When they saw him coming they threw the flowers on the ground and fled. Almost the entire stand of pink lady's-slippers had been destroyed.

VIRGINIA BLUEBELLS (*Mertensia virginica*) is of the forget-me-not family and grows in the Northern Hemisphere. It was named after the German botanist Karl Mertens (1764–1831). At first pink, the flowers turn blue, and, if left alone, spread quite rapidly. The plants grow to about two feet and are readily transplanted into a flower garden.

CANADA MAYFLOWER or false lily of the valley (*Maianthemum canadense*) is of the lily family. It is a low, almost creeping plant with small erect white flowers which make a lovely ground-cover in the woods.

WILD BLEEDING HEART (*Dicentra eximia*) of the bleeding heart family is an American species and can now be seen in many American and English gardens. Its cousin DUTCHMAN'S-BREECHES (*Dicentra canadensis*) is equally popular and spreads easily in a woodland spot. Its flowers are creamy white.

WOOD BETONY (*Pedicularis canadensis*) of the snapdragon family, is also known by the unpretty name of "lousewort" because it was thought that European cattle became infected by it. It happens to be one of my favorites, perhaps for no other reason than it varies in color from yellow to brown to red. It grows to about sixteen inches, and makes an interesting spot of color in a wild-flower garden.

DWARF IRIS (*Iris cristata*) of the iris family grows in rich woodland soil, a dwarf variety of the Old World iris with a particularly interesting design. It is only eight inches tall and can be used in the front of a garden, in a rock garden, or almost like a colorful groundcover.

SOLOMON'S-SEAL (*Polygonatum canaliculatum*) of the lily family, is the largest variety of this plant. First its greenish hanging blossoms and later its purple berries, and its curved and long leaves make it a most attractive plant that will come into your garden by itself if you have left the original soil alone. But it is also easily transplanted.

FALSE SOLOMON'S-SEAL (*Smilacina racemosa*) is also of the lily family, and is similar in growing habits and leaf formation, but has a raceme of white flowers at the end of the plant. This is often called plume, which in the fall turns purplish. At all times an interesting plant, it has remained along many roadsides although it originally grew in woods.

MAYAPPLE (*Podophyllum peltatum*) is of the barberry family and has become another all-time favorite of many gardeners because it grows almost anywhere, spreads easily, and needs no care or prodding. The fruit looks like a small yellow apple and has often been eaten by small children with (sometimes) disastrous effects

Indians gathered Solomon's-seal in autumn, cut the root into small pellets or rings which were pounded into a powder used to clot bleeding wounds.

Mayapple will multiply quite spectacularly. The lovely cream-white flower grows under a large umbrella-like leaf.

196

on the digestion. American Indians used it as a cathartic. Curiously even some botanists call this native of the New World by the name mandrake. The real MANDRAKE (*Mandragora officinarum*) is of the nightshade family. It is a wild plant that grows in the Middle East and around the Mediterranean. For three thousand years it has been known as a love potion, also an anaesthetic (Dioscorides) and a personification of evil spirits. It is even mentioned in Genesis 30:14–16. It was thought to be both male and female and to have grown from the semen of hanged men. All this and more makes it difficult to understand why our beautiful mayapple should be compared with it, although there seems to be some resemblance between the leaves of the plants.

WILD GINGER (*Asarum canadense*) of the birthwort family, got its name from the gingerlike smell of the rhizome when broken. It has a beautiful dark brown flower which is difficult to find under the leaves, but grows abundantly in spring woods and makes a ground cover worthy of every woodland garden.

VIOLET (*Viola missouriensis*) of the violet family is a light-blue variety with triangular leaves and grows in what is called "bottomlands" but can be transplanted into an eastern woodland garden. Other woodland violets are the wild yellow violet, the birdfoot violet, and the sweet-smelling small white violet which may be grown even in sunny spots.

SPRING BEAUTY (*Claytonia virginica*) of the purslane family is one of the loveliest of spring flowers. Another variety, called *Claytonia caroliniana*, blooms in early summer even in mountains.

STAR-OF-BETHLEHEM (*Ornithogalum umbellatum*) of the lily family is a European and Mideastern plant. It was already known to Dioscorides who said that the bulbs, both raw and boiled, were good eating. It has long been grown in gardens here and abroad, but can be found wild in dry woodlands and now even on road-

197

sides. Its long grass-like leaves can easily be mistaken for common grass; therefore it is best to transplant it just after it has bloomed.

JACK-IN-THE-PULPIT (*Arisaema triphyllum*) of the calla family is an American plant, to this day used by some American Indians who pound the half-dry or dry corm into a powder for rheumatism, asthma, and muscular pain. It is also called "Indian turnip" because it was used for food, but not before the corm was dried and roasted—another example of the amazing ways in which simple people knew how to experiment and find the right way to use a plant.

Although this list by no means tells *all* about transplantable early woodland flowers, it may begin to lead you to your own experiments with plants you can find in the woods. Varying with the location, in summer and autumn you will find such lovely plants as:

WILD GERANIUM, also called crane's-bill—from the resemblance of the long beak of the pistil to the crane's—(*Geranium maculatum*) of the geranium family is a relative, or perhaps the origin of the *pelargonium*, the geraniums which grace so many of our windowboxes as well as winter windows. The flowers are lavender-purple and make a fine showing wherever they are transplanted.

BANEBERRY, or COHOSH (*Actea pachypoda*) of the buttercup family is another perennial of the Northern Hemisphere and especially delightful in a garden. At first its flowers look like small pieces of lacy white fireworks; then, in the autumn, fruit appears which looks like doll's eyes, and this is in fact its other popular name. There is also a red baneberry that has deep red fruit with a similar design. I have had very good luck with it in well-drained, somewhat acid garden soil under filtered sunlight. This is one of the plants with which one learns. I had one in my mixed garden and planted another one under pine trees, only to discover that the second plant did not come into bloom after the first year. It is now once more transplanted under filtered light and in less pine-needle covered soil. I always hope there is another chance.

SNAKEROOT (*Cimicifuga racemosa*) of the buttercup family is also called bugbane because it doesn't smell nice even to insects. This is another North American native that was much used by Indians and later by white settlers for all sorts of things—from rattlesnake bites to croup, and from gonorrhea to impotence. Another name is rattletop, because as the seeds ripen they make a rattling sound in the breeze.

BEE BALM, or Oswego tea (*Monarda didyma*), is of the mint family and one of the few true red wildflowers in existence. There are also lavender-pink, white and purple *monardas*; all respond to neglect and multiply profusely. I started the lavender-pink variety some years ago in my herb garden, also in another spot where I grow some special ferns, and year after year friends come to dig up some of the plants for enjoyment equal to mine— that is, until bergamot, as this variety is called, takes over. But this is part of the fun of growing all kinds of plants; when a plant gets too prolific you can begin sharing it with friends.

WOOD or PHILADELPHIA LILY (*Lilium philadelphicum*) of the lily family is a native of our dry woods and one of the plants that is harder and harder to find. Only fifteen years or so ago we used to see quite a few along our shaded roadsides. Now they have retired more deeply into the woods and become a rare and precious specimen.

FRINGED ORCHIS (*Habenaria fimbriata*) of the orchid family is another spectacular plant that grows in late summer. I have found it only in New Hampshire at the side of a wet upland meadow.

It was so beautiful that I didn't want to take it up even if I could have done so, for I was far away from home. I understand that it is best transplanted in late fall into a partially shaded rich soil. Packed in wet moss it might travel well. Good luck, if you find it!

THIMBLEWEED (*Anemone cylindrica*) of the buttercup family is a charming yellow-green flower that turns into a thimblelike fruit. It is easily transplanted and grown in somewhat acid soil, and a surprisingly delicate addition to any garden. One could imagine that a collection of anemones, from wood to rue, with a number of varicolored cultivated anemones to the thimbleweed would make a rather unusual and interesting assemblage in the right kind of garden from early spring to autumn.

TURTLEHEAD (*Chelone glabra*) of the snapdragon family is a rather majestic native American plant with a white-and-pink-tinged flowerhead. There is also a deep pink, almost purple turtlehead (*Chelone obliqua*) that is more rare and delicate. Both grow in somewhat swampy areas, or just in wet soil, and in wet ditches in late summer and autumn. The name was derived from the flower's resemblance to a turtle's head—just another feat of the imagination.

BOTTLE GENTIAN (*Gentiana andrewsii*) of the gentian family, according to Asa Gray, was named after *Gentius,* king of Illyria, that somewhat obscure Greek-dominated region of what is now

The white turtlehead grows to six feet and could serve either as a background plant, or stand alone.

Yugoslavia. He discovered one of the varieties of the plant and its medicinal virtues which are mentioned by both Gerard and Parkinson. But this particular species seems to be a native of the region around the Tetons and has been used by Indians as a concoction for making a tonic. Many other varieties of gentians are known from other Alpine regions, and still others from low-lying places. I have found many in damp areas in New England. The flower, a deep, almost purple blue, always looks as though it is about to open but it never does. A white relative, *Gentian saponaria,* of similar growing habits, is more difficult to find.

Among the wild plants which grow in or near water are several that will enhance flowing or still water in your own garden. All are extraordinarily beautiful and exciting in their growing habits and colors.

MARSH-MARIGOLD (*Caltha palustris*) of the buttercup family is an early spring plant and grows in woods as well as on mountains. Planted in a brook, it will spread downstream; each year there will be more of the shimmering gold on top of the water. Gerard describes its "vertues" as "touching the faculties of these plants, wee haue nothing to say, either out of other men's writings, or our owne experience." As though beauty and freshness were not virtues enough!

BLUE FLAG (*Iris versicolor*) of the iris family is another perennial of the Northern Hemisphere described by Gerard and Parkinson and used as an eyewash by some American Indians. It grows in low-lying damp meadows, and is one of the most beautiful plants to behold. If you have a low and wet stretch of property and can't think what to do with it, a group of blue and yellow flag (the other variety of wild iris called flag) you could create a heavenly spot on your land. They are tough plants; and treated with care and devotion they should do very well for you.

WATER-LILY (*Nymphaea odorata*) of the water-lily family is white or pink, a native species, sends its rhizome to the bottom of a lake, pond, swamp, or even a slow-flowing stream where it will root and send its great flowers and leaves to the top. You can even create your own small lily pond.

PICKERELWEED (*Pontederia cordata*) of the pickerelweed family is usually found growing in the company of water-lilies and yellow pond-lilies, and its deep vibrant blue makes a stunning contrast to the white or pink or yellow flowers. It is easily dug out of the water (just be careful not to hurt its rhizome) and transplanted into your own pond. I have even seen it used as a single proud specimen in a bricked-in garden water basin. It is an American native; its name was given in dedication to a professor in Padua, Guillo Pontederia (1688–1756)—another example of how important and interesting our native plants were to Europeans as soon as they were discovered.

CARDINAL-FLOWER (*Lobelia cardinalis*) of the lobelia family is the other truly red wildflower of our woods and waters. It grows singly or in clumps, at the edge of brooks and swamps and even watery ditches. Despite the modesty of its location, it is one of the most spectacular native American plants. The story is told that some Canadian trappers first saw it in our northern wet woods, and because the color reminded them of a cardinal's sash they gave the flower the name of a prince of the Church. And it is indeed a princely plant which never fails to enchant a wanderer who comes upon it.

It is difficult to transplant, however, and will disappear if it doesn't like the spot in which you had hoped to make a new home for it. Unless you can find a plant close by, it is better to buy one from a grower of wildflowers or try to grow it from seed. I once bought a few seedlings from a nursery and all late summer and early autumn they bloomed ravishingly at the edge of a small swamp beyond my ferns. But then there came a dry spell, and the following year there wasn't a trace of them left. They may have seeded themselves down in a more permanently wet place, or died.

A similar disaster (with a happier ending, however) befell a friend who had transplanted a large clump in what appeared to be exactly the right place, only to find it gone the next year—but well established and happy on a neighbor's place where a cardinal-flower had never lived before! My friend was furious. Wasn't her water or soil good enough? But this is just another example of how a proud, beautiful plant prefers to choose its own domain.

GREAT LOBELIA (*Lobelia syphilitica*) of the lobelia family is a close relative of the cardinal flower with a similar design of its flowers, but is much easier to transplant and grow successfully. It does quite well in semishaded, somewhat acid and damp garden soil. Since lobelia is among the last flowers to bloom in late summer or early autumn, its beautiful blue color is a great bonanza among remaining green and evergreen plants. The American Indians regarded it as useful for chest pains, rheumatic conditions, catarrh, and, most important of all, syphilis—hence its botanical name.

SWAMP MILKWEED (*Asclepias incarnata*) belongs to the milkweed family and is a fairly common species seen at the edge of swamps and other wet places, and sometimes grows like a thick little shrub. Its outstanding appeal is the design of its exquisite pink flowers. Most people think of it as a weed and don't take a closer look—another example of how much beauty and pleasure pass us by in our unthinking and often arrogant carelessness. Like the regular milkweed which grows in the meadows, swamp milkweed can be transplanted.

WATER-HOREHOUND (*Lycopus americanus*), of the mint family, grows everywhere in the United States in low lying, wet or damp places. It has lovely tiny flowers. It might make a nice accent near a pond and people have transplanted it successfully. One of this species is the source of horehound candy.

There are, of course, many more woodland and water wildflowers we can bring into our gardens. Here, as everywhere else, it is the concept—the overall view, the plan—that counts. Begin with a small idea and a few plants at a time, and let the plants and the ideas grow with the years. And don't give up if a plant doesn't make it the first time. Woodland flowers will grow where they like, where they feel right and are comfortable and at home. Perhaps, in a way, they are the most rewarding plants of all: a link with the past, a promise for the future.

Similar to woodland flowers in ecology and habitat, but certainly not in color, form, or heritage, the ferns are among the oldest known plants on earth. Fossilized specimens millions of years old have been found in all the moderate climates of the world. Some were as large as trees, others were like the herbaceous plants we know today; all have a form of life and structure different from other plants. They have no flower, and reproduce by "spores" rather than seeds. Their leaves are called fronds, and, since time immemorial, their majesty and grandeur has added to man's awe of the wilderness.

Some ferns were sacred in Greece and Rome, and Dioscorides has described the medicinal value of those he knew. They inspired fear in the Middle Ages because no one could understand how a flowerless and seedless plant could reproduce itself. Surely it did so by black magic? Later herbalists ascribed many medicinal "vertues" to most ferns; and many Indian tribes boiled fern roots for starchy food and medicine—but they also thought that most ferns caused sterility. On the other hand, European settlers are said to have eaten ferntops like asparagus, or cooked them as herbs. Some Japanese ferns are still used in soup.

But in the introduction to his book, *Who's Who Among the Ferns,* published in 1909, W.I. Beecroft said: "It seems fitting that so many flowerless plants should so fully compensate for the absence of flowers by the beauty of their foliage."

It has been remarked that there are thousands of wildflowers in our region, but considerably less than 200 ferns; and would it not be much easier to collect ferns than wildflowers? It would be—if more people understood ferns more and loved them better.

Even more than wildflowers, ferns remind us of the silence and the coolness of the woods and the still untouched wilderness in which they keep on growing and multiplying. Some have a splendor of design equalled only by some of the trees beneath which they live. Their color ranges through almost all the shades of green. Each frond unfolds in its own way—some so tiny that they are difficult to see; others to majestic heights, dwarfing the other plants around them. Then come the tiny globules on the underside of the fronds, miniscule on some, big and fat on others, with thousands of tiny spores inside from which new plants will come in their own good time. Some exude a sweet scent (like my own hay-scented field of ferns); others must be rubbed between one's fingers to give up their aroma. Most die down in the winter with the rest of the land, but some are evergreen and stay with pine and spruce and hemlock to remind us that winter is by no means a dead season.

Some ferns are coarse, interrupted fern, cinnamon fern, ostrich fern, evergreen wood fern, Christmas fern, sensitive fern, and polypody, to mention some of the best known. Others are delicate and finely drawn: New York and Massachusetts fern, lady fern, hay-scented fern, marsh fern and silvery spleenwort. Others have unusual and distinctive forms: bracken, royal fern and maidenhair fern. Still others are small and love to grow in the fissures of rocks: rusty cliff fern, maidenhair spleenwort; and others, in sandstone, in granite rocks, the green spleenwort, walking fern, heart's-tongue, limestone adder's-tongue in limestone. Some ferns don't look like ferns at all: heart's-tongue and walking fern, purple-stemmed cliffbrake, Hartford fern.

No amateur knows them all, but everyone can find most of them sooner or later. Many need shade or semishade; some grow in sweet soil, but most prefer acid soil; and many grow in garden loam with no more attention than any other healthy plant. Also there are excellent guidebooks available today with the help of which one can find and study all the known species.

Many woodland ferns can still be seen at our roadsides: Christmas fern, wood and lady ferns, hay-scented ferns; and many others have persisted through the picking of careless passersby or the yearly cutting of road crews. But they grow smaller and smaller, until someday soon they too will disappear as so many wildflowers already have.

Some states, for example, New York, have put *all* ferns on their conservation list. None may be picked. Indeed the danger of their disappearing was great. For many years florists used wild ferns in their flower arrangements, and butchers decorated their trays of meat and poultry. If the fronds had been carefully *cut,* the ferns might not have been destroyed. But thousands were ripped out fast, and sometimes the whole plant torn up. Still, every year, gardeners can help save the plants that will otherwise disappear forever.

Most more or less common ferns transplant easily and well if just a little care is taken, a little knowledge learned. Build a green garden with ferns and other plants that live well with them: wildflowers, jack-in-the-pulpit, bee balm and bergamot. I even have a few lilies in my green garden, and it is doubly exciting to see them suddenly come into their bright colors against the cool green all around them. Put different ferns together: Christmas, maidenhair and wood fern, or whatever you can find that will help to make the texture of your garden more exciting.

In another, sunnier spot I have planted ostrich and royal ferns that grow tall and mighty; but in the same place I put some saxifrage which blooms in early spring and then disappears. I did have a little trouble with the hay-scented ferns; they were almost impossible to keep from spreading everywhere. However, a small wall of rocks fixed that.

Some ferns, such as Christmas, evergreen woodfern (also called marginal woodfern) and blunt-lobed woodsia, are evergreen in most areas and therefore well suited as underplanting with shrubs and trees. There was a "hole" in my foundation planting because the two laurels that were there had grown too far forward (as they have a way of doing) and the back was bare. There is now a big evergreen woodfern between them, and all is plumply filled.

Sometimes there is nothing you have to do, and there suddenly appears a hay-scented fern in the crotch of a tree right next to your house. Some people would call this fern a sport. But its fresh green looked simply grand against the gray bark.

When you have decided that you want ferns in your garden, go into the woods as you would for wildflowers, with a shovel and pail, and dig deeply so that none of the roots are left behind. Then make a hole larger than the ball of roots and put some peat moss into it. Then plant the fern, put more peat moss on the outside. And when everything is done, step firmly around the plant because, like shrubs and many garden flowers, ferns cannot tolerate air around their roots. Although some people have had good luck with transplanting fully grown ferns, it is more prudent to dig for them in early spring, before the fronds are fully unfurled, or in the autumn when they are fading.

And then, if you are lucky and have proved that you have the right soil and the right attitude toward them, new ferns will appear from nowhere. (A sensitive fern did just that under my pines.) To help you recognize a few of the shapes you will encounter during your adventure with ferns, here are some points for recognition:

Just as soon as the earth begins to warm, the tiny curled-up heads of the hay-scented and other ferns appear; the embryonic form of the leaves can already be seen.

CINNAMON ferns are at first tightly packed. The leaves at this stage are called "fiddleheads," and are often cooked by European and some American gourmets even today. Their taste is delicate and not like anything else. As the ferns grow, a cinnamon-like "club" appears in the middle of the fronds. This is a very common fern in the United States. I have transplanted a few in the front of my garden, against all advice from experts. But so far, so good—the roots were tightly packed with pine bark which holds water better than even peat moss, and my ferns have come back to full glory two springs in a row although there is no water anywhere nearby.

CHRISTMAS fern, the evergreen wonder, begins with tightly curled hairy heads. As soon as these appear, the still green but now somewhat messy leaves from last year may be cut away. Lush fresh leaves come up from the ground.

SENSITIVE fern does not look like a fern at all. It has thick, fairly coarse fronds. It cannot stand frost and quickly disappears, leaving behind only the fertile spike; but it will reappear next year.

MAIDENHAIR fern is perhaps the most unusual and loveliest of all. It announces its arrival somewhat later in spring than the other ferns by a curled spiral that unfolds into an almost flowerlike delicate plant which, if one is lucky, may grow to considerable width and height. It likes shady and somewhat damp spots, or at least well-drained soil though not necessarily soil that is acid. A variety of maidenhair fern was sacred to the Romans who dedicated it to Venus, the goddess of love who had arisen from the sea. The fern looked silvery under water, but came up dry. (The same must have happened to Venus.) I have tried this with a piece of my fern, but it came up as wet as anything.

Taking the marginal woodfern (or simply wood fern) as an example, the marvelous process of fern reproduction becomes better understood. On the underside of the fronds, first visible as tiny green spots, or sporangia, are what we would today call "packages" of tiny spores which are filled to bursting. When the spores have ripened in the late summer or early autumn hundreds of thousands and sometimes millions of them are catapulted outward.

When the spores find the right watery or damp spot, each develops into a prothallus, a single cell that proceeds to put a tiny root into the ground, and then begins to build itself, cell by cell, including sex organs microscopically minute in size. When the skin of the male organ bursts, the female organ begins exuding a scent agreeable to the male and the two combine. An egg develops, first anchored within the female part, sending a root into the earth and a stem upward. When this structure becomes independent of the "mother" it grows many roots, stems, and fronds. A new plant appears; a new fern graces the earth.

One single solitary cell, by a godlike turn of magic, becomes one of the graceful ferns of our world.

FIELD, MEADOW, AND ROADSIDE FLOWERS

Since time immemorial many of the meadow flowers were used for food and drink and medicine for they, too, were among the herbs; men knew them and loved them, and gave many of them sacred and devotional meaning.

Even the dandelion which the gardeners despise was the subject of lovely poetry by James Russell Lowell (1819–1891):

> *Dear common flower, that grow'st beside the way,*
> *Fringing the dusty road with harmless gold.*

209

And, have you ever seen a meadow in early spring covered with BLUETS (*Houstonia caerulea*) of the bedstraw family, also called quaker-ladies, a sea of white or light-blue that might help your own somewhat low-lying acid soil meadow? They are said to be not too easy to transplant, and the seeds are best sown as soon as frost is gone—or still better, in the fall. Bluets can also be rooted in sand, but this becomes complicated from one season to the next. However, wouldn't they look nice if you succeeded before much else is in bloom?

CINQUEFOIL (*Potentilla canadensis*) of the rose family is also called five-finger for the obvious reason that it has five leaves. It is light yellow. Many cultivated varieties of *Potentilla* are known to grow in gardens, so why not try to transplant the wild one? It may be found in late spring in the open, often at the sides of the roads we travel.

BEARDTONGUE (*Pentstemon grandiflorus*) is of the snapdragon family, a grand and showy plant of which several hybrids have been made into garden flowers. The purple variety is much less common than the white, which grows abundantly on many of our roadsides; and although it is best to reproduce it from seed, a friend of mine has successfully transplanted both colors. Just remember, always dig deeply, keep it moist, and plant it quickly in your garden.

BIRD'S-FOOT TREFOIL (*Lotus corniculatus*) of the bean family is a plant of European origin and much used as groundcover to hold the banks of newly built roads. It will serve equally well on a bare, sunny slope in your garden. The flowers are a strong golden yellow; it is easy to transplant and needs little care.

BLUE-EYED GRASS (*Sisyrinchium campestre*) of the iris family, is a charming plant with tiny blue flowers; and since it usually grows in fields or meadows in clump-like fashion, one can dig up a piece of ground and bring it home. However, the usual recommended form of propagation is by seed.

210

Blue-eyed grass can become quite full if left to its own devices in rich soil.

Black-eyed Susans

DEPTFORD PINK (*Dianthus armeria*) of the pink family is a charming and delicate plant that may invade a wildflower and even a flower garden of its own volition if the conditions are right. In the wild it is often seen together with blue-eyed grass in dry open places. The *Dianthus* family is one of the oldest known, first to Theophrastus and Dioscorides through other medieval herbalists, to Gerard and Parkinson who praised it for its beauty but not much more.

MAIDEN PINK (*Dianthus deltoides*) also of the pink family is mentioned by Gerard as a garden pink. To this day it is extremely popular in English gardens; has here escaped into our wilderness and naturalized in meadows, roadsides, and in open woods. I have encountered it in the Adirondacks, in July, as a great sheet of pink, and I don't remember a prettier sight anywhere. By all means, dig up some plants if you find them, and put them into your garden.

EUROPEAN BELLFLOWER (*Campanula rapunculoides*) of the bluebell family, another European import since the seventeenth century, now grows at roadsides and in thickets and is an imposing sight indeed. Usually it is cut down by road crews, but it always comes back the next year. It may be propagated by seeds and cuttings; or, simply by digging it up when the bloom is done. It is closely related to the harebell or Scottish bluebell which may also be found in similar conditions but is much smaller (to four feet, and usually somewhat less).

STAR THISTLE (*Centaurea cyanus*) of the sunflower family, called cornflower in England because it grows in cornfields there, is found here in wheatfields, or at roadsides. It probably is the ancestor of the bachelor's button so popular in our gardens. It might be fun to try to transplant some near a cultivated cousin if, that is, you are willing to experiment with this sort of thing (three to four feet, often lower).

SPIDERWORT (*Tradescantia virginiana*) of the spiderwort family is an American native with a beautiful, deep-blue color. It has been transformed into a very popular garden plant which also appears in white and pink. Our wild variety is easily transplanted, and will do well in garden soil. It may be found along roads and railroad embankments, and is one of the most successful flowers for a garden (eighteen inches to two feet).

LUPINE (*Lupinus perennis*) of the pea family was well known and already used in Egypt for food, and continues to be used in this way all around the Mediterranean. Gerard reports that Dioscorides recommended boiling it in rainwater to make a cleansing lotion for the face. Here, however, enters a mystery: Lupines also grow wild in our North and Far West; and I saw a whole stretch of them near the White Mountains. A few years ago, lupine seeds many thousands of years old were found in Oregon —and still germinated. And another among the fascinating questions of history is this: Were our lupines somehow brought to our Northwest? At any rate, the wild lupine had been transformed into the garden lupines by some clever spirits. So by all means, if you find wild ones, try to bring them into your garden. The young seedlings are easily transplanted (2 feet high and more).

CHICORY (*Cichorium intybus*) of the sunflower family, *is* a weed of the roadside and meadow—with the most beautiful blue color anywhere among wild plants. It is mentioned here not because it can be or should be transplanted, but because it should *not* be ripped out and thrown on the garbage pile. Chicory already grew in Egypt thousands of years ago, and is used as food there to this day. There are cultivated species with shoots blanched for salads, and the roots can be dried and used in coffee as is often done in France. Chicory is closely related to endive. It grows tall and proud (to five feet and more) and if you have it in your wild meadowland, be grateful.

GIANT PURPLE LOOSESTRIFE (*Lythrum salicaria*) of the loosestrife family grows in wet meadows, along streams, and other bodies of water, at the same time as Chicory, making the horizon purple with its flowers. It *can* be transplanted if one takes extreme care not to allow it to overrun cultivated and wild garden spots. But if you have a low-lying and wet piece of land which can be separated from the rest by a small stone wall or ditch it might well pay you to try (five feet).

FIREWEED (*Epilobium angustifolium*) of the evening-primrose family, also called Great willow herb, is a majestic plant which grows in dry clearings and burnt-out areas. This is a North American plant discovered by Thoreau, the great lover of the wilderness. To come upon it as I have, along several roadsides in the Adirondacks and in New Hampshire, is an unforgettable experience. Fireweed should be transplanted only in the spring, and if you can put it in front of dark evergreens in a likely dry place, you may be able to enjoy its glory (six feet).

TURK'S-CAP LILY (*Lilium superbum*) of the lily family is another of nature's wonders, with its brown-spotted orange blossoms of which as many as 40 may grow on a single stalk. Several friends of mine have simply dug up and transplanted a good many into their gardens where they grace the special beds that were made for them. This lily is a native American (eight feet).

WILD ROSE (*Rosa palustris* or *virginiana*) of the rose family, has many different species which only seasoned botanists are able to distinguish. One grows in the sandy soil of Cape Cod, along the dunes; others just come and live with you, and if you have the slightest respect for the wishes of the wild—leave them be. They take a while to bloom; but when they finally do, they are lovely amid other wildflowers. I wouldn't suggest transplanting them. Roses are easy enough to come by for a garden; just leave the wild ones alone (two to three feet).

NEW YORK IRONWEED (*Vernonia noveboracensis*) of the sunflower family is a beautiful deep-purple plant which often grows with goldenrod, another American native, and flourishes in open meadows. It is useful in a sunny spot in the wild garden, or

Seaside goldenrod (Solidago)

Salad burnet is very decorative and useful for salads, though not as well known as other herbs.

An outstanding border idea is this mixture of poppies and white iris, to be replaced later by blooming plants now green in the foreground. As soon as the poppies have disappeared, other perennials will take over. Most people place annuals in the front of a border because many grow low and bloom all summer long.

Tulips in spring

he pasque flower, a
ood rock-garden item
cause of its stature.

xifrage should be
ansplanted into rock
sures and will there-
re do quite well in a
ck garden with not
o much sun.

Johnny-jumps-ups, sweet, appealing, and an excellent ground-cover.

*Wild bleeding heart is
easily transplanted and
grows well amidst
other flowers.*

*Fringed orchids, one
of the multiple-headed
wild orchids.*

Pinxter (wild azalea)

Black snakeroot is a stunning plant, often growing to eight feet. It becomes extremely ornamental toward the back of a garden, or as I have it, planted near a rock and ferns.

The dramatic development of milkweed flowerheads to seed-pods. Each seed has wings which carry it away at the slightest breeze.

Close-up of a rhododendron head

A housefront in London, painted in "Trompe l'oeil." Only the windowbox full of geraniums in the foreground is real.

Garden loosestrife (in England also called golden loosestrife) is a stunning plant not enough seen in our gardens. It has naturalized in North America but is worthy of our attention in cultivation.

Mid-century hybrid, a stunning orange lily which a friend of mine grows in her vegetable garden.

*The nightblooming ce-
reus opens only once fo
a very short time, and
then fades until anothe
year, another night.*

*The bottle gentian is
easily transplanted and,
once established, needs
little or no care.*

I have succeeded in growing several butterfly weeds in a mixed herb and wildflower garden. It is always exciting to watch in its various stages of growth.

Hawthorn in bloom

Celmisia, a New Zealand import

meadow, and is easily grown from seed or cuttings taken before it blooms. It self-sows readily and will, therefore, in a short time make a ravishing showing when not much else is in bloom (five to six feet).

BUTTERFLY WEED (*Asclepias tuberosa*) is of the milkweed family and one of the most desirable plants either in a wild or a cultivated garden. It grows in open meadows and at roadsides. It is also called pleurisy root because American Indians used it to cure pleurisy. Like all members of this family it is not easily transplanted except when very young, and takes several years to bloom (two feet).

NEW ENGLAND ASTER (*Aster novae-angliae*) of the composite family grows in fields, meadows, and along roadsides, and is the ancestor of many cultivated asters. It is easily transplanted by division, and will self-sow freely. Put it in your garden or meadow; it will cover empty spots rapidly and with great aplomb.

FRINGED GENTIAN (*Gentiana crinita*) of the gentian family is among the most beautiful flowers in creation, a member of a family which grows in many parts of the world and in Alpine regions; it is used by Indians for its tonic qualities. It grows on railroad tracks, in open fields and meadows, also in wet woods; and when you find it, it takes your breath away. But *don't* try to transplant it. Fringed gentian is a biennial and can be grown only

There is no telling whether fringed gentian will stay with you once it has bloomed. The chances are it won't, but will disappear from your garden and come up again in some entirely different place.

from seed. There is no telling whether it will stay with you once it has bloomed. The chances are it won't, it will disappear from your garden and come up again in some entirely different place.

One year a friend in Connecticut told me that a farmer had a whole meadow of fringed gentian that I must see. But I had to go on, and the following year I was told that there was not a single fringed gentian left. One and all, they had disappeared as though a magic wand had been waved over them. Nor did I ever again find those that I had seen and photographed. Year after year people plant seeds, the flowers come up once, and then the ripe seed is blown about by the wind and the flowers are gone.

Of course you can transplant daisies, black-eyed susans, and many of their relatives such as coneflowers and goldenrod, and many, many more of the meadow and roadside flowers, and they will enrich your own meadows and gardens. But the beautiful Queen Anne's lace of the parsley family, also called wild carrot, and mentioned by Pliny as having grown in Crete, is almost impossible to transplant. It grows everywhere, the most queenly and graceful of flowers; and although you may pick it freely, you cannot own it in your garden. If it grows in your meadows, be glad and worship its beauty.

Queen Anne's lace

Today, everywhere in the country and adjoining almost every community there are growers, nurseries and garden stores. Those with whom I have done business, particularly those that deal in wildflowers, include:

Ruth Hardy's Wildflower Nursery, Falls Village, Conn. 06031
Leslie's Wildflower Nursery, Methuen, Mass. 01844
Putney Nursery, Putney, Vt.
Vick's Wildgardens, Inc., Box 115, Gladwynne, Penna.

There seem to be few wildflower nurseries that sell seeds. Mr. Leslie in Methuen, collects and sells seeds not only of our own wildflowers but also those of Alaska (these would probably germinate in our own colder climates, high elevations, and rock gardens).

In order to help you preserve and thereby increase the plants of our wilderness, a few general rules apply which could be simply summed up: *don't pick anything* you find in the woods, or along roadsides which have been cut through woods.

The following list is a combination of plants on the New York Conservation list, and on that of the New England Wildflower Preservation Society. Every state in the Union has its own conservation list which is available through local Garden Clubs, Horticultural Societies, and State Conservation agencies. If you're not sure you'll succeed, leave these where they are:

I. TREES AND SHRUBS

Alder, Black—*Ilex verticillata*
Azalea—*Rhododendron,* all native:
> Clammy or Swamp Azalea—*Rhododendron viscosum*
> Great Laurel—*Rhododendron maximum*
> Mountain Azalea—*Rhododendron roseum*
> Pinxter—*Rhododendron nudiflorum*
> Rhodora—*Rhododendron canadensis*

Bayberry—*Myrica pennsylvanica*
Dogwood, White—*Cornus florida*
Holly, American—*Ilex opaca*
Laurel—*Kalmia,* all native
      Bog Laurel—*Kalmia poliofolia*
      Mountain Laurel—*Kalmia latifolia*
      Sheep Laurel—*Kalmia augustifolia*

II. FLOWERS AND OTHER PLANTS

A. *Spring and Early Summer*
    Arbutus, Trailing—*Epigaea repens*
    Baneberry, Red—*Actaea rubra*
    Baneberry, White—*Actaea alba*
    Barren, Strawberry—*Waldsteinia fragarioides*
    Beach Heather—*Hudsonia tomentosa*
    Bead Lily—*Clintonia borealis*
    Bearberry—*Arctostaphylos uva-ursi*
    Bellworts—*Uvularia,* spp.
    Bird's-foot Violet—*Viola pedata*
    Bittersweet—*Celastrus scandens*
    Black Haw—*Viburnum prunifolium*
    Bloodroot, Red Puccoon—*Sanguinaria canadensis*
    Bluebead Lily—*Clintonia borealis*
    Blue-Eyed Grass—*Sisyrinchium,* spp.
    Blue Flag—*Iris versicolor*
    Bunchberry—*Cornus canadensis*
    Calla, Wild—*Calla palustris*
    Calypso—*Calypso bulbosa*
    Canada Violet—*Viola canadensis*
    Checkerberry—*Gaultheria procumbens*
    Columbine—*Aquilegia canadensis*
    Creeping Snowberry—*Gaultheria Hispidula*

Dogtooth Violet, Fawn Lily—*Erythronium americanum*
Dutchman's breeches—*Dicentra cucullaria*
Early Saxifrage—*Saxifraga virginiensis*
Fairy Wand—*Chamaelirium luteum*
False Miterwort—*Tiarella cordifolia*
False Solomon's Seal—*Smilacina racemosa*
Foxglove, wild—*Gerardia flava*
Fringed Polygala—*Polygala paucifolia*
Fume-Root or Pale Coridalis—*Corydalis sempervirens*
Gaywings—*Polygala paucifolia*
Ginger, Wild—*Asarum canadensis*
Ginseng, Dwarf—*Panáx trifolium*
Indian Cucumber Root—*Medeola virginiana*
Jack-in-the-Pulpit—*Arisaema triphyllum*
Labrador Tea—*Ledum groenlandicium*
Lady's-Slipper—*Cypripedium,* all spp.
Liverleaf—*Hepatica americana*
Marsh-Marigold—*Caltha palustris*
Mayapple—*Podophyllum peltatum*
Meadow Beauty—*Rhexia virginica*
Milkweed, Four-leaf—*Asclepias quadrifolia*
Miterwort—*Mitella diphylla*
Monkey Flower—*Mimulus ringens*
New Jersey Tea—*Ceanothus americanus*
Paintbrush, Painted-Cup—*Castilleja coccinea*
Pale Corydalis—*Corydalis sempervirens*
Partridgeberry—*Mitchella repens*
Pink Catchfly or Wild Pink—*Silene caroliniana var. pennsylvanica*
Pinxter-flower—*Rhododendron nudiflorum*
Pitcher-plant—*Sarracenia purpurea*
Pogonia—*Pogonia ophioglossoides*
Rhodora—*Rhodora canadense*
Robin Runaway—*Dalibarda repens*

Scarlet Painted Cup—*Castilleja coccinea*
Showy Orchis—*Orchis spectabilis*
Solomon's Seal—*Polygonatum biflorum*
Spring Beauty—*Claytonia*, spp.
Squirrel Corn—*Dicentra canadensis*
Sweet Bay—*Magnolia virginiana*
Trillium, All native
> Great White Trillium—*Trillium grandiflorum*
> Nodding Trillium—*Trillium cernuum*
> Purple or Wet-Dog Trillium—*Trillium erectum*
> Snow Trillium—*Trillium nivale*

Trout Lily, Eastern—*Erythronium americanum*
Twinflower—*Linnaea borealis var. americana*
Twisted-Stalk—*Streptopus roseus*
Violet—*Viola*
> Arrow-Leafed Violet—*Viola sagitatta*
> Bird's-Foot Violet—*Viola pedata*
> Canada Violet—*Viola canadensis*
> Downy Yellow Violet—*Viola pubescens*
> Early Yellow Violet—*Viola rotundifolia*
> Smooth Yellow Violet—*Viola eriocarpa* or *Gray Viola pennsylvanica*

Wake-Robin—*Trillium*
Wild Calla—*Calla palustris*
Wild Columbine—*Aquilegia canadensis*
Wild Lupine—*Lupinus perennis*
Wood Anemone—*Anemone quinquefolia*
Wood Sorrel—*Oxalis montana*
Yellow Stargrass—*Hypoxis hirsuta*

B. *Summer and Fall*
> Arrowhead—*Sagittaria* spp.
> Beechdrops—*Epifagus virginiana*
> Bottle Gentian—*Gentiana andrewsii*

Butterfly Weed—*Asclepias tuberosa*
Buttonbush—*Cephalanthus occidentalis*
Canada Lily—*Lilium canadense*
Cardinal Flower—*Lobelia cardinalis*
Clammy Azalea—*Rhododendron viscosum*
Coralroot—*Corallorhiza*, all spp.
Fringed Orchis—*Habernaria*, all spp.
Gentian—*Gentiana*, all native
       Fringed Gentian—*Gentiana crinita*
       Fringe-Tip Closed Gentian—*Gentiana clausa*
       Short-Fringe Closed Gentian—*Gentiana clausa*
       Stiff Gentian—*Gentiana quinquefolia*
Ginseng, Dwarf—*Panax quinquefolium*
Grass-of-Parnassus—*Parnassia glauca*
Grass Pink—*Calopogon pulchellus*
Harebell—*Campanula rotundifolia*
Indian Pipe—*Monotropa uniflora*
Lady's-Tresses—*Spiranthes*, all spp.
Lily—*Lilium*, all native
       Canada Lily—*Lilium canadensis*
       Turk's-Cap Lily—*Lilium superbum*
       Wood Lily—*Lilium philadelphicum*
Lobelia, Great Blue—*Lobelia siphilitica*
Lotus, American—*Nelumbo lutea*
Mad-Dog Skullcap—*Scutellaria lateriflora*
Marsh Pink—*Sabbatia stellaris*
Marsh Pink, Large—*Sabbatia dodecandra*
Milkwort—*Polygala polygama*
Mountain Fringe, also called Climbing Fumitony—*Adlumia fungosa*
One Flowered Pyrola, also called Wintergreen—*Moneses uniflora*
Orchids—*Orchis*, all native
Pine Sap—*Monotropa hypopitys*

Pinkstar, Upland, also called Rose-Pink—*Sabbatia angularis*
Pipsissewa, Green—*Chimaphila umbellata*
Pipsissewa, Mottled or Spotted—*Chimaphila maculata*
Pond-Lily—*Nuphar microphyllum*
Purple or Seaside Gerardia—*Gerardia martima*
Rattlesnake Plantain—*Goodyera pubescens*
Sabbatia—*Sabbatia,* all spp.
Sea-Lavender—*Limonium carolinianum*
Shinleaf—*Pyrola elliptica*
Spotted Wintergreen—*Chimaphila maculata*
Sundew—*Drosera,* spp.
Swamp-Loosestrife—*Decodon verticillatus*
Swamp Rose-Mallow—*Hibiscus moscheutos*
Sweet Pepperbush—*Clethra alnifolia*
Turtlehead, Balmony—*Chelone glabra*
Virgin's-Bower—*Clematis virginiana*
Water Lily, White or Sweet-Scented—*Nymphaea odorata*
White Snakeroot—*Eupatorium rugosum*
Wild Bean—*Apios americana*
Wild Bergamot—*Monarda fistulosa*
Wintergreen—*Gaultheria procumbens*
Wood Lily—*Lilium philadelphicum*
Yellow False Foxgloves—*Gerardia,* spp.

CHAPTER EIGHT

HERBS, VEGETABLES, AND BERRIES

PERHAPS it is their age-old tradition that sets herbs apart from other plants and gives them a special air—almost a feeling of importance and elegance. Nature has endowed herbs with an almost mystical appeal that goes far beyond their practical use.

> *For sight inherits beauty, hearing sounds,*
> *The nostrils sweet perfume;*
> *All tastes have hidden room*
> *Within the tongue; and feeling feeling wounds*
> *With pleasure and delight.*

With these charming lines of the mystic poet Thomas Traherne (1637–1674) the English herb expert and writer, Mrs. C. F. Leyel, introduces her book *Cinquefoil* in which she describes the "herbs" most pleasing to the five senses. If we had the time or the expertise, each of us could find the plants that please us most. Unfortunately around the word "herb" exists a confusion of tongues, a veritable tower of Babel built almost at the beginning of time.

Archaeologists and historians continue to be astounded. Fossilized seeds and plants are being found in excavations and rocks thousands of miles apart; roses in Oregon and Montana, lupine in Washington, water lilies in Tibet, others in Russia and Mesopotamia; all are thousands—and some millions—of years old. All are called "herbs," and so are all other flowering plants which die down to their roots in winter. A more contemporary term is "herbaceous," but the meaning is the same. Among the exceptions, of course, is the rose, but it is called a herb for its more than decorative uses.

From the list of herbs found in the library of the Assyrian King Ashurbanipal (668–625 B.C.) to the herbals of the fifteenth, sixteenth, and seventeenth centuries almost everything was called a herb and given specific properties. And we should not forget the amazing lore of North American Indians who seem to have found a use for everything that grew out of the sacred earth. For cooking, drinking, tanning and dyeing, the enhancement of the sexual life, vanities and vapors, almost all plants had a specific use or significance.

Many of the delightful stories are, as we now know, merely old wives' tales and not more valid than some European peasants' application of spiderweb to a sore. Others hold a good deal of merit and truth. Also, many flowering plants have symbolic meanings, some of which have not yet quite disappeared among the innocent or gullible. Angelica, for example, still means "inspiration" perhaps because its Latin name is *Angelica archangelica.* Borage was the medieval symbol for courage, and so it remains in several European countries. Heliotrope, first dedicated to Apollo, means love and in astrology is the herb of the sun. Horseradish is the bitter herb "bondage" in the Jewish Passover; lavender is the good-luck symbol for a woman, and also the astrological herb of Mercury; marjoram is the mascot for lovers, mint, the plant of Jupiter and hence power;

224

rue is the medieval symbol for morality and mercy, although Shakespeare made it stand for magic and witchcraft. Sage is the herb of Zeus, health, and longevity; thyme is the symbol of courage and activity, and so on almost ad infinitum. The rose, of course, has always been the grand symbol of passion.

A mystery remains: How did early Egyptian physicians find out that poppies produced opium, or Mexicans that digitalis could be made from foxglove, or the Rocky Mountain Indians that the bark of cascara made an excellent purgative later called *cascara sagrada* (the sacred bark) by early Spanish settlers?

Nor do we know how seasoning was discovered. Perhaps some man who was roasting a piece of meat covered it with a leaf to keep it clean, or protected, and then realized that the leaf had given the meat a new and pleasant flavor.

The early settlers in America brought their ideas with them from almost all parts of Europe and tended their herbs with loving care, some still for medicinal purposes, but mostly for condiments and food. But except for the Shakers who grew herbs commercially in New Hampshire and Massachusetts until 1950, the excitement about herbs died down. During the first world war, it is true that some hard-to-come-by exotic medicinal ingredients were grown in private and public gardens. In the intervening years, however, only the garden clubs and a very few passionate afficionados continued to talk about herbs.

But now that so many Americans are traveling abroad and learning about the pleasures of gourmet foods (and no respectable gourmet could possibly do without culinary herbs) this kind of special gardening has once more become a fashionable pursuit.

Today we can agree that the word "herbs" means plants for culinary use—almost to the exclusion of all others. One of the best-known nurseries in our northeast recommends for cooking only five varieties: Chives, marjoram, sage, tarragon, and thyme. To these a real cook would add basil, which is much used in

Italian cooking and in the preparation of many meats; and I would include rosemary, which is wonderful for flavoring, and also lavender and heliotrope for their lovely scent. But these are not hardy in the northeast, where they should be potted in the autumn and taken indoors. Lavender deserves to grace every herb garden or perennial border. The design of the flowers is charming, and the leaves have the sweetest smell. They are often dried and used in sachets and potpourri. Oregano has a misleading name: it is really wild marjoram (Oreganum vulgare) and

This photograph, courtesy of the Press Bureau of Colonial Williamsburg, shows the herb garden of "John Blair Kitchen," designed in the traditional English manner with brick paths and edges, the plants arranged in a totally orderly way. Note the small shrubs which accent the two central beds on both sides, and the clipped boxwood hedge which separates the garden from the kitchen and the neighbors. Reproducing this design today would take an enormous amount of labor, and, alas, almost nonexisting professional help. However, one could conceivably lay out a herb garden in similar shapes but with much less area to cover.

usually sold in a mixture of similar herbs. *Oreganum mexicana,* on the other hand, is a perennial in warm zones and an annual in the colder ones. Mexicana is widely used in Latin countries: in pizzas, pasta, and chili con carne. Thyme planted between flagstones adds a bit of color to an otherwise indifferent walk. As soon as the plant gets too big, it can be divided and used to start another fragrant spot. Thyme also makes an excellent edging plant for a perennial or herb garden. Another variety, lemon thyme, may be walked on. It will grow well in cracks between

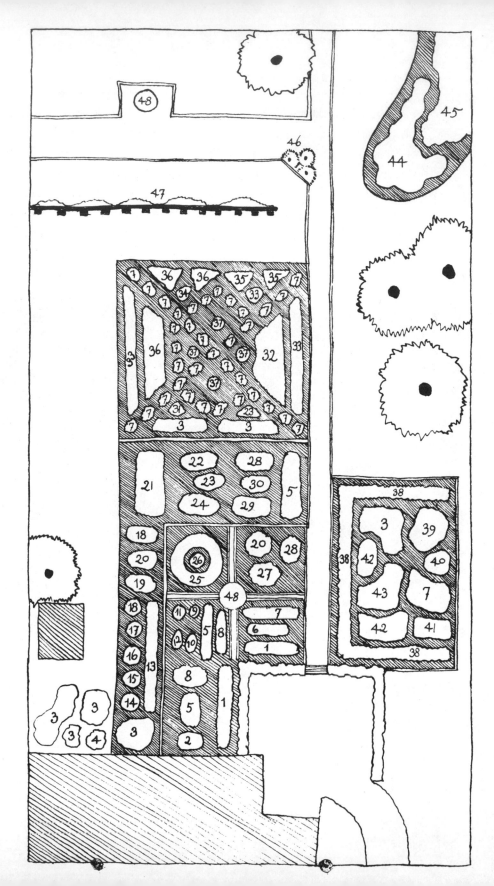

The herb gardens at Mystic Seaport in Connecticut, are probably furbished with plants and seeds which the whalers brought from all over the world. It is kept up today as a reminder of the importance of herbs in the life of early America. (Sarah Weintz)

1 curly onion
2 egyptian onion
3 julip mint
4 angelica & lemon balm mint
5 crimson thyme
6 salad burnet
7 english thyme
8 wild strawberries
9 hyssop
10 tarragon
11 asparagus
12 sage
13 chives
14 tall yarrow
15 woad
16 mugwort
17 wormwood
18 southernwood
19 bible leaf
20 lavender
21 woolly thyme
22 wild thyme
23 gray santolina
24 lemon geranium

25 creeping cranebill geranium
26 true myrtal
27 catnip
28 lemon thyme
29 balm scented geranium
30 lady's mantel
31 lemon verbena
32 nasturtiums
33 germander
34 rue
35 creeping yarrow
36 calender flower
37 rosemary
38 lambs ears
39 red bee balm
40 fox glove
41 silver king
42 canadian violet
43 camomile
44 flowering kahl
45 red geraniums
46 evergreen shrubs
47 rambler roses
48 sundial

stone, brick, or flagstones so long as there is enough soil to hold its roots. Every step becomes a moment of pleasure, for the lemony scent stays with you for quite awhile.

The advent of fluorescent light gardening has made it possible to grow other herbs during the cold months. Parsley and chives do exceedingly well, and provide fresh flavor from window to cooking pot or dish.

When it comes to starting a herb garden, almost anything goes. Your own plan will depend on the space available and the number of herbs you think you cannot do without. The restorations in Virginia's Williamsburg show the delectable and extravagant designs of herb gardens of the seventeenth and eighteenth centuries, and even today some people are ambitious enough to plan in the grand manner. One contemporary herb garden has six segments of identical size cut into the lawn. (It requires more work to keep the grass out of the beds than to tend them.) The tip of each segment is planted with large and tall herbacious flowers—lupine, delphinium, and others. (A less ambitious gardener might well use this idea to great visual advantage.) However, a small square surrounded by flagstones will give ample space for the basic herbs you need. And so will a space cut out from a lawn in which rocks help to set the plants apart. Some people are even satisfied with a couple of potted herbs near the kitchen door. If you wish to preserve a more traditional look, you might place an edging of bricks or a brick walk around your bed of herbs.

The spacing of the plants inside the herb graden is quite important, perhaps even more so than in other kinds of gardening. It is always a good idea to plant more than one of a species, both for crosspollinizing and insurance. Some species need more room than others to prevent their growing together; some become scraggly with age and should be cut back or replaced with young

230

plants; some have beautifully shaped leaves and flowers and should be given ample room. As in all other planting, if at all possible, you must project the final size and form of a plant.

The following chart will give you a good selection of herbs for your garden. If you are a novice and unsure as to which plants to use, almost any nursery will allow you to smell a leaf or let you crush it between your fingers to get the full fragrance.

To make this chart more useful and help you make an immediate choice for your garden of herbs—small or larger, if you have the room—here are the groups within which you might wish to make your choice:

I. CULINARY HERBS

A. Food: Basil, burnet, caraway, chives, coriander, dill, fennel, lovage, sweet and pot marjoram, mint, pepper, spear and apple, rosemary, saffron crocus, sage, savory, thyme.

B. Drink: Bee balm, borage, burnet, clove pink, mints, sage, verbena, sweet woodruff, wormwood.

II. SCENT

Heliotrope, lavender, rosemary, southernwood.

III. APPEARANCE

Purple-leaved basil, burnet, chamomile, foxglove, heliotrope, rosemary, saffron crocus, winter savory, several kinds of thyme, sweet woodruff, wormwood.

I have omitted the medicinal herbs because, in general, housewives and gardeners no longer make potions for luck and love.

HERB CHART   A = Annual   B = Biennial   P = Perennial

COMMON NAME *Botanical Name*	Origin	Kind	Location	Soil	Propagation	Height	Use
BASIL *Ocimum basilicum*	India	A	○	ord.	seed	18″	Cooking, especially with tomato dishes. Also comes with purple leaves.
BEE BALM (Oswego tea) *Monarda didyna*	United States	P	○ or ●	any	seed, div.	4′	Leaves make aromatic tea.
BORAGE *Borago officinalis*	Rome	A	○	ord.	seed	2–3′	Flowers and leaves give cucumber-like flavor to summer drinks. Flowers very attractive.
BURNET *Sanguisorba minor*	Europe	P	○	ord.	seed, div.	1′	Salads and cool drinks. Graceful plant.
CARAWAY *Carum carvi*	Asia Minor	B	○	ord.	seed	30″	Of the carrot family, seeds have aromatic flavor, used in cooking & breads. Oil used in *Kuemmel.*

Name	Origin	A/P		Soil	Propagation	Height	Uses
CHAMOMILE *Matricaria chamomilla*	Rome	A	O	ord.	seed	15″	Helps other plants grow. In Europe flowers are used for a tisane for washing blonde hair.
CHIVES *Allium schoenoprasum*	China	P	O	ord.	seed, div.	10″	Delicate onion flavor of leaves, much used in cooking and salads.
CLOVE PINK *Dianthus caryophyllus*	Greece	P	O	ord. well drained	seed, cutt.	10″	Flowers have lovely fragrance; for flavoring wine and vinegar.
CORIANDER *Coriandrum sativum*	Rome or Greece	A	O	good	seeds	2′	Delicious flavor of seeds; condiment and confections.
DILL *Anethum graveolens*	Egypt	A	O	ord.	seed	2′	Leaves used for flavor in cooking, or with sour cream and salads. Both leaves and seeds for flavoring pickles.

COMMON NAME / *Botanical Name*	Origin	Kind	Location	Soil	Propagation	Height	Use
FENNEL, SWEET / *Foeniculum officinalis*	Egypt	A	O	ord.	seed	3–4′	Seeds for condiment, leaves for their anise-like flavor; stems may be eaten like celery.
FOXGLOVE / *Digitalis purpurea*	Eurasia	B	O	ord.	seed	to 4′	Leaves source of digitalis.
HELIOTROPE (GARDEN) / *Valeriana officinalis*	Europe and Asia	P	O	good	seed, div.	c 5′	Beautiful fragrance, charming, tiny flowers.
HYSSOP / *Hyssopus officinalis*	Bible lands	P	O	poor soil	seed	2′	Condiment and liqueur flavoring (leaves). Pretty, small flowers.
LAVENDER / *Lavandula officinalis*	Mediterranean	P	O	rocky dry	seed, cutt.	1½–3′	Beloved for the fragrance of flowers. Dried for sachet and perfume.
LOVAGE / *Levisticum officinale*	Greece & Rome	P	O	rich, moist	seed	3–4′	Celery flavor of leaves and stem for soup and salads.

Name	Origin	A/P	Sun	Soil	Propagation	Height	Uses
MARJORAM, SWEET *Marjorana hortensis*	Eastern Mediterranean	A in North	○	ord.	seed, cutt.	8–12″	One of most fragrant and popular herbs. Spreads in garden. Use in cooking.
MARJORAM, POT *Majorana onites*	Mediterranean	P	○	light lime	seed, div.	same	Same, except has more thyme-like flavor.
MINT, APPLE *Mentha rotundifolia*	Mediterranean	P	○	moist	div. cutt.	20–30″	Combines flavor of apples with mint. Used as above for flavoring.
MINT, PEPPER- *Mentha piperita*	Egypt, Mediterranean	P	○	rich, moist	div. cutt.	c 2′	Much used for tea and flavoring. In medicine, source of menthol.
MINT, SPEAR- *Mentha spicata*	Egypt, Mediterranean	P	○	moist	div. cutt.	same	Used for mint sauce; oil for chewing gum.
PENNYROYAL (American) *Mentha pulegium*	United States	P	○ or light ●	moist	div.	low	Good tea for coughs and colds, but must be used with caution; some people allergic.

COMMON NAME / Botanical Name	Origin	Kind	Location	Soil	Propagation	Height	Use
ROSEMARY / Rosmarinus officinalis	Mediterranean	P	O	well drained	lime	3–6'	Very popular for meat and dressings.
SAFFRON CROCUS / Crocus sativus	Mediterranean	Bulb	O	any		low	Orange stigma, when dried, make the saffron. Used in cooking for flavor and color. Blooms in autumn, thus giving us late color.
SAGE, CLARY / Salvia sclarea	Southern European mountains	B	O	any	seed	3'	Leaves good in omelettes and for flavoring wine and beer. Plants should be replaced after second year of bloom.
SAVORY, SUMMER / Satureia hortensis	Eastern Mediterranean	A	O	good loam	seed	18"	Condiment with meats and vegetables.

Name	Origin			Soil	Propagation	Height	Remarks
SAVORY, WINTER *Satureia montana*	Mediterranean mountains	P	○	light sandy soil	seed, cutt.	2′	Good condiment, not as sweet as summer savory. Makes a good plant for accent.
SOUTHERNWOOD (OLD MAN) *Artemisia abrotanum*	Mediterranean	P	○	ord.	div.	2–5′	Grown for fragrance of leaves.
TARRAGON *Artemisia dracunculus*	Mediterranean	P	○ & some ●	ord.	div. cutt.	2′	Distinctive flavor. Much used in salads and cooking.
THYME (COMMON) *Thymus vulgaris*	Mediterranean	P	○	light, well drained	seed cutt. div.	6–10″	Very popular for seasoning; famous as source of honey. Tiny leaves attractive in border.
THYME, MOTHER OF *Thymus serpyllum*	Mediterranean	P	○	light, well drained	seed	very low	One variation; lemon thyme grows well between flagstones. Several colors of flowers and shades of green leaves.

COMMON NAME Botanical Name	Origin	Kind	Location	Soil	Propagation	Height	Use
VERBENA, LEMON *Lippia citriodora*	Tropical America	Shrub P	○ & in-doors	good	cutt.	tall	Leaves used for lemony taste in tea. Not hardy in North; bring indoors.
WOODRUFF, SWEET *Asperula odorata*	Rhine	P	○ or half ●	near woods and heath	rooted pieces	8″	Famous in German May wine; may be used in other drinks. Makes charming groundcover under taller plants.
WORMWOOD *Artemisia absinthium*	Mediterranean	P	○	poor soil	seed, cutt.	2–4′	Used in liqueur absinthe; makes fine strong accent in herb garden or other places.

NOTE: *We have here omitted* oregano *which is a trade name for a mixture of various herbs.* Oreganum vulgare *is used. This is the pot or wild marjoram.*

Some plants in our vegetable platters or salad bowls did not originate in the wilderness; they are called "cultigens"—plants invented long ago by some blithe and clever spirit through experimentation and crossbreeding. One of these "invented" plants is lettuce. For once, it seems quite inconceivable that it was in any way derived from that stringy and unattractive plant of our roadsides called wild lettuce (*lactuca canandensis*); the leaves of this plant are nothing to brag about and a very far cry from the beautiful crunchy and heavenly green heads we know today.

But even lettuce is not a contemporary plant. Pliny tells the story, based on earlier writings, of how the Emperor Augustus (63 B.C.–14 A.D.) had become seriously ill and no one knew what to do to help him. Finally the physician Musa suggested that the emperor eat lettuce. Although others disagreed, he followed Musa's advice and recovered. And lettuce became so popular in Rome that a method was discovered to preserve it. Pliny called it "oxymel," a mixture of vinegar and honey. Both Aristotle and Dioscorides extolled leek for strengthening the voice; but before that, the Egyptians and later the Druids thought that the layers of all onions represented the many lamina of the Universe.

Melons are said to have aroused the ire of the Elias by giving him a stomachache; the pea was a favorite of the Nordic god Thor. American Indians, as we all know, gave tomatoes, potatoes, and corn to the world.

Botanically speaking, a great many of our vegetables are annuals and must be grown fresh each year. This makes a friend of mine lament: "If only my vegetable garden didn't look like a truck garden as soon as things are up and eaten." This being so, most people who insist on having their own vegetables try to have them grow away from the house, or at least from the front; for the more you eat, the more disorderly the garden becomes.

239

An onion in flower.

Salad bowl, a noncrisp type of lettuce. All kinds of lettuce may be grown in good, fairly rich garden soil. It is a cool season crop, although it needs full sun. Since it grows rapidly—forty-five days or so from seed—it may also be sown indoors under fluorescent light. You then can have a bowl full of fresh, crisp lettuce in the middle of the winter.

On the other hand, even here there are visual compensations. There is little that is more lush-looking than a leaf of beet or spinach, more beautiful to look at than an onion or a leek in bloom, more graceful than asparagus gone to seed, or the stalks of corn after it has reached our dinner table.

A few exotic and attractive suggestions not seen in the average garden:

Good-King-Henry (*Chenopodium bonus-henricus*) also called Mercury, is sometimes grown for salad greens, but is most remarkable for its spinach-like leaves. It was a pot-herb in the Renaissance, and is now seen only in elaborate herb gardens, owners of which have historical interests.

Rhubarb, an Asiatic perennial "herb" grows in good garden soil, but for best results should be planted in a trench filled with well-rotted cow manure within one foot of the top to which four inches of topsoil are added. The plants are then put in, and another four inches of soil put around the roots. Since this is a large plant, it should be set into the ground four to five inches apart. Rhubarb is a permanent crop that will stand several annual cuttings. It is best planted in the vegetable garden, but it is also used as background planting in some flower gardens.

Butternut squash takes a great deal of room in a garden, and since it is a vine rather than an upright plant, it could be grown against a fence, on rocks or wherever it will not interfere with other plants. This is a winter squash which should be left until fully ripe and can then be kept in a warm, dry cellar for later use. Summer squash grows into a bushy plant and can well be grown in a vegetable garden. One of its varieties is zucchini which produces a great deal of fruit and is able to feed a fairly large family.

Horseradish belongs to the mustard family and has one of the most pungent roots in the vegetable kingdom. Known to and disliked by Dioscorides, Pliny, and all subsequent herbalists and botanists who disliked its effect on the breath and digestion, it is not to be confused with the ordinary radish which belongs to a quite different family.

Just remember one very basic fact: In the anticipation of growing glorious crisp lettuce, shiny tomatoes, sweet corn, crunchy radishes, you will almost always plant too much—and at the end of the season be left with produce no one has had the appetite to eat unless, of course, you wish to freeze or pickle or preserve vegetables such as cucumbers, tomatoes, and rhubarb. Perhaps there is a farmer somewhere in everyone's blood. Age-old traditions and habits are slow to die.

One friend who owns a successful advertising business in a town near his home insists, year after year, on planting every possible kind of lettuce: romaine, boston, iceberg, bib and saladbowl. But whatever you plan, first take a pencil and paper and figure out *what you want, how much,* and how to interrelate the various crops. Also, there are some very good and simple books which contain excellent practical advice.

In the Sunday *New York Times* of March 8, 1970, there was an outstanding piece by Rhoda S. Tarantino titled "How Many Vegetables for a Family of Four?" Rightly she called the whole thing a "puzzlement" because there are so many variables: soil, temperature, rainfall, exposure to sun. Nor is it possible to accurately predict yields in advance.

But she suggests a plot of twenty by forty feet for a family of four. (I wouldn't want to be the one to turn over that much ground.) However, any area of this size need not be plowed by a professional but could be handled by a couple of strong backs, skillful arms, sharp shovels or spades, forks and a hoe for turning over the ground, and then a rake to smooth out the earth and help remove weeds, stones, and pebbles. For making the rows in which seeds and seedlings are to be planted, a pointed hoe or even just a stick could be used, since seeds should be planted shallowly.

Some people like to fence in their vegetable gardens, and often a cutting garden is planted on one side of the garden or in between rows. But the soil should be tested before planting, for it should be sweet, not acid, and lime and manure are often needed.

But why not plant some of the better-looking vegetables in a regular flowerbed? Or, build a few simple boxes which could be painted a pleasant color and put almost anywhere, so long as they are six to eight inches deep and hold the right kind of soil. Paths of flagstones or brick could be laid between them and thus create a pattern rather than a jumble. Or, one could even make a virtue of a calamity by putting annuals into the rows as the vegetables are taken into the kitchen. In the case of lettuce and cabbage, one would plant two crops in the growing season and thus almost avoid the holes between plants.

It is always a good idea to plant perennial vegetables on one side, so that they are not disturbed by the cleaning-up processes of subsequent years.

To protect vegetables from grubs and weeds and save time and labor for the gardener, it is good practice to cover the ground between the rows of vegetables with black plastic, straw, or even grass cuttings. And if you don't wish to share your hard-earned produce with rabbits and woodchucks, you must fence in your vegetable yard with chicken or other small-mesh wire, buried into the ground at least a foot deep and two or three feet above it —deep enough so that the ever-voraciously hungry critters can't burrow under the fence, and high enough so they can't jump over it.

Since I cannot tell what you like or how much you will eat, you will find help in the excellent bulletin, "Suburban and Farm Vegetable Garden," Home and Garden Bulletin No. 9, which you can order for thirty cents from the Superintendent of Documents, U.S. Government Printing Office, Washington, D.C. 20402. It contains all the information on vegetable growing that

Quantity of seed and number of plants required for 100 feet of row,
depths of planting, and distances apart for rows and plants

Crop	Requirement for 100 feet of row		Depth for planting seed	Distance apart		
	Seed	Plants		Rows		Plants in the row
				Horse- or tractor-cultivated	Hand-cultivated	
			Inches	*Feet*		
Asparagus	1 ounce	75	1–1½	4–5	1½ to 2 feet	18 inches.
Beans:						
Lima, bush	½ pound		1–1½	2½–3	2 feet	3 to 4 inches.
Lima, pole	"		1–1½	3–4	3 feet	3 to 4 feet.
Snap, bush	"		1–1½	2½–3	2 feet	3 to 4 inches.
Snap, pole	4 ounces		1–1½	3–4	"	3 feet.
Beet	2 ounces		1	2–2½	14 to 16 inches	2 to 3 inches.
Broccoli:						
Heading	1 packet	50–75	½	2½–3	2 to 2½ feet	14 to 24 inches.
Sprouting	"	50–75	½	2½–3	"	"
Brussels sprouts	"	50–75	½	2½–3	"	"
Cabbage	"	50–75	½	2½–3	"	"
Cabbage, Chinese	"		½	2–2½	18 to 24 inches	8 to 12 inches.
Carrot	"		½	2–2½	14 to 16 inches	2 to 3 inches.
Cauliflower	"	50–75	½	2½–3	2 to 2½ feet	14 to 24 inches.
Celeriac	"	200–250	⅛	2½–3	18 to 24 inches	4 to 6 inches.
Celery	"	200–250	⅛	2½–3	"	6 inches.
Chard	2 ounces		1	2–2½	"	6 inches.
Chervil	1 packet		½	2–2½	14 to 16 inches	2 to 3 inches.
Chicory, witloof	"		½	2–2½	18 to 24 inches	6 to 8 inches.
Chives	"		½	2½–3	14 to 16 inches	In clusters.
Collards	"		½	3–3½	18 to 24 inches	18 to 24 inches.

Crop	Requirement for 100 feet of row		Depth for planting seed	Distance apart		
	Seed	Plants		Rows		Plants in the row
				Horse- or tractor-cultivated	Hand-cultivated	
			Inches	Feet		
Cornsalad	"		½	2½–3	14 to 16 inches	1 foot.
Corn, sweet	2 ounces		2	3–3½	2 to 3 feet	Drills, 14 to 16 inches; hills, 2½ to 3 feet.
Cress:						
Upland	1 packet		⅛–¼	2–2½	14 to 16 inches	2 to 3 inches.
Water	"		⅛–¼	2–2½	18 to 24 inches	4 to 6 inches.
Cucumber	"		½	6–7	6 to 7 feet	Drills, 3 feet; hills, 6 feet.
Dandelion	"		½	2½–3	14 to 16 inches	8 to 12 inches.
Dasheen	5 to 6 pounds		2–3	3½–4	3½ to 4 feet	2 feet.
Eggplant	1 packet	50	½	3	2 to 2½ feet	3 feet.
Endive	"	50	½	2½–3	18 to 24 inches	12 inches.
Fennel, Florence	"		½	2½–3	"	4 to 6 inches.
Garlic	1 pound		1–2	2½–3	14 to 16 inches	2 to 3 inches.
Horseradish	Cuttings	50–75	2	3–4	2 to 2½ feet	18 to 24 inches.
Kale	1 packet		½	2½–3	18 to 24 inches	12 to 15 inches.
Kohlrabi	"		½	2½–3	14 to 16 inches	5 to 6 inches.
Leek	"		½–1	2½–3	"	2 to 3 inches.
Lettuce, head	"	100	½	2½–3	"	12 to 15 inches.
Lettuce, leaf	"		½	2½–3	"	6 inches.
Muskmelon	"		1	6–7	6 to 7 feet	Hills, 6 feet.
Mustard	"		½	2½–3	14 to 16 inches	12 inches.
Okra	2 ounces		1–1½	3–3½	3 to 3½ feet	2 feet.
Onion:						
Plants		400	1–2	2–2½	14 to 16 inches	2 to 3 inches.
Seed	1 packet		½–1	2–2½	"	"
Sets	1 pound		1–2	2–2½	"	"

Crop	Requirement for 100 feet of row		Depth for planting seed	Distance apart		
	Seed	Plants		Rows		Plants in the row
				Horse- or tractor-cultivated	Hand-cultivated	
			Inches	*Feet*		
Parsley	1 packet		1/8	2-2½	"	4 to 6 inches.
Parsley, turnip-rooted	"		1/8-1/4	2-2½	"	2 to 3 inches.
Parsnip	"		½	2-2½	18 to 24 inches	"
Peas	½ pound		2-3	2-4	1½ to 3 feet	1 inch.
Pepper	1 packet	50-70	½	3-4	2 to 3 feet	18 to 24 inches.
Physalis	"	25-40	½	2-2½	1½ to 2 feet	12 to 18 inches.
Poke	"		½-1	3-3½	3 to 3½ feet	3 feet.
Potato	5 to 6 pounds, tubers		4	2½-3	2 to 2½ feet	10 to 18 inches.
Pumpkin	1 ounce		1-2	5-8	5 to 8 feet	3 to 4 feet.
Radish	"		½	2-2½	14 to 16 inches	1 inch.
Rhubarb		25-35		3-4	3 to 4 feet	3 to 4 feet.
Salsify	1 ounce		½	2-2½	18 to 26 inches	2 to 3 inches.
Shallots	1 pound (cloves)		1-2	2-2½	12 to 18 inches	"
Sorrel	1 packet		½	2-2½	18 to 24 inches	5 to 8 inches.
Soybean	½ to 1 pound		1-1½	2½-3	24 to 30 inches	3 inches.
Spinach	1 ounce		½	2-2½	14 to 16 inches	3 to 4 inches.
Spinach, New Zealand	"		1-1½	3-3½	3 feet	18 inches.
Squash:						
Bush	½ ounce		1-2	4-5	4 to 5 feet	Drills, 15 to 18 inches; hills, 4 feet.
Vine	1 ounce		1-2	8-12	8 to 12 feet	Drills, 2 to 3 feet; hills, 4 feet.
Sweetpotato	5 pounds, bedroots	75	2-3	3-3½	3 to 3½ feet	12 to 14 inches.
Tomato	1 packet	35-50	½	3-4	2 to 3 feet	1½ to 3 feet.
Turnip greens	"		¼-½	2-2½	14 to 16 inches	2 to 3 inches.
Turnips and rutabagas	½ ounce		¼-½	2-2½	"	"
Watermelon	1 ounce		1-2	8-10	8 to 10 feet	Drills, 2 to 3 feet; hills, 8 feet.

anyone can possibly need. You will decide the size of your own vegetable garden by juggling the produce and the space it takes until you have arrived at the smallest practical area for the most food.

The following is the important Table 2 from the booklet. The botanical names have been omitted, perhaps for no other reason than that few but the most expert care that the Latin name for artichoke is *Cynara scolymus*.

Berries certainly taste better fresh than when bought at the market. Perhaps the most widely known and loved of all is the strawberry (*Fragaria*). It was dedicated to the nordic goddess Freia or Friga, from whom the Virgin Mary inherited it in the Middle Ages. But already Pliny described it in his usual somewhat exaggerated fashion as one of the wild fruits of Italy, as did the poet Virgil. Throughout the Middle Ages the strawberry appeared in paintings and manuscripts. John Parkinson describes it in detail, and claims that the leaves are "always" used in drinks, lotions, and gargles. The fruit, always popular at the table, was even then mixed with sugar, claret wine, milk or cream, and the water distilled from the fruit made a concoction for "the passions of the heart."

Jonathan Swift is supposed to have said: "God doubtlessly could have made a better berry, but doubtlessly he never did." Several of the noble families of France and England emblazoned their crests with the flower and the fruit. Today, many varieties are grown everywhere in southern and moderate climates; but the best tasting of all is still the tiny wild *Fraise de bois*, which grows in our woodlands as it does in those of Europe and in the European Alps.

Today even the wild strawberry has been cultivated and can be found in herb gardens and among the plants of flower gardens, sometimes among vegetables. Its cultivation is not difficult; it grows in any good garden soil, but should be protected from weeds by straw placed between the blooming plants. Cheesecloth or wire should be put over them when they begin to come into fruit, to prevent birds from eating the crop before you do.

There are two native kinds of blueberries in the eastern U.S.: high-bush which grow in acid soil, and the low-bush which grow in sandy soil and among rocks from Maine to Florida. Blueberries must not be confused, as they often are, with huckleberries to which they are related. Huckleberries are black and have none of the good taste of blueberries.

The high-bush variety can be and is widely cultivated and hybridized, which increases the size of the fruit. If the wild variety does not satisfy you, or if your open land is devoid of them, by all means buy a few bushes from a nursery; but be sure to cover them either with nylon netting or cheesecloth as soon as the berries appear. Birds love them even more than we do.

Another berry-bearing plant long known in Europe is the raspberry. It belongs to an immense genus of 400 or more plants. Its botanical name is *Rubus idaeus,* which is the one known to Parkinson and among those cultivated here by commercial growers and ambitious home gardeners. There are several varieties. Indian Summer and September, for example, are recommended for the home grower. The soil in which raspberries are to grow should be prepared two or three years in advance to eliminate all weeds, and must be provided with manure; the soil should be plowed deeply and pulverized. Exact directions for planting and disease control are contained in Cornell Extension Bulletin 719, New York State College of Agriculture, Cornell University, Ithaca, New York. Full-bearing shrubs need to be contained in a special place of a garden and carefully staked.

Vineyards are known to have already been grown in Sumer, more than five thousand years ago; they must have come to Palestine from Egypt, for it is said in Psalms 80:8, "Thou has brought a vine out of Egypt, thou has cast out the heathen and planted it." In Cretan and later Greek art, paintings of decorations of grapes abound. And did not Homer describe the vineyards of Alcinous in great detail? It seems as though wine, vineyards, and drinking were favorite parts of the life of the ancients and so they are into our very own day. Dioscorides described the grape and its uses in great detail, although Pliny was unsure whether the effect of drinking was injurious or beneficial.

In our day, wild grapevines and, of course, cultivated vines are found all over the world. A gardener can have fun with growing his own grapes. To start a new vine, a rooted cutting is usually planted; when the vines grow up and begin to bear they should be held up by a trellis and bound to wire.

Wild grapes are found almost everywhere, and although their fruit does not have the taste of cultivated varieties they grow rapidly and often fill in an undesirable spot where nothing else will grow. They trail over rocks, and because they embrace other shrubby plants they must be watched. Like honeysuckle, in time they can kill a mountain laurel or even a small tree.

> *An ambitious gardener can create lovely designs with his strawberry patch; one friend of mine set them in tiers, forming a rather impressive-looking hill.*

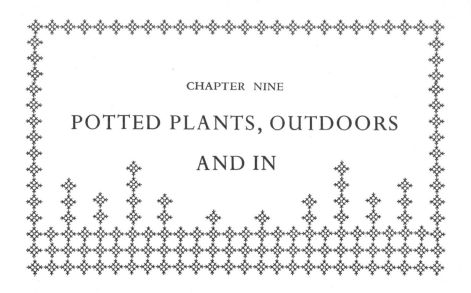

CHAPTER NINE

POTTED PLANTS, OUTDOORS

AND IN

LIKE so many other good ideas, gardening with potted plants is a very old pursuit. The Egyptians filled boxes and pots with colorful flowers and placed them on the walks around their houses. The paved courts of the Greeks were similarly adorned, as were also the marble terraces of their temples. (In the ruins of the Temple of Hephaistos, flower pots and sherds have been excavated.) Later, many of the battlements of medieval castles and fortresses all over Europe were decorated with flowerpots. This has lasted through the entire history of gardening and down to our own day.

On terraces, walls, walks, and for the decoration of the edges of living spaces, passageways and corners; in window boxes, planters, birdcages, baskets, all sorts and shapes of ceramic containers, potted plants can be used everywhere. A particularly interesting and attractive piece of earthenware, metal, or even wood, planted with geraniums, begonias, petunias, small evergreens, ivy, or any other suitable plant will add color or texture to an otherwise gray and empty expanse.

A gardener too lazy or too busy to turn over a great deal of earth and keep on working all spring and summer and fall could conceivably create an outstanding effect with nothing more than potted plants around his house—without being any less of a gardener for it. I have often thought that this is exactly what I should do with my small front terrace, and forget about digging, planting, sweating, worrying about bugs and moles, and all the other creatures which make a gardener's life miserable. Then, too, many fussy plants don't like it in this spot or that and refuse to show their true color no matter how assiduously I have cared for them. How much easier it would be to move them to

Plants in baskets and wisteria make for a literal "hanging garden."

places *they* want—if they were in pots, and, therefore, portable.

Perhaps some day, when I am older and wiser and my joints crack even louder than they now do, I will do as the Greeks did—and enjoy color and scent outside of only potted plants. This is not to say that all work and care connected with container planting may be omitted. Exposure to sun and shade, soil, fertilization, insect control, and watering are just as important to potted plants as they are in all other kinds of horizontal and vertical gardening—often even more so. But there is still another advantage inherent in potted plants: You can take many plants out of their containers, dig them into your garden, and then, when the outside growing year is done, put their roots back into captivity and take them indoors again for another long season of pleasure.

Everywhere the geraniums (*Pelargonium*) of the geranium family—red, pink, or white—seem to be the most beloved flowers of all. This originally African plant has traveled everywhere, from the window boxes of the peasants all over Europe, to all kinds of arrangements in gardens, to the *parterres* of the great castles; from the multitudinous bloom of the well-kept and nourished plants in thousands and perhaps millions of American gardens and houses, to a forlorn and dusty little flower pot on the fire escape of our unforgivable slums.

Ancient Athenean flowerpots. (Agora Excavations)

There now seem to be at least two hundred and fifty species, but the most popular in our climate belong to four groups: Lady Washington—showy, colorful, and easy to propagate, as are almost all other kinds of geraniums; fish geranium—a continuous bloomer with often variegated leaves; ivy geraniums with ivy-like leaves which can be trained along wires or stakes; and finally the desirable scented geraniums that smell like mint, apple, rose, cinnamon, and so on. Of these the rose geraniums are the most often seen. But it would be fun to grow several of these in a collection of various scents.

One of my friends has on his front terrace a huge cement container full of red geraniums; another friend has lined the steps of his terrace with clay pots; still another put her pots into an antique wire basket; and another decorated a steep natural stone wall with square wooden containers together with chrysanthemums in clay pots, and put them on different levels.

Put geraniums into a mixture of top and potting soil in bright sunshine, and they will almost never stop growing and blooming. Take a cutting in July or August, put it in sand or water (I prefer the latter because you can *see* when the roots begin to form) and plant it in the ubiquitous four-inch pot. A friend keeps her collection of geraniums (several scented ones among them) in front of her house on a flagstone slab; someone else hangs them in baskets from large brackets at the corner of her

The epitome of successful pot gardening is found in the middle of London, where several streets vie with each other, year after year, in making the fronts of their houses bloom. The few feet of space are between sidewalk and house.

Chrysanthemums on an impro-
vised "table" made from a piece
of flagstone.

Garden furniture makes perfect
pedestals for almost any outdoor
plant.

This old iron fire bucket filled to
the brim with hens and chickens
looks stunning on a terrace.

house; still another friend has large pots standing in front of the entrance to a cabin in the woods. But the most elegant flowerpots of all come from Italy and their design adds immeasurably to the pleasure of a terrace, porch, steps, and the flowers.

But geraniums are certainly not the only plants for potting out of doors. Any plant that will stand the climate—myrtle, even a birch tree or wisteria or rosebush—can be cultivated in pots. Pot your favorites first. I enjoy my pot of modest begonias all summer long, setting them off the ground on top of a clay tile for looks as well as to keep out worms and rabbits.

And because I never really want to do much with annuals but needed a bit of color at a corner of my house, I utilized a stand (gift from a friend) which had been used in France for storing cooking pots in graduated sizes. I used it for potted plants instead, and it gave me pleasure all summer long. The flowers flourished, there were no weeds, and everyone who entered the door felt warmly welcomed by this actually rather silly invention.

During the Winter

The simplest way to grow plants indoors is around windows. The fact that some plants do best in full sun (geraniums, begonias, lantana) and others in partial sun (Thanksgiving and Christmas cacti, and some of the leafy plants) or in almost no sun at all (African violets or cyclamen in an east window) makes it possible to have almost a greenhouse in nothing more elaborately horticultural than a living room. Kitchen windows often do nicely (so long as the leaves don't get spattered with grease) or any other room in the house except bedrooms—fresh-air fiends open windows in weather that can kill the green and growing things in one fell swoop.

Besides all the fun of the tending and watching live flowers when all is dead and still outside, the design, color, and form of plants can add immeasurably to the decorative scheme of a room and not only enliven but lend a vibrant and continuous feeling of life. Year after year a friend gives me a pink cyclamen which I hugely enjoy next to a blue glass jar. I am so used to this combination that it has become a very special kind of symbol.

Another friend puts her deep-red geraniums on glass shelves inside a south window and this arrangement, repeated year after

The Victorian era outdid itself in indoor planting as it did in other areas of architecture and decoration.

year, has become almost something like *her* special escutcheon. A gorgeous Amaryllis emblazons nothing more exciting than a kitchen corner that consists of two windows. A contemporary living room without much color in its walls and floor is immeasurably brightened by a trough in front of its windows which is filled with cacti, herbs, and many other plants; on a ledge built in front of it rests a beautiful Japanese pot with croton, a tropical plant with green leaves interlaced with red markings. If there were nothing else of interest in this room, the plants alone would give it a lift.

I have experimented with a white azalea in a black Japanese pot, and it looked so very much better than it would have in the brown clay pot in which it came. But I made a horrendous mistake well worth remembering and guarding against: I neglected to ask the florist whether this was a hardy azalea or merely a greenhouse plant. When I planted it outdoors in the following spring, it promptly gave up its beautiful ghost.

Japanese pottery is often an improvement over our Western ware—especially since a regular flowerpot is porous and constantly loses water to the atmosphere.

Year after year I enjoy a Thanksgiving cactus that always comes into bloom at the right time. Its flowers are similar to those of the better known Christmas cactus except for their color: this one has salmon-pink flowers that make my room sing. Hoya, also called "wax plant," has the most delicately pink clusters of blossoms in the axils of its leaves. It is a vine, sweetly fragrant, and belongs, of all things, to the milkweed family; butterfly weed and the purple-flowered milkweed of our meadows are native American wildflowers, but hoya comes from Asia and Australia.

Many people grow flowers from bulbs indoors. Croci, narcissi, hyacinths can be put in glasses or dishes filled with pebbles and treated (as, for example, special hyacinth containers in which the roots develop in the dark) so as to assume almost continuous bloom throughout the winter. But after they have bloomed, don't expect to get another showing outdoors. The bulbs will take two or three years to renew their flower-producing ability outdoors, and will never really amount to very much. Personally I hate to throw out any plant material that shows the tiniest sign of life, but I have never been successful in this area. Lilies of the valley are self-renewing corms, not bulbs, and so may well be worth a try.

Other people like to make small gardens in bottles or in huge brandy glasses. Here one can work with native materials—mosses, grasses, pipsissewa, and other small wild plants. If the air and soil are kept moist by putting a pane of glass over the rim of the bottle or glass, they will do well. A friend of mine made beautiful Christmas presents that way. She took the glasses back every autumn to—as she put it—"refresh" the little "garden."

It takes a special knack to work inside small confines; a great deal of patience and the willingness to go out into the woods to find new materials. But by all means, if you have time and the

258

love for this charming way of gardening, try it. Other people like to make aquatic gardens in an aquarium or terrarium. The difference between the two is that in the first, plants and fish live happily together and give children much pleasure; the second, usually made in an aquarium without fish or frogs, is similar to the brandy glass idea only much larger. Both create points of interest in almost any room, and are excellent activities for children because they teach them early how to work with living plants.

The true aristocrats among plants, however, grow in hothouses —large or small, elaborate or simple, erected separately in a garden or yard, or attached to the house. They can even be built into windows, but should jut out from the house to allow plants light from three directions.

Few of us can afford the kind of large, separate greenhouses which may be seen on some of the very old estates in Great Britain. The geranium section of the great greenhouse of the Botanical Gardens in Dublin is truly overwhelming; so are the greenhouses of our own botanical gardens and great estates or growers. Although most of us cannot emulate them, occasional visits can teach us much and at least spur our own efforts. I shall never forget my visit to a grower in Rhinebeck, New York, where flourish millions of anemones in all colors, sizes, and varieties.

More likely within the means of the average gardener are small greenhouses attached to the main building which can be more easily heated by a central heating plant, heating cables inside the flowerbeds, or even just space heaters with a thermostat that goes on at night when the house temperature gets too low. A ventilating device is important, and so is shade when the sun gets too hot in the autumn or in early spring.

An American greenhouse—
really a kind of sunporch attached to the house.

One of the many orchids that
can be grown only in warm, humid conditions.

If you decide on a greenhouse, make sure it has
provision for shade as well as sun.

Here may be grown plants too delicate to take the cold weather outside—geraniums, begonias, succulents, and many others which you can enjoy outdoors in the summer or wish to propagate from cuttings for outdoor planting for the following year. Greenhouses also enable you to enjoy strictly tropical plants far too delicate for outdoors in any but the hottest climates, or just for a short period in the colder ones, plants such as orchids and the like. Among these are also begonia pendula of the begonia family; the showy and beautiful spineless cacti called *Epiphyllium* of the cactus family; or some of the thirty species of *Episcia*—also called flame violet, a relative of African violets —American herbs from the tropics with luscious leaves and lovely red flowers. The latter are typical hothouse plants and can stand only very little, if any, exposure outdoors.

The extraordinary nightblooming cereus of the cactus family, which originated in South America and the West Indies, has given me one of the memorable nights of my life. A friend of a friend had succeeded in growing one to the point of blooming, and a party had been arranged to watch its waxy and almost etherial petals open. There we were, photographing each succeeding moment, until at two o'clock in the morning the flower finally opened in all its spectacular glory.

And then there are the African violets (*Saintpaulia*) of the Gesneriaceae family in many colors—with leaves of different texture, from glossy smooth to variegated rough—which grow only indoors and in a shady spot (although they can sometimes stand short exposures outdoors during hot and humid August days, but always in the shade). Another friend of mine with an unbelievably green thumb for African violets, grows them by the hundred under fluorescent lights in an especially built commercially available fixture which she keeps in a light and well ventilated room.

This brings me to that enormously fun-giving horticultural

261

pursuit of growing things under artificial light. Today this has become a large industry that creates better-looking and practical stands and almost constantly improved lamps which give forth ever more ultraviolet light.

One neighbor provides fresh vegetables for his family during the brutal months of January, February and March. Another specializes in primulas; she grows so many varieties that even a botanist might gape incredulously at the bounty. Another grows all the seedlings she wants to set outside in the spring; she is a truly rabid gardener, with an extraordinary amount of knowledge and skill. Each April she comes up with a colossal number of plants from the bounty of her fluorescent fixtures in the basement. In fact fluorescent gardening can be done anywhere, and what fun it is! Even I have succumbed.

I had a useless north window in my small pantry and decided to make it into a tiny experimental station—which sounds stuffier and more impressive than it turned out to be. The point is that anyone with hammer, nails, and a folding rule can come up with something that will work.

I also learned a few facts. Trying to grow wildflowers from seed indoors and under lights is an uncertain procedure, to say the least. All I could raise was a measly little butterfly weed, and as soon as I set it out into the ground—it died. Fringed gentian, thimbleweed, bloodroot, pink turtlehead, wild ginger, trailing arbutus, and pink-crimson shooting star didn't even show a cotyledon. I have broadcast the remaining seeds of these plants into my woody spot, and am waiting.

Many wildflower seeds take a long time to germinate, and are much fussier than the seeds of cultivated plants. And why shouldn't they be: habituated to a cover of molded leaves and pine needles in acid soil, conditions almost impossible to duplicate artificially.

My wildflower seeds are in two-inch pots on the upper two shelves. On the lower shelves I had better luck. Here, planted in peat pellets containing the necessary nutrients (available in farm and garden stores) I grew foxglove, lavender, sweet william, parsley, ageratum, delphinium, lupine, carnation, poppy and nicotiana. The pellets were set in baking tins on top of marble chips (any kind of small-size gravel will do) to help retain moisture. When the foxglove, nicotiana and delphinium had fairly large leaves I transplanted them into small clay pots and then, when it was warm enough, outdoors. They are doing quite well. Some I shared with young friends who were just as curious as I to see what would happen.

On the lower shelf at the right is a Venus's-flytrap (*Dionaea muscipula*) one of the insectivorous plants which aroused my curiosity. After it showed its minuscule white flowers, I gave it away. I remembered how much more beautiful is a pitcher plant, which grows in the wilderness and does not need a plastic tent to keep it moist. To the right on the same shelf are African violets which did just fine. I sprayed them with a misting bottle and covered them with plastic at night to retain the moisture. Now they are healthy blooming plants, proudly displayed on a shelf in my library.

Next year I shall know better. I will grow some herbs, chives, parsley, dill, and perhaps even basil to share their flavor with gourmet friends. I shall also try pinks, which a rock gardener par excellence collected for me, and a few Alpines that a friend had brought me from Switzerland. But I just might get into the same trouble with them as I did with last year's wildflower seeds. I now have them in the refrigerator, trying to duplicate their natural condition, at least for a while; then I will dig up some acid soil and crushed stone to see what artificial sunlight will do for them.

Another and better way to grow seeds (which I tried later) is to put them in baking pans filled with either vermiculite, "Jiffy Mix"—another new growing medium, or sphagnum moss, another excellent growing medium preferred by some gardeners. Then cover the pans with glass or plastic to keep them moist. In a very few days the tiny seeds will sprout. When the tops begin to touch the cover, take it off. Since the lights have a drying effect on the "soil," I misted it three times a day.

Since then I have transplanted several quite respectable tomato plants and a healthy lupine into two-inch pots. As soon as it gets warm outside (and the plants are bigger), they will go outdoors.

If you wish to try your hand at building this kind of grow-window, here are the specifications:

Having first figured out the size of the rough opening I would obtain by removing the old window frames and sash, I went to

My north window converted into a fluorescent-lighted min

the lumberyard and ordered two aluminum windows with sliding glass panes and screens. Then I built two frames of one inch by twelve inch pine boards, and screwed them together in the middle to have enough surface for the frames of the windows. I screwed my frames into the rough opening, and then the windows to the outside. I caulked all around, and had a young friend help me with a small overhang. We were able to use the copper flashing of the old window. Unfortunately I had not figured on the fury of northern gales that would drive water right through the light aluminum frames into the new window; neither had I figured on condensation leaking in. Now there is a larger roof and more thorough caulking. I still get some condensation at times, but newspapers sop it right up, and, anyway, it gives more humidity for the plants. (You can avoid all this by installing a second pair of windows, but this is much more complicated and expensive.)

greenhouse—before and after. Note baking tins chuck full of seedlings.

Then I installed four pairs of metal standards with brackets on which I placed two boards. On the underside of the top of the frame, and on the underside of the two boards (which are of course, movable) I attached fixtures with fluorescent bulbs specially made for plants. These are plugged into a box in the middle, which in turn is connected to an automatic timer. I leave the lights on for ten to twelve hours during the day and turn them off during the night. This might have been too much light for the wildflower seeds, which according to the design of nature need much darkness for sleep and might not be prepared to let a mere human change their time clock. But it did work for the other plants, which were, after all, of the cultivated kind and therefore more amenable to artificial treatment.

On the front panel (which is dark in the photograph because I wanted to show the effect of the fluorescent lights in the windows) hangs a group of tiny stainless-steel cultivating tools that a generous friend brought me from England. I keep the thermometer on one of the center panels, and all winter long, no matter how cold it got outdoors, the temperature inside my "greenhouse" never went below 60 degrees—which seemed to be just about right.

"Damping off" seems to occur more easily in a small garden under light than outdoors, though it does happen wherever seeds are grown in soil. A fungus in the growing medium kills the young plants and topples them over; and there is nothing you can do except throw the whole content of the pan, the flat, or the pot into the garbage. If you encounter this condition, try to grow the next batch of seeds in vermiculite; then, as soon as the tops of the seedlings show, water them with a weak solution of fertilizer. When the plants have grown their true leaves they can then be safely—or at least *more* safely—transplanted into a more permanent position. An alternate procedure is to get fresh potting soil, but cover it with a layer of vermiculite. Then keep your fingers crossed, and pray. Damping off can occur if you water too much.

No conversation about potted plants would be in the least complete without mentioning bonsai, the age-old Japanese way of dwarfing flowers and trees, both deciduous and evergreen. Many of these tiny works of art have been grown and worked with for many generations of gardeners and are truly astounding products of the Japanese love for small-scale perfection. Time was when some of the true Japanese bonsai could be imported into the United States. Now, however, the Department of Agriculture forbids the importing of plants without extensive fumigation, and so it has become necessary for bonsai lovers to start their own plants.

With patience and forbearance, many of the most common evergreens can be dwarfed. Started in tiny pots, with their roots clipped back, constantly watched, and then, when the plants are big enough, transplanted into earthenware or clay dishes—and pruned, and pruned, and pruned—the most interesting shapes can finally be achieved.

A friend of mine who is a bonsai specialist tells me that perhaps the most rewarding American evergreens are hemlock, for its naturally tiny needles are in keeping with the small scale of the plant; also taxus, or yew, one of the most indestructable of

A bonsai, under a foot tall, with an excellent growth of moss in a hexagonal Japanese pot. The bare limbs are intentionally left to suggest a natural tree.

all conifers. Pinch the new growth continually to make sure that no branchlet ever grows perfectly straight—anathema to a good bonsai.

Juniper is a good traditional bonsai subject. But those that I have seen are usually not up to snuff. One reason, perhaps, is that only when the mature, scale-type foliage of a juniper emerges does it look "right." The native junipers you are likely to find growing in New England meadows and out of outcroppings begin with juvenile prickly foliage; and so long as the plant is kept miniaturized, the more likely it is to keep up the baby "plumage." Your bonsai juniper is apt to wind up looking like a Joshua Tree, but try if you like. The ropy bark of juniper can become quite pretty with age.

In Japan there exists a particular kind of pine (five-needled) that is ideal for bonsai, for it is no hardship for the needles to grow naturally under one inch in length. In this country, jack pine or perhaps dwarf mughus are acceptable substitutes. A friend of mine had a beautiful mughus bonsai that had been naturally dwarfed (thanks to neglect in its nursery can); now, with its new growth pinched back each spring, it is slowly taking on the look of a much older tree.

Indeed, the Japanese seem to have two types of bonsai pines. The first, as described above, a replica of the mature specimen; the second is simply an example of a tree that has had to contend with the limitations of nature. In other words, you can take white or red pine (both fairly long-needled varieties) and train it into the same wind-swept, picturesque form that is usually associated with seaside or mountain specimens. Such a tree is not trying to "be" anything except itself, but is perhaps the purest kind of bonsai.

If you are a flower-lover, try native crab apple and shad-blow trees. They will not bloom until the branches have been repeatedly pruned back to encourage side shoots, and until their roots have developed sufficiently to carry the nutrients essential for bud formation. Or dig a seedling of albizzia (sometimes called mimosa) and let it come into bloom while it is still small.

A few general rules on bonsai: They should not be indoors constantly. Any species that is normally outdoors in winter should be left out (still in its pot, of course). Dig a small trench, preferably under shrubs or at the base of a stone wall where the wind is not too strong, line the bottom with dry leaves and bury the plants, pot and all, in some mulch (dry leaves, bark chips, pine needles) that does *not* retain water. The idea is to keep the pot from freezing and thawing too quickly; roots can freeze as hard as stone with little damage, so long as the drop is not sudden. Keeping the already sparse foliage from drying wind and sun is also a "must," as is screening to avoid rabbit and rodent damage.

This wintering outside is necessary for miniatures of trees and shrubs you might want to flower in the spring, but I have seen junipers and (naturally) albizzias doing very well indoors. A New York Japanese supply house keeps its selection of pines and atlas cedars inside display windows, but they always look un-gainly and pale. Bonsai should have full sun for at least half the day in summer, need frequent watering and a soil mixture that does not retain too much moisture and drains readily.

Be sure to repot or at least trim the roots once each year, especially in the case of pines, and make every effort to clip off "taproots" or any roots that go straight down. The perfect bonsai has lateral surface roots that spread outward an inch or so before going under.

The subject is really as complex as you care to make it, and there are a number of quite excellent books on the market. But do beware of any text if the illustrations suggest that all you need do is lop a few branches off a nursery-bought evergreen and put a little ceramic horse in the pot. Such cute things are impositions on the tree, not an attempt to help it display its true essence—the proper goal of all true bonsai.

Before you invest in potted plants, or grow them outdoors in the summer and then bring them inside, you should ask several questions. The first, of course, is whether you really do want plants inside? Are you prepared to care for them, and do you have the interest and the time? Are you willing to study the need of each plant for light, air, food, and water, and are you ready to put *their* needs above other requirements of your daily life? (Better a tall tree in your backyard than a dead cyclamen on the windowsill!)

Have you seen enough of them, in other people's houses, in green- and hothouses, in florists' shops, to know which appeal to you most for color and design, and for which your house has the needed conditions? Are you an experimenter who doesn't mind failure if it comes; are you a student and learner and willing to take advice? For although all these questions apply to outdoor gardening as well, nature's own conditions set the pace outside; indoors, you have to create many of them yourself.

You should also understand the very basic conditions under which plants can grow indoors and prosper. Most of our houses are too hot and too dry in the winter, and coolness and proper humidity are essential for almost all but the most tropical plants. You should learn not to water either too little or too much, for every plant inside your house may have a different need. Too, you can either overfeed your plants or starve them to death. Like children, plants will gobble up everything you give them. Overfeeding the roots might make them rot and seems a good deal worse than starving them a little. And don't think that insects won't pester plants indoors just as they do outside. Aphids, red spiders, white flies, and scale must be dealt with—not only because they make the house plants sick, but they can also infect their neighbors.

For those who are willing (and able) there are foliage houseplants, including some beautiful ferns; flowering houseplants in an unbelievable range of shape, color, and even scent; there are vines, herbs, and minature fruits, and succulents, evergreens, and flowering shrubs. And there are pots, dishes, planters, stands, and tables and windows; some you can buy, and many you can make, using your imagination, to fit the spaces into which the plants belong.

If you happen to fall in love with a certain kind of plant, indulge in collections. Succulents make interesting masses of green shapes, often with additional color; herbs will help perfume the air around them; primroses will give you masses of color, as will African violets. Geraniums will bloom their heads off if you just give them a little love. Gardenias and camelias, and lemon trees and oleander will add grandeur, scent, and size to your rooms. Fuchsias will make lively pendulums, hanging from baskets, and so will one of my favorites, the spiderplant, which is grass-like and graceful and continues to put forth new plants in amazing profusion.

On the following pages is a list of the most popular indoor plants that will serve as a basis for your own choices. Before you become too involved, however, try to see them in growers' hothouses, and talk to friends who have had experience with them. Another warning: don't try to grow too many plants. If you do, they may grow you out of your own living space or crowd your small hothouse and fluorescent fixtures so badly that you end up with a hopeless jumble.

I. FLOWERING PLANTS

AFRICAN VIOLETS (*Saintpaulia*) of the Gesneriaceae family, are among the most popular indoor plants, produce single or double flowers in white, pink, and many shades of blue and violet, even combinations of color. They grow in regular soil mixture, and should be kept fairly moist; they prefer being watered and

fertilized from the bottom and only a little from the top. If
dusty or dirty, the leaves can be washed with soap and water,
but must be allowed to dry in shady places. Indirect light is
best, or fluorescents.

AMARYLLIS (*Amaryllis*) many are of the lily family, are tropical bulbs
with highly unusual habits. The flower will grow in full sun or
shade, in moderate humidity and temperature. Bulbs have to be
planted with about two-thirds showing. After the spectacular
pink flower has bloomed (larger bulbs sometimes produce two
flowers) the leaves will appear. When the leaves get yellow they
are cut off, and the plant kept dormant in a cool place for as long
as you like. When you wish it to grow again, begin to water it.
I put my amaryllis outdoors in the summer.

BEGONIA (*Begonia*) of the Begoniaceae family has watery stems and
continuously produces white or pink flowers, outdoors in the
summer and indoors when it gets cold. The plants need a good
deal of watering, grow profusely and can be divided easily when
they outgrow their pot or overgrow a flowerbed into which they
were planted for the warm season.

BEGONIA, TUBEROUS (*Begonia tuberhybrida*) may be planted outdoors, but also does well in a north window. When the flowers
are finished, allow the plant to rest. Otherwise start them indoors
in mid-March, in boxes or pots, in potting soil and set them outdoors after all danger of frost is passed.

CAPE PRIMROSE (*Streptocarpus*) of the Gesueriaceae family produces
trumpet-like flowers, grows in subdued daylight, cool temperature, and high humidity in winter. It may be grown in moist
soil in summer.

CHRISTMAS CACTUS (*Zygocactus truncatus*) of the cactus family is a
succulent with many fleshy branches which serve as leaves, and
has lovely pink flowers at Christmas time. Water moderately
when not in bloom, and often while blooming. Grows in either

272

direct or filtered sunshine. Put outdoors in shaded place during summer.

There is also a variation of Christmas Cactus called Thanksgiving—a cactus with flowers that are more salmony in color and which does not seem to grow as big. It blooms in late November. Both species are easily propagated by cutting a branch the length of three "leaves" and putting it in water. They will root and make more plants in a short time.

CINERARIA (*Senecio cruentus*) of the composite family may be grown from seeds in May for winter bloom, or in the autumn for spring bloom. But this is not easy; and if you like the massive flowers in blue or one of the many other colors the plants can produce, get one from a florist. If you are lucky and work hard, you may be able to keep new plants blooming.

CUPID'S BOWER (*Achimenes*) of the Gesueriaceae family has red or blue flowers shaped like petunias. It grows from rhizome planted between March and May and must be kept in a sunny window. Plant flowers in summer. After they are finished, dig up rhizome and keep in dry place at low temperature.

CYCLAMEN (*Cyclamen persicum*) of the Primlaceae family should be put in an east window, and kept moist; prefers water from the bottom. Take plant outdoors to a shady spot where the leaves will remain green but the rest of the plant can rest. Some clever gardeners are able to get another season of bloom, but so far I have never been able to do so. I keep them indoors until they get too measly to be enjoyed. At this moment, however, I do have a two-year-old plant that does show signs of new life.

EPISCIA (*Episcia*) of the Gesueriaceae family is often potted in hanging baskets. Care is similar to African violets. Keep soil moist, and grow in indirect light.

GARDEN BALSAM, TOUCH-ME-NOT (*Impatiens balsamina*) of the Balsam family grows easily from seed or cuttings, blooms after about three months and never stops. Pinch tips off for better branching. Grow in sunny or semisunny window during winter; outdoors in sun or semishade.

GARDENIA (*Gardenia*) of the Rubiaceae family grows in full sun and humus soil, needs a warm room, and is usually rather difficult to grow even with the greatest care because it is a Southern plant. But some people are lucky and have the beautiful, fragrant, china-like blossoms in spring.

GERANIUM (*Pelargonium*) see discussion on page 252.

GLOXINIA (*Sinningia*) of the gesneriaceae family grows from tubers, is almost stemless, and has beautiful flowers of brilliant colors. Keep soil moist; place in indirect sunlight with medium temperature.

JERUSALEM CHERRY (*Solanum pseudo-capsicum*) of the Solanaceae family can be grown from seed and in direct sunlight. It produces a round orange or scarlet fruit the size of a cherry. But plant lasts only one year and then must be discarded. Be careful when handling, as the fruit is poisonous if eaten.

KALANCHOE (*Kalanchoe blossfeldiana*) of the Crassulaceae family is a succulent and has scarlet flowers in late winter and in early spring. Very good-looking, and grows in full sun. Needs three weeks of long nights for success.

LADY'S-EARDROPS (*Fuchsia*) of the Onagraceae family is a very popular plant, with a pendulum of blue and red flowers. Plant in potting soil, keep moist, and grow in subdued light. Remove ends of stems often to allow it to branch out. May be propagated by seeds or cutting. Put outdoors in summer.

LANTANA (*Lantana*) of the Verbenaceae family flowers continuously, each flower in several colors. See page 255. Grows from seed or cuttings, indoors and out. I have found that if I cut the stems back when I put the plants indoors, they will begin to bloom again—and more profusely than ever.

274

OLEANDER (*Nerium oleander*) of the Apocynaceae family is a stunning plant that blooms in early summer, and sometimes all summer long, and can withstand colder temperatures than most house-plants. Grow in full sun, *but beware of eating; one leaf can kill a man.*

ORCHIDS (Cane orchid—*Dendrobium nobile;* Florist orchid—*Cattleya mossiae;* Lady's-Slipper orchid—*Paphiopedilum insigne*) of the Orchidaceae family are among the best for the amateur indoor gardener. Plant in pure moss or fern root, water weekly, grow in subdued daylight at moderate temperature and high humidity. These beautiful and flashy plants, however, are better grown in a hothouse and they require a good deal of care, for their leaves should be moistened daily; the plants watered once a week.

PASSIONFLOWER (*Passiflora*) of the Passifloraceae family has four hundred species, most native to the Americas. It is a vine with beautiful flowers. Not hardy outdoors in the north, but is fairly easily grown in hothouses and makes a spectacular sight. Use garden soil; fairly humid atmosphere.

It is also possible to grow lemon and orange trees indoors. The varieties most likely to succeed are Otaheite orange, Poderosa lemon, and Meyer lemon which will grow in subdued daylight and cool temperatures. If they do well, they take up a good deal of room.

II. FOLIAGE PLANTS

Note: Although many plants in this category also bloom, they are most often grown for their dramatic foliage rather than for their flowers.

ALUMINUM PLANT (*Pilea cadierei*) of the Urticaceae family has thin foliage with aluminum markings. A species called Artillery plant (*Pilea microphilla*) got its name because when the plant is shaken the flowers discharge a cloud of pollen. It needs direct sunlight, warm temperature, and low humidity. Clip to help branching.

ARAUCARIA (*Araucaria*) is Norfolk Island pine renowned for the symmetry of its branches. Keep it moist in humus soil, in indirect sunlight, and at a moderate temperature.

BEGONIA (*Begonia rex*) is different from the species noted under Flowering Plants. This one, grown for its large leaves, does best in moist humus soil, warm temperature and indirect sunlight. Will grow during summer months in a shady window or on a porch.

BROMELIAD (*Aechmea*) Urn Plant, *Billbergia, Bromelia, Cryptanthus,* Earthstar, *Neoregalia,* and *Vriesia,* of the Bromeliaceae family, distinguished from each other by differently shaped and sometimes striped leaves, are among the easiest plants for indoor growing. Leaves hold water and do well in light or shade. Humus soil is required. When plants mature, brilliantly colored spikes of flowers grow from the central pool of water inside the plant. They last for several months.

CAMELLIA (*Camellia*) of the Theaceae family is actually a southern shrub that cannot be grown in the north except in greenhouses. It has beautiful foliage and gorgeous flowers, is grown from cuttings, and needs slightly acid soil. Should not be attempted by home grower, but makes great decorative plants for living rooms.

CAST-IRON PLANT (*Aspidistra*) of the Lily family is one of the toughest plants for indoor use. It may not *thrive* on neglect, but will only rarely die from it. If taken care of, it will have large glossy leaves. It requires potting soil, shade or subdued sunlight, temperature not too hot and not too cold, and medium humidity.

CHINESE EVERGREEN (*Aglaonema*) of the Arum family has dark green leaves growing from canelike stems, will flourish for years in the dark part of a room, and grows in water or in humus soil. When stems become too long, cut and reroot.

276

CROTON (*Codiaeum*) of the Euphorbiaceae family is called simply "Foliage plant" through the Middle West, a popular and beautiful plant with variegated evergreen leaves, highly decorative. It needs warmth, regular watering, bright sun.

DEVIL'S IVY (*Scindapsus*) of the Araceae family has small roots on stems by which it climbs. There are several species originated in East India and Malaysia, which means that originally they were tropical plants and need warmth and humidity here. Grows more slowly than *Philodendron,* which see.

DRAGON PLANT (*Dracaena*) of the Lily family is a slow grower, but retains its foliage for a long time. There are several species with spots or bands of different colors. It needs indirect sunlight, regular potting soil, warmth, and low humidity.

DUMB CANE (*Dieffenbachia sequine*) of the Araceae family is a spectacular plant with large variegated leaves. Several species are available. Regular potting soil, indirect sunlight, warm temperature, and low humidity are required. This species has poisonous leaves which, when eaten, cause temporary loss of speech.

FATHEADED LIZZIE, also called IVY TREE (*Fatshedera Lizei*), a crossing of English Ivy and Fatsiajapouic of the Araliaceae family is an evergreen shrub with ivy-like leaves. It needs support while growing, regular potting soil, moisture, full sun, and a cool temperature.

FERNS: MAIDENHAIR (*Adiantum wrightii*); WOOD FERN (*Nephrolepis*); BIRD'S-NEST FERN (*Asplenium nidus*); SPIDER FERNS (*Pteris*); and HOUSE HOLLYFERN (*Crytomium falcatum*). All these are highly decorative houseplants, sometimes used in low containers for table decoration where they get subdued light. They need a warm temperature and high humidity. Maidenhair looks very much like the wild plant and its Latin name refers to its water-shedding ability. Therefore it must be a descendant of the Mediterranean species dedicated to Venus.

ASPARAGUS FERN (*Asparagus plumosus*) is particularly enjoyable indoors, a cultivated fern that grows happily in a cool place when freely watered. In fact it is a feathery South African *vine* and mostly grown commercially for florists. Just buy one, and enjoy it.

FIG (*Ficus radicans* or *Ficus pumila*) of the Moraceae family, variegated, rooting, or climbing, are highly desirable indoor plants which grow in warmth or cold. Another species called Rubber plant (*Ficus elastica*) is equally adaptable to varying conditions and therefore popular. However, the leaves should often be wiped with a wet cloth. Grow any of these plants in regular potting soil and diffused sun.

FLAME NETTLE (called thus in England) or COLEUS (*Coleus*) of the Mint family is an interesting and easily grown plant with many colors of leaves and patterns. Grow it in regular moist potting soil, full sun, warm temperatures, and medium humidity; easily grown in small hothouse or even on a windowsill. Pinch out tips for fuller growth.

IVY (*Hedera*) of the Araliaceae family is an old favorite and grows easily and fast but dislikes constant dryness. Therefore it should be sponged occasionally. Can be trained to grow in all sorts of shapes. There are several specics, all are good houseplants. Train early by pinching off ends. Grow in potting soil, full sun, cool temperature, and medium humidity.

MOSES-IN-THE-CRADLE (*Rhoeo discolor*) of the Commelinaceae family is a cluster of stiff, lancelike leaves, metallic on top, glossy purple on bottom. Grow in regular soil mixture, indirect sunlight, medium temperature, and medium humidity. (Another writer calls this plant MOSES-IN-THE-BOAT, perhaps because the tiny white flowers are borne in boatlike bracts.)

PALMS of the Palmaceae family are mostly so huge that they would not make houseplants; however, two species, *Phoenix roebelini,* a pygmy, and PARLOR PALM (*Collinia elegans*) can be used as potted plants. Eventually they may also outgrow the height of a

278

room, but in the meantime they will fill a dim corner and give you some green. They need warm temperature and moderate humidity.

PEPEROMIA (*Peperomia sandersi*) of the Piperaceae family, bears leaves in rosettes with deep red stems. Heartshaped leaves are deep green to bluish with bands of silver radiating from centers. Plant in potting soil, grow in direct sunlight, warm temperatures, and low humdity.

PEPPER ELDER (*Peperomia*) of the Piperaceae family, bushy compact plants, slow-growing, with ornamental foliage. There are several species of various design and color. Grow in regular potting mixture, allow soil to dry between watering, but not to much. They need sunlight, a warm temperature, and low humidity.

SCREW PINE (*Pandanus*) of the Pandanaceae family, develops long arching leaves, shaped like sword blades arranged spirally around the trunk. Use potting soil, indirect sunlight, warm, dry atmosphere.

SNAKE PLANT (*Sansevieria*) of the Lily family, develops clumps of erect, narrow leaves. A popular houseplant, needs little care and will grow in dim light as well as in full sunshine. Needs moderately warm atmosphere, and low humidity.

SPIDERPLANT (*Chlorophytum*) is a perennial herb of the lily family. It grows easily, almost rampant, sending out stems with tiny white flowers at the end of which new plants grow. When the roots are exposed they may be planted during the winter in potting soil, outdoors in the summer. The plant grows extremely well in ordinary garden soil, and can be taken up in the autumn to make new plants for indoors. It is said that this plant grows best in a cool greenhouse, but I have mine growing in a sunny south window and it keeps on coming. It needs fairly frequent watering. Outdoors I put the pot in a basket; indoors I drape the leaves in front and in back of a shelf.

SWEETHEART VINE, much better known as *Philodendron,* of the Avaceae family is one of the best known indoor plants. There are several species: *Ph. scandens, Ph. Oxycardium, Ph. dubium, Ph. panduraeforme, Ph. pertusum, Ph. squamiferum,* and more, all grow better under the adverse conditions of a house than almost any other potted plants. Grow in potting soil, keep moist, in indirect sunlight and low humidity. Some forms of philodendron require stakes against which to grow, others need no support. There are several kinds of philodendron leaves, almost solid, and then cut, narrow and wide, some long, some short, some simple, others complicated in design. It is important to wash the leaves once a month with soap and water, otherwise special foliage waxes are needed to prevent their drying out.

UMBRELLA TREE (*Schefflera*) of the Avaliceae family, comes from Australia. Outdoors it grows twenty to thirty feet. Indoors it will be much smaller, and is easy to grow. Has slender, glossy green leaves; needs indirect sunlight, warm temperatures, medium humidity.

WANDERING JEW (*Tradescantia fluminensis*) of the Commelinaceae family is one among several species, all with leaves so similar that they are difficult to distinguish. Plants trail; often leaves have white or pinkish streaks. Easy to propagate by cutting off tops of stems, and pot. Pot in ordinary soil, grow in indirect sunlight, moderate temperatures, and humidity.

III. SUCCULENTS

Succulents are basically those plants which have had to adapt themselves to growing in arid regions such as deserts by storing what little water they receive in their leaves. The category now called "succulents" is one that is able to survive long droughts. They make good houseplants, for they need little care; they are used to cold nights and hot desert days. Most of them come into spectacular bloom. I know several young people who love to collect them and find their sometimes weird shapes appealing. They can be grown in hothouses and on windowsills. They can be bought in most florist shops; but if you happen to travel in Arizona or Southern California, it would be fun to dig some up and bring them home in no more protective a container than a plastic bag.

Among the best and most popular succulents are: BARBADOS ALOE (*Aloe vera*); BARREL CACTUS (*Echinocactus*); ECHEVERIA RETUSA, ECHINOCEREUS, FEROCACTUS, KALANCHOE BLOSSFELD-IANA, ORCHID CACTUS (*Epiphyllum hybridum*); PARTRIDGE-BREASTED ALOE (*Aloe variegata*); PEANUT CACTUS (*Chamaecereus silvestrii*); PEBBLE PLANT (*Lithops*); PINCUSHION CACTUS (*Mammillaria bocasana*); PRICKLY PEAR (*Opuntia microdasys*), and TRICHOCEREUS.

I have had experience with echeveria which grows in Mexico and Southern California. It is one of the most satisfactory plants I know. Once you find or buy this plant and put it in sandy soil it will grow in no time at all, and tiny pink flowers on long thin branches will appear. If you want more, just take a leaf, or a piece of blooming branch, lay on top of a tray or pot and it will grow new plants. The small new plants make lovely gifts for sick and old people who hugely enjoy this extraordinary plant. I also enjoy kalanchoe, which needs to be grown in the sun. In the middle of winter this plant will burst forth with hundreds of tiny red blossoms. Take it outdoors in the summer to a shady place where it can rest and renew itself for another season of happy blooming.

IV. BULBS

As briefly mentioned before, the forcing of bulbs to give forth with bloom in the dreariest days of winter is a rewarding pursuit.

Crocus and freesia (with its beautiful sweet scent); grape hyacinth, hyacinth, daffodils, and paper-white narcissi, snowdrops, scillas, and even tulips can make a lovely showing on your living room windowsill or kitchen window. All you need do is put them among pebbles in a low dish or crock. Only hyacinth bulbs, which are large, need special containers available in your garden store. They have a lovely shape, pinched in the middle so that the bulbs sit on top and the roots grow down into water—which has to be renewed every few days to keep the roots coming. Some gardeners recommend lukewarm rather than cold water and darkness until the roots get long.

This list of indoor plants has been compiled with the help of United States Department of Agriculture, Bulletin No. 82, *Selecting and Growing Houseplants;* the handbook of the Brooklyn Botanic Garden, *House Plants;* and a most useful little publication from England, *Be Your Own House Plant Expert,* which you might be able to order from your local bookstore, or from the British Book Center, Inc., in New York City. These publications as well as the others listed in the Bibliography herein will help you decide which plants you are prepared to grow in the specific conditions of your own house.

A SHORT GLOSSARY OF INDOOR PLANTING TERMS

Humidity. The relative humidity in heated or air-conditioned homes is 40 to 50 percent—often much less. This is too dry for many plants. The humidity can be raised by putting plants over the kitchen sink where water flows almost constantly. By grouping plants together, the air surrounding them is usually more humid than in the rest of your house and will help all. You can set plants above a tray of gravel or peatmoss which is kept wet. (I do this in my seed window.)

If possible, install humidifiers in your heating or air-conditioning system. It'll be better for you too. If you have registers in your baseboards, pots or tray of water set above or in front of them will increase the humidity of your rooms. But this does not usually add to the stylishness of your décor. For plants that require very high humidity, a hothouse is best. Sometimes a covered terrarium will help, at least for small plants.

Potting. There are two kinds of pots available today, the old-fashioned clay pots (used since remote antiquity) and the contemporary plastic pots, usually white or green. Both have advantages and disadvantages. Clay pots allow the plants to "breathe"; but they break easily and are heavy. Plastic nonporous pots may let water collect below the roots and help them to rot. On the other hand, they are much lighter than clay pots and don't break as easily. I have tried both kinds, and have concluded that clay pots are the more "natural" containers for flowers.

Double Potting is sometimes recommended to increase the humidity around a plant. A clay pot is set in another, larger nonporous pot containing peatmoss or vermiculite which is constantly kept moist. Thalassa Cruso, the well-known authority on house plants, calls double potting the process of planting two layers of bulbs on top of one another so that a double quantity of flowers may be obtained.

Potting Soil consists of a variety of mixtures formulated for the needs of various types of plants, and made by growers and the owners of large greenhouses for *their* needs. For the average aficionado of house plants, however, potting soil is available in packages of several sizes which contain the necessary ingredients for most plants. Add vermiculite or perlite—small mica particles that enhance the soil's water-retention abilities. Topsoil and peatmoss, also available in packages and bags, are rich enough in nutrients to make good potting soil. At times a portion of sand may add to the texture of the medium. Garden soil or loam that has been worked and added to, will suffice in many cases.

For example, I had put a new spiderplant in a sunny spot in

my garden during the summer and wanted to pot it when the weather got cold. I simply dug the plant up with sufficient soil to fill the pot, and added vermiculite. The plant is doing fine. When it comes right down to it, there are as many theories about soils and soil additives as there are growers.

Water and Fertilizers. Too much watering is more dangerous to plants than watering too little, as already discussed before. Most of the feeding of houseplants can thus be done by adding fertilizers, which come in liquid and powdered form in a variety of packages with minute directions on their labels. Another simple way of watering is to immerse the pot in a sink with just enough water to reach to the top of the pot (*not* over it and into the soil) and leave the pot soaking for fifteen to twenty minutes. As a matter of fact this is a good lazy method, because the soil stays moist for quite a while, which is actually better than sharp streams from a watering can.

Flowering succulents such as Christmas and Thanksgiving cacti need very sparse watering until they show signs of blooming. Then they must be watered at frequent intervals until the blooming time is done. A friend who is an outstanding gardener shared a secret with me: When it is near blooming time, he feeds his Christmas cacti with a solution of one teaspoon of saltpeter to one quart of water. But try to get saltpeter at your local drugstore! It has been banned because some young fools used it for evil purposes. However, an out-of-the-way, old-fashioned pharmacy may still have some. All you need is two or three ounces per year.

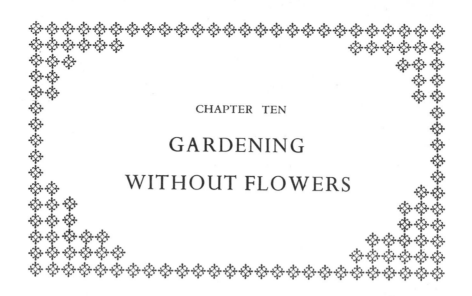

CHAPTER TEN

GARDENING

WITHOUT FLOWERS

Despite all obstacles
Which hinder the path
Of the rushing brook:
All water dividing
Around banks and ledges,
In the end,
In the end flow
Exultantly together.

"SEPARATION", UNKNOWN JAPANESE AUTHOR

EVEN before the last war and in ever-increasing numbers since then, Americans have been visiting Japan and returning elated by the gardens which for thousands of years have been an integral part of Japanese life. Around the temples, private houses, and public buildings the Japanese have planted gardens with the deepest meaning; every stone, every path, every pebbled walk, every tree and shrub were placed in a position of special significance. To the oriental mind, a garden leads the way to a view of life, to meditation, to peace, to serenity and inner understanding.

285

Americans have made a habit of supporting the object without the spirit—bringing medieval castles stone by stone from England, furnishing old houses with European and Oriental antiques (authentic or imitations). We reach out to create new and spectacular effects, not necessarily because they are tasteful but because they are now in fashion. I by no means want to belittle the many Japanese gardens which now dot our countryside; but I do wonder why we find it so necessary to duplicate things the tradition and history of which we don't really understand.

A nearby neighbor, for example, who isn't even interested in gardening but has the money to pay for it, suddenly wants a Japanese garden—and probably for no other reason than because right now it is the *chic* thing to do.

I have visited the great Japanese garden in Ireland, said to be the largest in the world outside Japan; it is complete with red bridges, lanterns, and statues of Buddha, and also astounding plantings. If no more, it is a horticultural curiosity of the first order . . . and it left me cold, perhaps because it was such an obvious tourist attraction. But there *are* a few Japanese garden architects who have created wonders, authentic and beautiful works of art which are signposts of the great culture from which they came.

I also know the Japanese Stroll Garden at the Hammond Museum in North Salem, New York. This garden is not a curiosity but a meaningful addition to the museum. I cannot say whether it is a garden in the true tradition of the Japanese; I *can* say that whenever I go there to photograph I feel inspired; and sometimes when I am troubled with myself and my world I come away with a new sense of peace, acceptance and hope.

> *Ah, do not swat them,*
> *The sad flies,*
> *Forever wringing their thin hands.*
> ISSA

There are many techniques in Japanese gardening that can greatly add to our own Western sense of material and space. Even if not every one of them gives us cause for meditation, many spring from lively imagination and good sound garden knowledge that should be recognized and understood. Other friends of mine have adapted Japanese garden ideas to *their* way of life—to fit the contour of their land, and even to the amount of gardening time they have to spare.

For one Japanese "secret" is that a garden built of trees, shrubs, gravel, stone and sand needs a great deal less constant attention than a perennial (much less annual!) border. And although nearly all trees need pruning here and there, and sand raking, and even the flattest pebbles don't always stay in place after a hard rain, the amount of labor needed to set these elements right again cannot compare with the constant snipping, cultivating, replanting, and fertilizing any other kind of garden requires.

In a Zen garden, an area of sand raked in flowing motions represents water. Even if you didn't know that, it is still a beautiful expanse of gray and glittering particles of minute stones which keep on changing during the day and night. It can give you pleasure as does the texture of sand on the edges of the sea. Even if you might not have any interest in finding sixteen large stones to represent the Rakan, the disciples of Buddha, one single tall rock placed on its end on a bed of gravel will lend a sense of power and grandeur difficult to achieve in any other way.

> O *snail*
> Climb *Mount* Fuji
> But *slowly, slowly.*
> ISSA

The stone too will alter as the light constantly changes to reveal new planes and colors, new edges and shapes.

Your sense of color will be inspired by the choice of the kind of stones and pebbles you use. Many of the flat stones have been washed by river waters, or can be found at the edge of the sea on some of the New England island beaches; the smaller pebbles that can now be bought at good nurseries, come in different sizes from fairly large to tiny and in many shades from snow white through ranges of beige and cream. (In any case, my preference runs to the gray or beige water-worn stones that come from riverbeds or Japanese gardening supplies stores. These are flat, and thus sink into the soil more slowly, and are usually far more "natural" looking than an eye-jolting expanse of snow-white crushed quartz or marble). I had no problem getting a few bags to put between my flagstones, and our local nurseryman told me they came from quarries in New Jersey and Connecticut. They are rolled and polished by efficient modern machinery, and glitter like jewels.

A Japanese bridge support which a friend was lucky enough to find (and which could be replaced by an old American mill-stone) is set like a piece of sculpture into ordinary beige gravel against a background of low-growing evergreens and rock. And if you wanted to make of your back door something more interesting than a mere instrument of utility, flagstones surrounded by more gravel with evergreens at one corner will give status and elegance to an otherwise not very important part of your house. If you happen to have a small brook on your place, channel it to hop down over large rocks. This is one of the most pleasant country sounds I know—water flowing and jumping in the shade of a gulley.

And how much Japanese ideas can do for large and small trees and evergreen shrubs! I have seen a small weeping hemlock planted against an old tree, and the shining needles stand in contrast to the gray bark behind. An arresting effect. Dwarf rhododendrons can be planted in an area adjoining a lawn; pine bark between them does not allow weeds to crop up. A similar

288

Heavy slabs of steppingstone laid into a bed of gravel make walking easy and safe. I have always admired how the owner of this garden had the good sense to plant a fern at the side of the steps. (Design: Vito Fosella)

Even pieces of dead wood—straight or with contorted shapes which direct the eye—have place and meaning in a well-designed garden. (Stephen S. Simon)

effect is obtained with rounded evergreens spaced between an outcropping of rocks—a different kind of rock garden, and one that needs no work except an occasional pruning to keep the round shapes in good trim. And how graceful a bit of creeping juniper embracing a rock set apart from another large stone by a tasteful and practical expanse of pine bark!

The Japanese have developed a great number of evergreen trees and shrubs, and for very good reasons. Some of the slender blooming specimens such as crab apple, flowering quince, weeping cherry, or any other of the lovely weeping and flowering trees can give your garden grace and form as little else will.

SMALL EVERGREENS
Low-growing or spreading, suitable for a garden of texture and shapes

ARBORVITAE (*Thuja*): low-growing varieties—*Eicoides, Globosa, Pumila, Umbraculifera.*

CEDAR (*Cedrus*): varieties—*Aurea pendulata, Pygmea, Comte de Dijon.*

CRIPTOMERIA (*Cryptomeria*): varieties—*Bandi-Sugi, Pygmea, Spralis elongata, Jindai-Sugi, Vilmoriana.*

DOUGLAS FIR (*Pseudotsuga*): varieties—*Densa, Prostrata.*

FALSE CYPRESS (*Chamaecyparis*): varieties—*Elwoodi, Ericoides, Filifera* (this is a large genus and there are more low-growing and well-shaped species too numerous to mention here).

FIR (*Abies*): varieties—*Hudsonia, Compacta.*

GIANT SEQUOIA (*Sequoiadendron*): varieties—*Pygmea, Prostrata.*

HEMLOCK (*Tsuga*): varieties—*Horsford dwarf, Minuta.*

JUNIPER (*Juniperus*): varieties—*Globosa, Expansa, Pfitzerania, Nana.*

PINE (*Pinus*): varieties—*Globosa, Prostrata, Compacta* (these are among the several species of pine of which there are a good many and can be selected by the form of their needles).

PLUM-YEW (*Cephalotaxus*): varieties—*Prostrata, Peduncalata prostrata.*

REDWOOD (*Sequoia*): varieties—*Prostrata.*

SPRUCE (*Picea*): varieties—*Capitata, Globosa, Minutifolia, Pumila, Inversa, Prostrata, Nana.*

YEW (*Taxus*): varieties—*Amersfort, Compacta, Repandens, Aurescens.*

And if you have no idea at all what to do with a small hill on which nothing will ever grow, plant some miniature evergreens and surround them with gravel. If the incline is not too steep, the trees' roots will hold the gravel and your problem will be solved.

But, of course, you don't have to eliminate flowers completely just because you want to take care of a simpler garden. At the Hammond Museum garden, for example, a long, curved row of alyssum winding down a hillside signifies a dry stream in the Japanese manner. The effect is stunning. You could also create a similar result with buttercups, wild phlox (*Phlox divaricata*) and even yarrow, daisies, or any other fast-spreading wildflower. These won't last as long as the alyssum, which blooms through almost the entire growing season; but, for that matter, if you have nothing more than rocks and bare earth, why not try a "stream" of ferns to create the feeling of a cascading river?

You can even carry the whole idea of verisimilitude one step further and create—as I have seen done in Rye, N.Y.—a miniature landscape where granite, blasted loose from a swimming pool excavation, and fertile soil were molded into diminutive ravines, tiny crags and outcroppings, and piled to suggest mountains. Moss and arenarzia form the grass; naturally dwarfed evergreens provide the trees, none more than a foot tall. The larger plants are toward the front, so that the landscape seems to recede by several miles in less than five feet.

In the crevice of a large stone with which you don't know what to do, plant a bit of grass. It won't grow so high that you have to mow it, and the green leaves will relieve the surface and monotony of the stone.

One group of plants seldom seen in gardens of the northeast, but well known and much used in Europe and beginning to be admired for their great beauty, are the ornamental grasses. I saw them for the first time at the Blue Mount Nurseries in Monkton, Maryland. One of the owners, Richard Simon, took me to Baltimore to show me some of their plants in a garden designed for ornamental grasses alone. It was the lightest, airiest, weaving spectacle one can imagine. I couldn't resist getting a couple of species for myself and they are doing very well in full sun. In another couple of years, when they are fully grown, I may remove most of the nearby flowers.

BLUE FESCUE (*Festuca glauca*) is evergreen, has a bluish or grayish (or both) foliage, blooms in June (although the bloom of most ornamental grasses is not always their greatest attraction) and won't grow much over a foot high. Full sun, good garden soil (which incidentally applies to all species mentioned here).

Fountain grass

FOUNTAIN GRASS (*Pennisetum alopecuroides,* also called *P. japonicum*) has a bloom that sways gracefully in the lightest breeze. The plant fills quite a bit of space when fully grown, and is therefore a very practical plant not only for lazy gardeners but also for those who have too many empty spaces. It grows to about thirty inches.

ORNAMENTAL OATS (*Avena sempervirens*) blue-gray and semievergreen, has a habit of spreading, and grows to about two feet.

PAMPAS GRASS (*Cortaderia selloana*) grows very tall with showy plumes and is not hardy north of Baltimore; but if you do live south of that region, one single plant will cover the side of your house above the first story. Extremely dramatic.

There are other ornamental grasses about which you may wish to know more. *House and Garden* magazine had a beautiful piece about them in the August 1967 issue which you may be able

Wild rice

to find in your local library. Since the Bluemount Nurseries are wholesalers, they cannot sell you a single plant, but they might be able to tell you which nurseries carry their stock.

Another favorite of mine is wild rice (*Zizania aquatica*) which I saw growing at the edge of the lake at the Hammond Museum's Japanese Stroll Garden. It is extremely graceful and appealing as its thin wands are reflected in the water—a good idea if you have a pond or lake on your property. It grows wild in many of our marshes and can be easily transplanted.

By all means, if you like peonies, buy yourself a shrub, the tall growing variety, and put it in a corner of your garden. Or, if you own a small or large body of water, plant iris in dense rows; not, of course, the tall heavy garden variety but the delicate blue or yellow flags, or a species that grows thin and tall like Dutch iris or *Iris reticulata*. Long after the bloom is gone, the sword-like leaves of the plant will give you a neat and clean accent. Or plant chrysanthemums next to a stone walk. They last a long time in the autumn, usually blooming until the first frost.

By all means, plant a willow or other sinuous-trunked tree to reflect in your brook, pond, or pool. Little else is as satisfying as the movement of a tree seen reflected in water.

Suddenly you will see deeply into the woods, not because you have cleared them so diligently, but because every shape has its own meaning, its own design, and its own relationship with the shape next to it. The naked branch of a willow tree, swaying gently in the breeze, will make a veil of tiny and gentle surprises of slim forms and interlocking spaces; birches will suddenly look mysterious when seen against the sun, showing every pore in their bark.

For when you begin to design a garden such as these, you will begin to *paint* with gray and brown and green; you will compose a picture of glittering stone and rolling rock; you will deal in contrasts of texture you had never known before, and add mystery and surprise to *your* patch of Earth.

But perhaps it is just in these new ways, these other colors, these contrasts of bark and pebble, these simple plains and surprising shapes that you will come into your very own. You are using gravel as groundcovers, and bark for grass. Your trees may not reach into the sky, but your tall pieces of rock will be as powerful as men standing still and looking inward. You may not, after all, have created a "Japanese" garden, but you still might come to understand that there is much that heaven has given for your own expanse of Earth and that the greatest attributes of your garden have come from the resources of your own spirit.

Birds make small sounds on leaving.
My garden sleeps awaiting their return.

Whenever someone proudly shows me his land, his gardens, his trees and flowers, I feel his sense of ownership, but something way down deep within me questions the word "mine." I do the same, of course, when I talk about the field of ferns below my house; I say *my* field of ferns. When I look at my small terrace and enjoy the sights of the laurels I have transplanted so long ago, I feel that they are *"my"* mountain laurels. When the wild azaleas down near the swamp are in their breathtakingly beautiful bloom, I feel *"my"* azaleas.

But do we really *possess* the good and generous Earth around us? Does the legal deed to our "property" mean that it is really ours?

I don't think so. This piece of Earth, this small bit of land, these native trees which were here long before I came will be here long after I have gone. These wild grasses, these woodland flowers, all that I cherish, do not belong to me. They are merely *lent* to me, placed into my hands in trust. I must care for them, protect and guard them; not so that they may be worth more in money when I am done, but worth more in beauty, in tenderness, in love. The work of my hands, the time I have spent, the good thoughts I may have had, were merely a tribute, a token in gratitude for the good fortune, the blessing, that I was allowed to share in my garden.

For it has put gladness into my heart.

BIBLIOGRAPHY

A SHORT NOTE ABOUT A LONG BIBLIOGRAPHY

THE reason for mentioning so many books is that in one way or another, I have used them all, learned from them, had fun with them and often inspiration.

In the Wilderness chapter, for example, I have not only listed the latest guide books which help with the latest available identifications (botanists, like other scientists, don't always agree on a name or even a method) but also older, out-of-print books which I was lucky enough to find and thoroughly enjoy. For many earlier writers had very personal feelings about the plants they described; they *cared*; they felt the wonder of some small yellow thing coming through the grass, the miracle of a frond of ferns, the grandeur and majesty of a tall tree. And although some of the names or classifications may have changed, the beauty of the plants has not.

Also, I believe in what is now called "inter-disciplinary study." You don't have to know about flower pots in ancient Athens to be a good gardener, but I always feel it increases my enjoyment to learn how and why the Sumerians began to appreciate the fruits of *their* soil.

CHAPTER ONE

THE PERSONAL TOUCH

American School of Classical Studies at Athens. *Garden Lore of Ancient Athens*. Princeton, N.J., 1963.

Anderson, Edgar. *Plants, Man and Life*. University of California Press, Berkeley, and Los Angeles, 1967.

Berrall, Julia, S. *The Garden*. An illustrated history. The Viking Press, New York, N.Y., 1966.

Fairbrother, Nan. *Gardens Since Eden. Horizon*. American Heritage Publishing Co., New York, N.Y., May 1959, p. 24ff.

Fairbrother, Nan. *Men and Gardens*. Alfred A. Knopf, New York, N.Y., 1956.

Gibbs, Rebecca Whitehead. *Gardens Through the Ages*. 1937.

Krutch, Joseph Wood. *The Gardener's World*. G. P. Putnam's Sons, New York, N.Y., 1959.

Lees, Carlton, B. *Gardens, Plants, and Man*. Rutledge-Prentice-Hall, Inc., Englewood Cliffs, N.J., 1970.

Metropolitan Museum of Art. *Gardens as Illustrated in Prints*. New York, N.Y., 1949.

Stroud, Dorothy. *Capability Brown*. Country Life, Ltd., London, 1950.

Thomas Jefferson's *Garden Book*, 1766–1824. The American Philosophical Society, Philadelphia, Pa., 1944.

Vaughan, Agnes Carr. *The House of the Double Axe*. Doubleday & Company, Inc., Garden City, N.Y., 1959.

von Miklos, Josephine; Fiore, Evelyn. *The Gardener's World*. The Ridge Press, Inc.; Random House, N.Y., 1969.

Wright, Richardson. *The Story of Gardening*. Dodd, Mead & Co., 1934; Dover Publications, Inc., New York, N.Y., 1964.

CHAPTER TWO

THE BASICS—BOTANY, HORTICULTURE, AND A BIT OF ZOOLOGY

Alexander, E.J. and Woodward, Carol. *The Flora of the Unicorn Tapestries,* reprinted from the Journal of the New York Botanical Garden, May–June 1941.

Babcock, Mary Reynolds. *First Aid for Flowers*. Farrar, Straus & Company, New York, 1954.

Bailey, L.H. *How Plants Get Their Names*. Dover Publications, 1963.

Bloom, Alan. *Moisture Gardening*. Faber & Faber Ltd., London, 1966.

Blunt, Wilfred. *The Art of Botanical Illustration*. Collins, London, 1967.

Brooklyn Botanic Garden. *Gardening in Containers; A Handbook*. Brooklyn, N.Y., 1958.

Brooklyn Botanic Garden. *Handbook on Garden Pests*. Brooklyn, N.Y., 1966.

Brooklyn Botanic Garden. *Handbook on Mulches*. Brooklyn, N.Y., 1957.

Brooklyn Botanic Garden. *Handbook on Propagation*. Brooklyn, N.Y., 1965.

Brooklyn Botanic Garden. *Handbook on Soils*. Brooklyn, N.Y., 1966.

Bucknell, Barry. *Do-It-Yourself in the Garden*. Pan Books, Ltd., London, 1967.

Burns, Mary-Ann. *Plant Anatomy*. Arlington Books, London, 1964.

Darlington, Arnold. *Plant Galls*. Blanford Press, London, 1968.

de Witt, H.C.D. *Plants of the World; The Higher Plants*. E.P. Dutton & Co., Inc., New York, N.Y., 1966.

Duffield & Company, *A Garden Book For Autumn and Winter*. New York, N.Y., 1924.

Editors of *Organic Gardening, The Organic Way to Plant Protection*. Rodale Books, Inc., Emmaus, Pa., 1969.

Editors of *Sunset* magazine and Sunset Books, *Basic Gardening Illustrated*. Lane Books, Menlo Park, Calif., 1966.

Edmond, J.B.; Senn, F.S.; Andrews, F.S. *Fundamentals of Horticulture*. McGraw-Hill Book Company, New York, N.Y., 1957/64.

Fernald, M.L. *Gray's Manual of Botany*. Rewritten and expanded, 8th edition. American Book Company, New York, N.Y., 1950.

Fogg, Jr., John M. *Weeds of Lawn and Garden*. University of Pennsylvania Press, Philadelphia, Pa., 1956.

Gleason and Cronpuist. *The Natural Geography of Plants*. Columbia University Press, New York, N.Y., 1964.

Greulach, Victor A. *Botany Made Simple*. Doubleday & Company, Garden City, N.Y., 1968.

Hay and Synge. *The Dictionary of Garden Plants.* Ebury Press, and Michael Joseph, London, 1969.

Headstrom, Richard. *Garden Friends and Foes.* Ives Washburn, Inc., New York, N.Y., 1954.

Hessayon, Dr. D.G. *Be Your own Lawn Expert.* Pan Britannica Industries, Waltham Cross, Herts, England.

House & Garden's Gardener's Daybook. Ralph Bailey, (ed.). M. Evans & Company, Inc., New York, N.Y., 1965.

Hull, George F. *The Language of Gardening.* World Publishing Company, New York, N.Y., 1967.

Hunt, Peter. *Herbaceous Plants, #1.* Ebury Press, London, 1965.

Hutchins, Ross E. *The Amazing Seeds.* Dodd, Mead & Company, New York, N.Y., 1965.

Hutchins, Ross E., *This Is a Flower.* Dodd, Mead & Company, New York, N.Y., 1963.

Hutchins, Ross E., *This Is a Leaf.* Dodd, Mead & Company, New York, N.Y., 1962.

Jaeger, Paul. *The Wonderful Life of Flowers.* George G. Harrap & Co., Ltd., London, 1961.

Klots, Alexander, B. *Field Guide to the Butterflies,* the Peterson Field Guide Series. Houghton Mifflin Co., Boston, Mass., 1951.

Lemmon, Robert S. *How to Attract the Birds.* Doubleday & Company, Inc., Garden City, N.Y., 1950.

Miscellaneous writers. *The Care and Feeding of Garden Plants.* American Society for Horticultural Science, National Plant Food Institute, and Prentice-Hall, Inc., Englewood Cliffs, N.J., 1955.

Morwood, William. *The Lazy Gardener's Garden Book.* Doubleday & Company, Inc., Garden City, N.Y., 1970.

New York State College of Agriculture. *Flowers from Seed,* by R.E. Lee; Cornell Extension Bulletin 981, Cornell University, Ithaca, N.Y., 1914.

Novak, F.A. *The Pictorial Encyclopedia of Plants and Flowers.* Crown Publishers, Inc., New York, N.Y., 1966.

Northen and Northen. *Ingenious Kingdom.* Prentice-Hall, Inc., Englewood Cliffs, N.J., 1970.

Reader's Digest. *Complete Book of the Garden.* The Reader's Digest Association, Ltd., Pleasantville, N.Y., 1966.

Reid, Douglas. *Botany for the Gardener.* Taplinger Publishing Co., Inc., New York, N.Y., 1967.

Scientific American; Plant Life. Simon & Schuster, Inc., New York, N.Y., 1957.

Simon, Maron; Elliott, John; Pierce, Dickson; Hendrix, Beatrice. *The Complete Garden Handbook.* D. Van Nostrand Co., Inc., New York, N.Y., 1950.

Sire, Marcel. *Secrets of Plant Life.* The Viking Press, Inc., New York, N.Y., 1969.

Slade, Daniel Denison. *Evolution of Horticulture in New England.* G.P. Putnam's Sons, New York, N.Y., 1895.

Smith, A.W. *A Gardener's Book of Plant Names.* Harper & Row, Publishers, New York, N.Y., 1963.

Smith, James Edward. *English Botany.* London, 26 vols., 1790–1808.

Taylor's Encyclopedia of Gardening. Houghton Mifflin Company, Boston, Mass., 1961.

Thrower, Percy. *Gardening and Garden Tools.* Educational Productions Ltd., London, 1958.

U.S. Department of Agriculture. *Ants in the Home and Garden;* Home and Garden Bulletin No. 28; Washington, D.C. (Revised 1967.)

U.S. Department of Agriculture. *Better Lawns;* Home and Garden Bulletin No. 51; Washington, D.C. (Revised 1962.)

U.S. Department of Agriculture. *Controlling Insects on Flowers;* Agriculture Information Bulletin No. 237; Washington, D.C.

U.S. Department of Agriculture. *Early American Soil Conservationists.* Washington, D.C., 1941, 1966.

U.S. Department of Agriculture. *Salt Tolerance of Plants;* Agriculture Information Bulletin No. 283; Washington, D.C., 1964.

U.S. Department of Agriculture. *Selecting Fertilizers;* Home and Garden Bulletin No. 89; Washington, D.C., 1963.

U.S. Department of Agriculture. *Water Facts;* Soil Conservation Service P.A. 337; Washington, D.C. (Revised 1964.)

Waitley, Douglas. *My Backyard.* David White Co., New York, N.Y., 1970.

Winkelmann-Rhine, Gertraude. The Paintings and drawings of Jan "Flower" Breughel, Harry N. Abrams, Inc., New York, N.Y., 1968.

CHAPTER THREE

ELEMENTS OF GARDEN DESIGN

Ashberry, Anne. *Gardens on a Higher Level.* Hodder and Stoughton, London, 1969.

Austin, Alfred. *The Garden That I Love.* Adam & Charles Black, Publishers, London, 1905.

Berrisford, Judith. *The Very Small Garden.* Faber & Faber, Ltd., London, 1968.

Brooklyn Botanic Garden. *Creative Ideas in Garden Design.* Brooklyn, N.Y., 1966.

Brooklyn Botanic Garden. *Gardens of Western Europe,* Brooklyn, N.Y., 1960.

Bush-Brown, James and Louise. *America's Garden Book.* Charles Scribner's Sons, New York, N.Y., 1939, 1952, 1958, 1965.

Clifford, Derek. *A History of Garden Design.* Faber & Faber, Ltd., London, 1962, 1966.

Connell, Charles. *Aphrodisiacs in Your Garden.* Taplinger Publishing Co., Inc., New York, N.Y., 1966.

Editors of *Sunset* Magazine and Sunset Books. *Ideas For Garden Color.* Lane Books, Menlo Park, Calif., 1965.

Editors of *Sunset* Magazine, and Sunset Books. *Garden Work Centers.* Lane Books, Menlo Park, Calif., 1968.

Genders, Roy. *Perfume in the Garden.* Museum Press, Ltd., London, 1955.

Genders, Roy. *The Cottage Garden.* Pelham Books, 1969.

Grant, John and Carol. *Garden Design Illustrated.* University of Washington Press, Seattle and London, 1954, 1958, 1967.

Hadfield, Miles. *The Art of the Garden.* Studio Vista, Ltd., London, 1965.

House and Garden, Garden Guide. Condé Nast Publications, Inc., New York, N.Y., 1967.

Hunt, Peter (ed.). *The Shell Gardens Book.* Phoenix House, London, 1964.

Hyams, Edward. *The English Garden.* Harry N. Abrams, Inc., New York, N.Y. (No date.)

Jekyll, G. *Colour Schemes in the Flower Garden.* Country Life, Ltd., London, 1908.

Jovet, Paul; Lowenmo, Runo; Jovet-Ast, S. *Fleurs de Jardin.* Fernand Nathan Press, Paris. (No date.)

Lawless, Emily. *A Garden Diary.* Methuen & Co., London, 1901.

Lawrence, Elizabeth. *Gardens in Winter.* Harpers & Brothers, New York, N.Y., 1961.

Leighton, Ann. *Early American Gardens.* Houghton Mifflin Company, Boston, Mass., 1970.

Masson, Georgina. *Italian Gardens.* Harry N. Abrams, Inc., New York, N.Y. (No date.)

Mathys, Heini. *Der Schoene Kleingarten.* Hallwag Verlag, Stuttgart, Germany, 1967.

Novak, F.A. *The Pictorial Encyclopedia of Plants and Flowers.* Paul Hamlyn, Ltd., London, 1966.

Nuese, Josephine. *The Country Garden.* Charles Scribner's Sons, New York, N.Y., 1970.

Page, Russell. *The Education of a Gardener.* Atheneum Publishers, London, 1962.

Roper, Lanning, editor of the Sunday *Times. On Gardens and Gardening.* London, 1969.

Sackville-West, V. *Garden Book.* Michael Joseph, London, 1968.

Schuler, Elizabeth. *Gardens Around the World.* Harry N. Abrams, Inc., New York, N.Y., 1964.

Thompson, Maurice. *My Winter Garden.* The Century Company, New York, N.Y., 1900.

CHAPTER FOUR

TREES, SHRUBS, AND VINES

Brockman, C. Frank. *Trees of North America.* A Field Guide, Golden Press, New York, N.Y., 1968.

Brooklyn Botanic Garden. *Handbook on Vines.* Brooklyn, N.Y., 1954.

Brooklyn Botanic Garden. *Dwarf Conifers.* Brooklyn, N.Y., 1965.

Brooklyn Botanic Garden. *Handbook on Flowering Shrubs.* Brooklyn, N.Y., 1964.

Beilmann, August P. *What Tree Shall I Plant.* Academy of Science, St. Louis, Mo.

Collis, John Stewart. *The Triumph of the Tree.* The Viking Press, Inc., New York, N.Y., 1954.

Cox, E.H.M.; Cox, P.A. *Modern Shrubs.* Thomas Nelson & Sons, Ltd., London, 1958.

Downing, A. J. *The Fruits and Fruit Trees of America.* John Wiley, New York, N.Y., 1853.

Faust, Joan Lee (ed.). *The New York Times Book of Trees and Shrubs.* Alfred A. Knopf, Inc., New York, N.Y., 1964.

Golden Nature Guide; A Guide to Familiar American Trees. Simon and Schuster, Inc., New York, N.Y., 1952.

Graves, A.H. *Winter Key to Woody Plants.* Published by the author, Wallingford, Conn., 1955.

Hay, Roy. *The Gardener's Round.* Macmillan and The *Times,* London, 1968.

Hellyer, A.G.L. *Shrubs in Color.* W.H.& L. Collingridge, London, 1965.

Hutchins, Ross E. *This Is a Tree.* Dodd, Mead and Co., New York, N.Y., 1964.

Kirkegaard, John. *Trees, Shrubs, Vines and Herbaceous Perennials.* Williams Bookstores Company, Publishers, Boston, Mass., 1916.

Matthews, F.S. *American Trees and Shrubs;* A Putnam Nature Field Book. G. P. Putnam's Sons, New York, London, 1915. (25th printing.)

Perkins, Harold O. *Espaliers and Vines.* D. Van Nostrand Co. Inc., Princeton, N.J., 1964.

Petrides, George A. *A Field Guide to Trees and Shrubs.* Houghton Mifflin Company, Boston, Mass., 1958.

Phillips, C.E. Lucas. *Climbing Plants for Walls and Gardens.* Heinemann, London, 1967.

Platt, Rutherford. *1001 Answers to Questions About Trees.* Grosset & Dunlap, Inc., New York, N.Y., 1959.

Platt, Rutherford. *American Trees.* Dodd, Mead & Co., New York, N.Y., 1962.

Platt, Rutherford. *The Great American Forest.* Prentice-Hall Inc., Englewood Cliffs, N.J., 1965.

Rayner, M.C. *Trees and Toadstools.* Rodale Books, Inc., Emmaus, Pa., 1947.

Rogers, Walter E. *Tree Flowers of Forest, Park, and Street.* Dover Publications, Inc., New York, N.Y., 1965.

Sargent, Charles Sprague. *Manual of the Trees of North America.* 2 vols. Dover Publications, Inc., New York, N.Y., 1961. (First printed in 1905.)

Symonds & Chelminski. *The Tree Identification Book.* William Morrow & Co., Inc., New York, N.Y., 1958.

Symonds, George; Mervin, A.W. *The Shrub Identification Book.* M. Barrows & Co., New York, N.Y., 1963.

Watts, M.T. *Master Tree Finder.* Nature Study Guild Publishers, Naperville, Ill., and Berkeley, Calif., 1963.

CHAPTER FIVE

WHAT FLOWERS SHOULD YOU CULTIVATE?

Anderson, A.W. *How We Got Our Flowers.* Dover Publications, Inc., New York, N.Y., 1966.

Barraclough, Daphne. *A Flower-Lover's Miscellany.* Frederick Warne & Co., Ltd., London, 1961.

Blunt, Wilfrid. *Tulipomania.* Penguin Books, Ltd., Harmondsworth, Middlesex, England, 1950.

Brooklyn Botanic Garden. *Trained and Sculptured Plants.* Brooklyn, N.Y., 1961.

Brooklyn Botanic Garden. *Breeding Ornamental Plants.* Brooklyn, N.Y., 1959.

Burke, L. *The Language of Flowers.* Price, Stern, Sloan Publishers, Inc., Los Angeles, Cal., 1965.

Creekmore, Hubert. *Daffodils are Dangerous.* Walker & Company, New York, N.Y., 1966.

Cuthbert, Mable Jacques. *How to Know the Spring Flowers.* William C. Brown Company, Publishers, Dubuque, Iowa, 1949.

Dyer T.F. Thiselton. *The Folklore of Plants*. D. Appleton Company, New York, N.Y., 1894.

Editorial Staffs of Sunset Books and *Sunset* Magazine. *How to Grow and Use Annuals*. Lane Book Co., Menlo Park, Calif., 1965.

Editors of *Sunset* Magazine and Sunset Books, *How to Grow and Use Bulbs,* Lane Book Co., Menlo Park, Calif., 1962.

Edland, H. *Roses*. The Viking Press, Inc., New York, N.Y., 1962.

Edland, H. *The Pocket Encyclopedia of Roses*. The Macmillan Company, New York, N.Y., 1969. (Revised edition.)

Educational Productions, Ltd., London, 1968. Bulbs.

Foley, Daniel J. *Garden Flowers in Color*. The Macmillan Company, New York, N.Y., 1945.

Hollingworth, Buckner. *Flower Chronicles*. Rutgers University Press, New Brunswick, N.J., 1958.

Genders, Roy. *Anemones*. Faber & Faber, Ltd., 1966.

Graff, M.M. *Flowers in the Winter Garden*. Doubleday & Company, Inc., Garden City, N.Y., 1960.

Haes, E.C. *Bulbs for Small Gardens*. Pan Books Ltd., London, 1967.

Hardwicke, Denis. *Flowers from Seed*. Pan Books, London, 1965.

Haring, Elda. *The Complete Book of Growing Plants from Seed*. Hawthorn Books, Inc., New York, N.Y., 1967.

Kerr-Dowden. *Shakespeares' Flowers*. Longmans Young Books Ltd., London.

Lemmon-Sherman. *Flowers of the World*. Doubleday & Company, Inc., New York, N.Y., 1964.

McFarland, J. Horace; Pyle, Robert. *How to Grow Roses*. J. Horace McFarland Co., Harrisburg, Pa., and The Macmillan Company, New York, N.Y., 1946.

Moreton, C. Oscar. *Old Carnations and Pinks*. George Rainbird, in association with Collins, London, 1955.

Nicholsen, Wallis; Anderson, Balfour; Fish; Finnis. *The Oxford Book of Garden Flowers*. Oxford University Press, London, 1968.

Pemberton, Rev. Joseph H. *Roses: Their History, Development, and Cultivation*. Longmans, Green and Co., London, 1920.

Phillips, G.A.R. *Aristocrats of the Flower Border*. Country Life, Ltd., London, 1948.

Polunin, Oleg. *Flowers of Europe*. Oxford University Press, London, 1969.

Rockwell, F.F. *The Book of Bulbs*. The Macmillan Company, New York, N.Y., 1946.

Sitwell, Sacheverell. *Old-Fashioned Flowers*. Charles Scribner's Sons, New York, N.Y., 1959.

Stevens, G.A. *Roses in the Little Garden*. Little, Brown and Company, Boston, Mass., 1926.

Subnik and Kaplická. *Cacti and Succulents*. Pail Hamlyn, London, 1968.

Taylor, R.L. *Plants of Colonial Days*. Colonial Williamsburg, Inc., Williamsburg, Virginia, 1952.

Tergit, Gabriele, *Flowers Through the Ages*. Oswald Wolff, Publishers, Ltd., London, England, 1961.

U.S. Department of Agriculture. *Spring-Flowering Bulbs*. U.S. Government Printing Office, Washington, D.C., 1958/66.

Wilson, Helen Van Pelt. *Perennials Preferred.* M. Barrows & Company, Inc., New York, N.Y., 1950.

Wilson, James W. *Flower Gardening: A Primer,* Van Nostrand Reinhold Company, New York, N.Y., 1970.

Wilber, Donald N. *Persian Gardens and Garden Pavillions.* Charles E. Tuttle Co., Tokyo, Japan, 1962.

Wyn, A.A. *The Little Book of Roses.* Hallwag Ltd., Berne, Switzerland, 1949.

CHAPTER SIX
ROCK, ALPINE, SEAFRONT, AND WATER GARDENS

ROCK

Adams, H.S. *Making a Rock Garden.* McBride, Nast & Company, New York, N.Y., 1912.

Anderson, E.B. *The Small Rock Garden.* Pan Books Ltd., London, 1965.

Foster, H. Lincoln. *Rock Gardening.* Houghton Mifflin Company, Boston, Mass., 1968.

Schenk, George. *How to Plan, Establish, and Maintain Rock Gardens.* A Sunset Book, Lane Book Co., Menlo Park, Calif., 1966.

ALPINE

Bloom, Alan. *Alpines for Trouble-Free Gardening.* Faber & Faber, London, 1961.

Brooklyn Botanic Garden Record. *Notes on Scree Building,* by Gerhard Sidow, Brooklyn, N.Y., 1970.

Hills, Lawrence D. *Alpine Gardening.* Faber & Faber, London, 1955.

Huxley, Anthony. *Mountain Flowers.* Blanford Press, London, 1967.

Konstandt, Oscar. *The Most Beautiful Alpine Flowers.* Thorsons, Publishers, Ltd., London, 1958.

Librairie Payot Lausanne. *Fleurs des Alpes.* 2 vols., Paris, France.

Vogel & Roshardt. *Die Shoensten Berglumen.* Hallwag, Bern, Orbis Pictus, 1956.

Weiss, Von Josef. *Blumen der Alpen.* Karl Robert Langewiesche, Verlag, Germany, 1957.

Wendelberger, Dr. Elfruns. *The Alps in Bloom.* Thorsons, Publishers, Ltd., London, 1958.

WATER PLANTS

Montauk Village Association. *The Salty Thumb.* Montauk, New York, 1967.

Hubbell, H.W.; Norman, M.G. *Treasures of the Shore, A Beachcomber's Botany.* The Chatham Conservation Foundation, Inc., Jack Viall, Printer, West Harwich, Mass., 1963, 1964, 1967.

Lounsberry, Alice. *Gardens Near the Sea.* The Plimpton Press, Norwood, Mass., 1910.

Mercer, F.A.; Hay; Roy. *Rock Wall and Water.* Vol. 4. The Studio Publications, London and New York. (No date.)

Zim, H.S.; Ingle, L. *Seashores.* A Golden Nature Guide, Golden Press, New York, N.Y., 1955.

CHAPTER SEVEN

BRINGING THE WILDERNESS CLOSE

Aiken, Senator George D. *Pioneering with Wildflowers.* Prentice-Hall, Inc., Englewood, N.J., 1968. (Revised Edition.)

Anthon, Henning. *The Pocket Encyclopedia of Wildflowers.* Blanford Press, London, 1965.

Archibald, David. *Wildflower* (Quick Key Guide to). Doubleday & Company, Inc., Garden City, N.Y., 1968.

Birdseye, C. & E.G. *Growing Woodland Plants.* Oxford University Press, New York, N.Y., 1951.

Bolin & Post. *Fleur des Prés et des Bois.* Fernand Nathan, Paris.

Coon, Nelson. *Using Plants for Healing.* Hearthside Press, Inc., New York, N.Y., 1963.

Coon, Nelson. *Using Wayside Plants.* Hearthside Press, Inc., New York, N.Y., 1957/60.

Craighead, Craighead and Davis. *Field Guide to Rocky Mountain Wildflowers.* Houghton Mifflin Company, Boston, Mass., 1963.

Creevey, C.A. *Harper's Guide to Wildflowers.* Harper & Brothers Publishers, New York and London, 1912.

Dana, Mrs. William Starr. *How to Know the Wildflowers.* Charles Scribner's Sons, New York, N.Y., 1904. Reprinted by Dover Publications, Inc., New York, N.Y., 1968.

Dietz, Marjorie J. *Favorite Wildflowers.* Doubleday & Company, Inc., Garden City, N.Y., 1965.

Durand, Herbert. *My Wildflower Garden.* G.P. Putnam's Sons, New York, N.Y., 1927.

Eifert, Virginia S. *Tall Trees and Far Horizons.* Dodd, Mead & Co., New York, N.Y., 1965.

Everard, Barbara, and Morley, Bryan D. *Wildflowers of the World.* G.P. Putnam's Sons, New York, N.Y., 1970.

Ewan, Joseph. *Rocky Mountain Naturalists.* The University of Denver Press, Colorado, 1950.

Fernald, M.L.; Kinsey, A.C.; rev. by Rollings. *Edible Wild Plants of Eastern North America.* Harper and Bros., New York, N.Y., 1958.

Fitter, Richard. *Your Book About Wildflowers.* Faber and Faber, London, 1960.

Gibbons, Euell. *Stalking the Wild Asparagus.* David McKay Co., Inc., New York, N.Y., 1962.

Grehan-Rickett. *The Odyssee Book of American Wildflowers.* The Odyssey Press, N.Y., 1964.

Grigson, Geoffrey. *Flowers of the Meadow.* Penguin Books, Middlesex, England, 1950.

Harris, Ben Charles. *Eat the Weeds*. Ben Charles Harris, Worcester, Mass., 1955.

Hatfield, A.W. *Pleasure of Wild Plants*. Taplinger Publishing Co., Inc., New York, N.Y., 1966.

Herbst, Josephine. *New Green World*. Hastings House, Publishers, Inc., New York, N.Y., 1954.

Hausman and Hinckely. *Beginner's Guide to Wildflowers*. G.P. Putnam's Sons, New York, N.Y., 1948.

Hinds, Harold R.; Hathaway, Wilfred A. *Wildflowers of Cape Cod*. The Chatham Press, Inc., Old Greenwich, Conn., 1968.

Hitchcock, A.S. Rev. by Agnes Chase. *Manual of the Grasses of the United States*. U.S. Government Printing Office, Washington, D.C., 1950.

House, Homer D. *Wildflowers of New York*. The University of the State of New York, 1918. 2 vols. (Also available in one volume edition.)

Hull, Helen S. *Wildflowers for Your Garden*. M. Barrows & Company, New York, N.Y., 1952.

Jaeger, Edmund C. *Desert Wildflowers*. Stanford University Press, Stanford, Calif., 1968.

Kingsbury, John M. *Deadly Harvest*. Holt, Rinehart & Winston, New York, N.Y., 1965.

Lemmon and Johnson. *Wildflowers of North America*. Hanover House, Garden City, N.Y.

Martin, W. Keble. *The Concise British Flora in Colour*. Ebury Press, and Michael Joseph, London, 1969. Second (revised) edition.

Mathew and Taylor. *Fieldbook of American Wildflowers*. G.P. Putnam's Sons, New York, N.Y., 1955.

Mathews, F. Schuyler. *Familiar Features of the Roadside*. D. Appleton and Company, New York, N.Y., 1897.

McClintock and Fitter. *Collins Pocket Guide to Wildflowers*. Collins, London, 1969.

McKenny, Margaret; Johnston, Edith. *A Book of Wayside Fruits*. The Macmillan Company, New York, N.Y., 1945.

Medsger, Oliver Perry. *Edible Wild Plants*. The Macmillan Company, New York, N.Y., 1939.

Miller and Whiting. *Wildflowers of the Northeastern United States*. G.P. Putnam's Sons, 1898.

Montgomery, F.H. *Native Plants of Northeastern United States and Eastern Canada*. Frederick Warne & Co., Inc., New York, N.Y., 1962.

Montgomery, F.H. *Weeds of the Northern United States and Canada*. The Ryerson Press, Toronto, Canada, 1964.

Newcomb, Lawrence. *Pocket Key to Common Wildflowers*. New England Wildflowers Preservation Society, Boston, Mass., 1963.

New England Wildflower Preservation Society Horticultural Hall. *Poisonous Plants of the Northeast, Native and Introduced*. Chart 1 and 2. Boston, Mass.

New York State Museum Bulletin. *Annotated List of the Ferns and Flowering Plants of New York State*. The University of the State of New York, Albany, N.Y., 1924.

Nicholson, Ary, McGregory. *The Oxford Book of Wildflowers*. Oxford University Press, London, 1965.

Peterson, R.T.; McKenny, M. *A Field Guide to Wildflowers*. Houghton Mifflin Company, Boston, Mass., 1968.

Rickett, H.W. *The New Field Book of American Wildflowers.* G.P. Putnam's Sons, New York, N.Y., 1963.

Rickett, H.W. *Wildflowers of the U.S.,* vols. I & II. McGraw-Hill Book Company, New York, N.Y., 1966/67.

Roberts, Harold and Rhoda. *Colorado Wildflowers.* Denver Museum of Natural History, Colorado, 1967.

Spencer, Edwin Rollin. *Just Weeds.* Charles Scribner's Sons, New York, N.Y., 1940.

State of California, Department of Natural Resources. *Point Lobos Wildflowers.*

Steffek, E.F. *Wildflowers and How to Grow Them.* Crown Publishers, Inc., New York, N.Y., 1963.

Stefferud, A. *How to Know the Wildflowers.* Henry Holt & Co., New York, N.Y., 1950.

Stokoe, W.J. *The Observer's Book of Wildflowers.* Frederick Warne & Co., New York, N.Y.

Stupka, Arthur. *Wildflowers in Color.* Harper & Row, Publishers, New York, N.Y., 1965.

Svolinsky and Barton. *Wildflowers.* Spring Books, London, 1963.

Taylor and Hamblin. *Handbook of Wildflower Cultivation.* The Macmillan Company, New York, N.Y., 1966. (Third printing.)

Thompson, C.J.S. *The Mystic Mandrake.* University Books, New Hyde Park, N.Y., 1968.

Van Doren, Mark (ed.). *Travels of William Bartram.* Dover Publications, Inc., New York, N.Y., 1955.

Vermont Botanical Club. *The Flora of Vermont.* Free Press Printing Co., Burlington, Vermont, 1937.

von Miklos, Josephine. *Wildflowers in Your House.* Doubleday & Company, Inc., Garden City, N.Y., 1968.

U.S. Department of Agriculture. *Conquest of the Land Through 7000 Years; Information Bulletin No. 99.,* Washington, D.C.

Waggerl, K.H. *Die Schoensten Blumen in Wiese und Feld.* Umschau Verlag, Frankfurt am Main, 1966.

Walcott and Platt. *Wildflowers of America.* Crown Publishers, Inc., New York, N.Y., 1953.

Wherry, Edgar T. *Wildflower Guide.* Doubleday & Company, Inc., New York, N.Y., 1948.

Whittle, Tyler. *The Plant Hunters.* Chilton Book Company, New York, N. Y., 1968.

Zim, M.S.; Martin, A.C. *Flowers,* A Golden Nature Book. Simon and Schuster, Inc., New York, N.Y., 1950.

FERNS

Audubon Center, Greenwich, Conn. *Ferns and Flowering Plants.*

Beecroft, W.I. *Who's Who Among the Ferns.* Moffat, Yord and Company, New York, N.Y., 1910.

Clute, Willard Nelson. *The Fern Allies.* Frederick A. Stokes, New York, N.Y., 1905.

Cobb, Boughton. *A Field Guide to the Ferns.* Houghton Mifflin Company, Boston, Mass., 1956.

Foster, F.G. *The Gardener's Fern Book.* D. Van Nostrand Co., Inc., Princeton, N.J., 1964.

Parsons, F.T. *How to Know the Ferns.* Dover Publications, Inc., New York, N.Y., 1961. (Originally published in 1899.)

Wherry, Edgar T. Ph.D. *The Fern Guide.* Doubleday & Company, Inc., Garden City, N.Y., 1961.

Wiley, Farida A. *Ferns of Northeastern United States.* Published by The National Audubon Society, New York, 1936/48.

CHAPTER EIGHT

HERBS, VEGETABLES, AND BERRIES

American Spice Trade Association. *A Treasury of Spices.* New York, N.Y., 1956.

Brooklyn Botanic Garden. *Handbook of Herbs.* Brooklyn, N.Y., 1958.

Clarkson, R.E. *Herbs—Their Culture and Uses.* The Macmillan Company, New York, N.Y., 1942.

Gerarde, John. *The Herball, or General Historie of Plants.* London, 1597.

Herb Grower Magazine, The. *Herb Teas and Tea Herbs.* The Herb Grower Press, Falls Village, Conn., 1960.

Herb Grower Magazine, The. *Herbs for Beauty.* The Herb Grower Press, Falls Village, Conn., 1962.

Herb Society of America. *A Primer for Herb Growing.* The Herb Society of America, Boston, Mass., 1952/54.

Hogner, Dorothy Childs. *A Fresh Herb Platter.* Doubleday & Company, Inc., Garden City, N.Y., 1961.

Kamm, M.W. *Old-Time Herbs for Northern Gardens.* Little, Brown and Company, Boston, Mass., 1938.

Krutch, Joseph Wood. *Herbal.* G.P. Putnam's Sons, New York, N.Y., 1965.

Leyel, C.F. *Cinquefoil.* Faber and Faber, London, 1957.

Leyel, C.F. *Herbal Delights.* Faber and Faber Ltd., London, 1937.

MacLeaod, Dawn. *A Book of Herbs.* Gerald Duckworth & Co., London, 1968.

Meyer, Clarence. *The Herbalist.* Rand McNally & Company, Condey Division, U.S.A., 1918, 1960. (Revised and enlarged.)

Morgenthau Fox, Helen, *Gardening with Herbs for Flavor and Fragrance.* Dover Publications, Inc., New York, N.Y., 1970.

Parkinson, John. *Paradisi in Sole, Paradisus Terrestris.* London, 1629, 1904 (facsimile).

Pedacio Dioscorides. Salamanca, Spain, 1570.

Schering Corporation. *Medicine and Pharmacy.* Schering Corporation, Bloomfield, N.J., 1956.

Scully, Virginia. *A Treasury of American Indian Herbs.* Crown Publishers, Inc., New York, N.Y., 1970.

Sharon Audubon Center. *Herbs in the Garden. The Herb Grower* Magazine, Falls Village, Conn.

Sounin, Leonie de. *Magic in Herbs.* M. Barrow, Inc., New York, N.Y., 1952.

Stearns, M.G. *Herbs and Herb Cookery Through the Years.* Old Sturbridge Village Booklet Series. Meriden Gravure Co., Meriden, Conn., 1965/67.

VEGETABLES AND BERRIES

Dahlgren, B.E. *The Story of Food Plants.* Field Museum of Natural History, Field Museum Press, Chicago, Ill., 1940.

Darrow, George M. *The Strawberry.* Holt, Rinehart & Winston, New York, N.Y., 1966.

Editors of *Sunset* Magazine and Sunset Books. *Vegetable Gardening.* Lane Book Co., Menlo Park, Calif., 1966.

Quinn, Vernon. *Vegetables in the Garden and Their Legends.* J.B. Lippincott Co., Philadelphia, Pa., 1942.

Simmons, A.J. *The Vegetable Grower's Handbook.* Penguin Books, Middlesex, England, 1948.

See also general books on botany, horticulture, and gardening.

CHAPTER NINE
POTTED PLANTS, OUTDOORS AND IN

Briscoe, T.W. *Orchids for Amateurs.* W.H. & L. Collingridge, Ltd., London, 1950.

Brooklyn Botanic Garden. *Bonsai, Special Techniques.* Brooklyn, N.Y., no date.

Brooklyn Botanic Garden. *Gardening under Artificial Light,* Brooklyn, N.Y., 1970.

Brooklyn Botanic Garden. *Stalk the Wilds for Unusual Bonsai.* Brooklyn, N.Y., 1969/70.

Budlong, Ware. *Indoor Gardens.* Hawthorn Books, Inc., New York, N.Y., 1967.

Cathey, Henry. *Indoor Garden for Decorative Plants.* U.S. Dept. of Agriculture, Washington, D.C., 1965.

Charry, Elaine, C. *Fluorescent Light Gardening.* Van Nostrand Reinhold Company, New York, N.Y., 1965.

Cruso, Thalassa. *Making Things Grow.* Alfred A. Knopf, Inc., New York, N.Y., 1969.

Fogg, H. Witham. *The Small Greenhouse.* Pan Books Ltd., London, 1965.

Hessayon, Dr. D.G. *Be Your Own House Plant Expert.* Pan Britannica Industries, Herts., England.

Hull, George F. *Bonsai for Americans.* Doubleday and Company, Inc., Garden City, New York, 1964.

Kiaer, Eigil. *Indoor Plants.* Blanford Press, London, 1967.

Lee, Elsie. *At Home with Plants.* The Macmillan Company, New York, N.Y., 1966.

Rector, Carolyn. *African Violets.* Blanford Press, London, 1951.

Simmons, Adelma, Grenier. *Herbs to Grow Indoors.* Hawthorn Books, Inc., New York, 1969.

Taylor & Gregg, *Winter Flowers in Greenhouse and Sun-Heated Pit.* Charles Scribner's Sons, New York, N.Y., 1969.

U.S. Department of Agriculture, *Insects and Related Pests of House Plants.* Home and Garden Bulletin #67, Washington, D.C., May, 1960.

U.S. Department of Agriculture, *Selecting and Growing House Plants.* Home and Garden Bulletin #82, Washington, D.C., June, 1962.

309

CHAPTER TEN

GARDENS WITHOUT FLOWERS

Brooklyn Botanic Garden. *Trained and Sculptured Plants.* Brooklyin, New York, 1961, 1968.

Brooklyn Botanic Garden. *Dwarf Conifers; A Handbook on Low and Slow-Growing Evergreens.* Brooklyn, N.Y., 1965.

Engel, H. David. *Japanese Gardens for Today.* Charles E. Tuttle Co., Inc., Rutland, Vt., and Tokyo, Japan.

Newson, Samuel. *A Japanese Garden Manual for Westerners.* Tokyo News Service, Ltd., 1968.

Newson, Samuel. *A Thousand Years of Japanese Gardens.* Tokyo News Service, Tokyo, 1959.

Saito, K.; Wada, S. *Magic of Trees and Stone.* Japan Publications Trading Company, New York, San Francisco, Tokyo, 1970. (4th print.)

Yoshimura Yugi and Halford, Giovanna M. *The Japanese Art of Miniature Trees and Landscaping.* Charles E. Tuttle Co., Inc., Rutland, Vt., 1957.

In addition to all the books just mentioned, I have also used and enjoyed others which have added to my understanding and love of nature; I hope you will find some of them, somewhere, sometime, and spend a few hours in their very good company.

ON NATURE

Borland, Hal. *An American Year.* Simon & Schuster, Inc., New York, N.Y.

Borland, Hal. *Sundial of the Seasons.* A Selection of Outdoor Editorials from *The New York Times.* J.B. Lippincott Co., Philadelphia and New York, 1964.

Borland, Hal. *The Seventh Winter.* J.B. Lippincott Co., Philadelphia and New York, 1959.

Borland, Hal. *This Hill, This Valley.* J.B. Lippincott Co., Philadelphia and New York, 1957.

Brooklyn Botanic Garden. *Conservation for Every Man.* Special Printing of *Plants & Gardens.* vol. 18, #2. Brooklyn Botanic Garden, Baltimore, Md., 1962.

Collins, Jr., Henry Hill. *The American Year.* G.P. Putnam's Sons, New York, N.Y.

Eisely, Loren. *The Mind as Nature.* Harper & Row, Publishers, New York, N.Y., 1962.

Gooch, Bernard. *The Strange World of Nature.* Lutterworth Press, London, 1950.

Lord, Russell. *The Care of the Earth.* The New American Library, Mentor Books, New York, N.Y., 1963.

Milne, Lorus and Margery. *Patterns of Survival.* Prentice-Hall, Inc., Englewood Cliffs, N.J., 1967.

Platt, Rutherford. *Our Flowering World.* Dodd, Mead & Co., New York, N.Y., 1947.

Platt, Rutherford. *This Green World.* Dodd, Mead & Co., New York, N.Y., 1949.

Teale, Edwin Way. *Autumn Across America.* Dodd, Mead & Co., New York, N.Y., 1956.

Teale, Edwin Way. *Journey Into Summer.* Dodd, Mead & Co., New York, N.Y., 1966.

Teale, Edwin Way. *North with the Spring.* Dodd, Mead & Co., New York, N.Y., 1963.

Teale, Edwin Way. *Wandering Through Winter*. Dodd, Mead & Co., New York, N.Y., 1966.

Thoreau, Henry David. *Walden*. Modern Library, Inc., New York, N.Y., 1950.

Thoreau, Henry David. *Thoreau On Man and Nature*. Peter Pauper Press, Mount Vernon, N.Y., 1960.

Thoreau, Henry David. *The Maine Woods*. Branhall House, New York, N.Y., 1950.

POETRY AND LITERATURE

Bacon, Francis. *Selected Writings*. The Modern Library, Inc., New York, N.Y., 1955.

Basho, Buson, Issu, Shiki, and many others. *The Four Seasons, Japanese Haiku*. Peter Pauper Press, Mount Vernon, N.Y., 1958.

Freene, Donald (compiled and edited by). *Anthology of Japanese Literature*. Grove Press, Inc., New York, N.Y., 1955.

Funk, Wilfred. *Word Origins*. Grosset & Dunlap, Inc., New York, N.Y., 1950.

Grover, Edwin Osgood. *The Nature Lover's Knapsack*. Thomas Y. Crowell Company, New York, N.Y., 1927.

Henderson, Harold G. (translations and commentary by). *An Introduction to Haiku, An Anthology of Poems and Poets from Hashu to Shiki*. Doubleday & Company, Inc., Garden City, N.Y., 1958.

Kreymborg, Alfred (ed.). *An Anthology of American Poetry, 1630–1941*. Tudor Publishing Co., New York, N.Y., 1941.

Noyes, George R. (revised and enlarged by). *The Poetical Works of Dryden*. Houghton Mifflin Company, Boston, Mass., 1950.

Randolph, Anson D.F. *Songs of the Woodlands, The Garden and the Sea*. New York, N.Y., 1859.

Rees, Ennis (translated by). *The Odyssey of Homer*. Random House, Inc., New York, N.Y., 1960.

Ross, J.B.; McLaughlin, M.M. (ed.). *Medieval Reader*. The Viking Press, Inc., New York, N.Y., 1949.

Shipley, Joseph T. *Dictionary of Word Origins*. The Philosophical Library, New York, N.Y., 1945.

Van Doren, Mark (ed.). *An Anthology of World Poetry*. Blue Ribbon Books Inc., New York, N.Y., 1934.

Wedeck, Harry E. (ed.). *Dark and Middle Ages Reader*. G.P. Putnam's Sons, New York, N.Y., 1964.

Wheeler, Candace. *Content in a Garden*. Houghton Mifflin Company, Boston, Mass., 1904.

WHEN AND HOW TO GET HELP

Brooklyn Botanic Garden. *Trees and Shrubs: Where to Buy Them*. Brooklyn, N.Y., 1963.

Stephenson, J.W. *The Gardener's Directory*. Hanover House, Garden City, N.Y., 1960.

And all the plant catalogues you can get hold of.

INDEX